SILENT PARTNERS

Silent Partners

*Women as Public Investors during Britain's
Financial Revolution, 1690–1750*

AMY M. FROIDE

OXFORD

UNIVERSITY PRESS

OXFORD
UNIVERSITY PRESS

Great Clarendon Street, Oxford, OX2 6DP,
United Kingdom

Oxford University Press is a department of the University of Oxford.
It furthers the University's objective of excellence in research, scholarship,
and education by publishing worldwide. Oxford is a registered trade mark of
Oxford University Press in the UK and in certain other countries

First Edition published in 2017

Impression: 1

Published in the United States of America by Oxford University Press
198 Madison Avenue, New York, NY 10016, United States of America

British Library Cataloguing in Publication Data
Data available

Library of Congress Control Number: 2016934361

ISBN 978-0-19-876798-5

Printed in Great Britain by
Clays Ltd, St Ives plc

Acknowledgments

I have invested just over a decade of my career to these women capitalists and in the process I have become happily indebted to many scholars, archivists, and institutions. I would like to thank the archivists and librarians who have assisted me with this project, most notably the staff of the Henry E. Huntington Library, the Folger Shakespeare Library, and the British Library, the National Archives at Kew, the Bank of England Archives, the London Metropolitan Archives, and the Nottinghamshire County Archives.

I very much appreciate the monetary investments some have made in me and my research. Much of the research for this book was funded by a Peter and Helen Bing Endowed Fellowship in 2007–8 and another short-term fellowship in 2010–11 from the Henry E. Huntington Library, as well as a short-term fellowship from the Folger Shakespeare Library in 2013–14. UMBC's History department provided me with funds for research trips to archives in Britain, as did the Herbert Bearman Foundation, which awarded me the Bearman Foundation Chair in Entrepreneurship for 2007–10. UMBC's College of Arts, Humanities and Social Sciences provided me with a semester off from teaching to finish writing a draft of this book in 2013.

I have had the pleasure of working at UMBC for the duration of this project. I could not wish for better colleagues and a better department in which to practice history. I especially want to thank the chairs of the History department while I have worked on this book: John Jeffries, Kriste Lindenmeyer, and Marjoleine Kars. All three have championed my scholarship, been supportive of sabbaticals and leaves, and helped me seek out funding for my research. I hope I do them credit. I am also fortunate to have had a number of student research assistants who have helped me find and analyze many of the sources I used in this book. Thanks in particular go to Jenny Parish, Teresa Foster, and Vicki Heath, who have all done UMBC and the History profession proud.

I have had the opportunity to present my research to many audiences and I want to thank the many scholars who provided ideas, suggestions, and advice. In particular, I would like to thank Ann Carlos, Anne Laurence, Margaret Hunt, Anne Murphy, and Rosemary O'Day for their support and assistance with this project over the years. I am grateful for the feedback I received from the USC-Huntington Seminar on Early Modern British History, the History department seminar at Johns Hopkins University, the Early Modern History workshop at Princeton University, and the Women's History seminar at the Institute for Historical Research at the University of London. I would like to thank the History department writing group (a.k.a my friends Kate Brown, Christy Chapin, Marjoleine Kars, Susan McDonough, Andrew Nolan, Meredith Oyen, and Dan Ritschel) for their careful reading of the drafts of two chapters. I am grateful to Cynthia Herrup, who at my first presentation on this topic told me I had found my next book. And I appreciate the time taken by the three anonymous readers for Oxford University Press, who suggested ideas for revision and saved me from a number of mistakes. Lastly, thanks to OUP editors Stephanie Ireland, Terka Acton, and Cathryn Steele for their excitement about and assistance on this project.

Some of my biggest debts are to those who have provided me with friendship, love, and moral support. Thank you to my mother and stepfather, Diana and Mike Oliver, my sisters, Holly and Amber, and their families. Continuing thanks and appreciation to Cynthia and Judith. And to my friends Ann, Anne, Mary Beth, Michelle, and Tristan, thanks for getting me through the rough spots. Lastly, much love to my little dividend, my daughter Sophie.

Table of Contents

List of Figures

List of Tables

1

Introduction: Women as Public Investors in England

It is the heady years of the Financial Revolution in London. Men sit in the coffeehouses of Exchange Alley, perhaps Garraway's or maybe Jonathan's, eagerly trading pieces of paper that promise a share in the East India Company or some other joint-stock venture. Look a little further through the haze of pipe smoke and you will notice a woman or two talking to a broker or handing over coin for a share. Next, head to Grocer's Hall in Princes Street, now home to the Bank of England. A number of carriages pull up in front of the building and when you stop to examine the passengers you note that every third or fourth one is female. One of the women enters the Bank to collect her quarterly dividend payment, while another sends in her maidservant. Follow the second one's coach. Its next stop is South Sea House. This time the mistress emerges and goes inside to transfer some stock. Stroll away from South Sea House and head toward one of the many lottery offices in the City. Stop in Stationer's Alley, Ludgate Street, at the one that advertises in the London papers their discrete premises for "gentlemen and ladies." You see both male and female customers bustle in and out buying tickets as well as groups of women purchasing shares of tickets together. Next head to one of the State lottery drawings at the City's Guildhall. Blue coat boys from the Christ Church charity school stand on the stage and draw the prize-winning tickets. The crowd holds its breath, waiting for the lucky numbers. Scan the assemblage and you will see many women watching the proceedings with rapt interest. Some are elegantly dressed and attended by servants, while others pop in between running errands for their mistresses, or selling goods on the Royal Exchange. While these women are distracted by the spectacle, other women move in close, deftly picking their pockets. Some people will leave the Lottery drawing as double losers. What you are viewing are the sites and opportunities of England's Financial Revolution. At first glance this may seem a masculine world, but look a little closer and you will see women—the silent partners of this revolutionary period in finance. If you stop to listen perhaps these women are not so silent after all. And in this book they are no longer silenced.

This book sets out to explore Englishwomen's relationship to and role within financial capitalism in the late seventeenth and early eighteenth centuries. A whole generation of Marxist feminist historians taught us that Britain's transition to capitalism had a negative, if not downright pernicious, effect on the economic (and overall) status of women.[1] While most scholars now favor a more nuanced version of this story, early modern women's relationship to capitalism still has not undergone a total reassessment. Until the last decade or so we have viewed capitalism as something that acted on or affected women, and not vice versa. Women's historians have been reluctant to consider that women participated in and were agents of capitalist enterprises, as much as capitalism was something that acted on them. We have not fully interrogated how some women may have benefited from capitalism and even sought out and welcomed the opportunity to participate in the capitalist economy. Women not only "adapted to capitalism," in the words of Pamela Sharpe, they also actively sought out the new financial opportunities it brought.[2]

This book posits that the financial independence of unmarried women, as well as married women's rights to separate property, allowed women to participate in and further England's Financial Revolution. When convenient, capitalism could be "gender blind"; all money was welcome in London's Exchange Alley. In her 2005 article "Coverture and Capitalism," Amy Erickson made a similar argument, positing that the legal freedom of spinsters and widows allowed them to swell the numbers of prospective investors during England's Financial Revolution and beyond.[3] This book will provide some of the evidence to strengthen Erickson's assertion that English financial markets were open to female capital, especially the money of femes soles. But we will also see that it was not just unmarried women who participated in the Financial Revolution, for married women circumvented coverture to engage in investing alongside their unmarried sisters.

This book seeks to show how Englishwomen's participation in early modern capitalism fits into, as much as it challenges, the economic history of women. Scholars have shown that women were active participants in the early modern English economy but often marginalized in low pay, low status jobs.[4] Women were not equal participants in the guild structures of English towns and were

[1] An overview of the pessimistic view of capitalism's effect on women in England and a discussion of the work of Alice Clark, Eric Richards, Keith Snell, and others, can be found in Janet Thomas, "Women and Capitalism: Oppression or Emancipation? A Review Article," *Comparative Studies in Society and History* 30:3 (1988), 534–49.

[2] Pamela Sharpe, *Adapting to Capitalism: Working Women in the English Economy, 1700–1850* (London: St. Martin's Press, 1996).

[3] Amy Louise Erickson, "Coverture and Capitalism," *History Workshop Journal* 59 (2005), 3.

[4] This pessimistic view of women's economic role over time is best represented by the work of Judith M. Bennett. *Ale, Beer and Brewsters in England: Women's Work in a Changing World, 1300–1600* (Oxford: Oxford University Press, 1996); "'History that Stands Still': Women's Work in the European Past," *Feminist Studies* 14 (1988), 269–83.

exceptions rather than the rule in high status, lucrative trades. This meant that by necessity women took advantage of new sectors of the economy that had not yet been formalized and dominated by men. Add to this the social stigma against genteel women working and those who needed to maintain themselves were faced with a dilemma.[5] How to retain their status and still support themselves? In this economic context, women's investment in the newly emerging market for stocks and shares makes a lot of sense. Women sought out investment opportunities because they needed more economic options and were smart enough to take advantage of new opportunities. Women adapted to, even embraced, the changes brought by the Financial Revolution in the late seventeenth and early eighteenth centuries because of their somewhat marginalized status in the English economy of the time.

The heart of this book is a socio-economic study of the women who placed their money into the new public funds that began to emerge in Britain during the 1690s; a period dubbed by P. G. M. Dickson the "Financial Revolution." The key elements of England's new financial system were the establishment of the Bank of England and the long-term national debt in the 1690s, as well as an active secondary market in securities.[6] This book will examine female investors in these new public investment opportunities including the Bank of England (chartered in 1694), public corporations such as the East India Company and the South Sea Company and lesser-known ones like the Mine Adventurers Company and the York Buildings Company, as well as the national debt. It is this latter area that has not yet seen much sustained investigation. One of the findings of this book is early modern English-women's embrace of government funds and growing role as public creditors.

Another of this book's contributions is to nuance the notion of a "female investor," showing that historically not all women have followed the same investing behaviors. The main stereotype about female investors in the present day is that they are risk averse but in the past this was not necessarily the case.[7] This study will show that there was no such thing as a generic "female

---

[5] For the difficulties of middling class women going into trade, see Margaret R. Hunt, *The Middling Sort: Commerce, Gender and the Family in England, 1680–1780* (Berkeley, CA: University of California Press, 1996).

[6] Anne L. Murphy, *The Origins of English Financial Markets: Investment and Speculation before the South Sea Bubble* (Cambridge: Cambridge University Press, 2009), 2; Carl Wennerlind, *Casualties of Credit: The English Financial Revolution 1620–1720* (Cambridge, MA: Harvard University Press, 2011), 7; Larry Neal, "How it All Began: The Monetary and Financial Architecture of Europe during the First Global Capital Markets, 1648–1815," *Financial History Review* 7 (2000), 123.

[7] Tahira Hira and Cäzilia Loibl, "Gender Differences in Investment Behavior" (Aug. 31, 2006) <www.finrafoundation.org> (accessed June 2015), Catha Mullen, "Real Data Suggest Gender Biases in Investing" (Feb. 5, 2014), and Suba Iyer, "Overcoming Gender Irrationality for Better Investing" (March 5, 2014), <blog.personalcapital.com> (accessed June 2015). These recent studies show that men take more financial risks than women, but authors also acknowledge that other factors such as marital status, age, education, and income level may be more important predictors of economic behavior than gender.

investor" during the Financial Revolution. Rather, women of different marital and social status invested for different reasons. They had varying levels of financial knowledge, skill, and comfort with risk.

This book will build on recent scholarship that has begun to examine women who invested in eighteenth-century England. Scholars have focused on whether women were passive or active investors and whether they were risk averse or open to engaging in financial speculation. This book contributes to these discussions by coming at these questions from new and different perspectives. Economic historians have focused on stock trading to show passive or active investing behaviors. In this book I broaden the criteria for assessing women's investing behavior by including whether women bought or sold stocks of their own volition, whether they changed or altered their portfolios, especially stocks they inherited, and how they made investing decisions.

This book also contributes to the history of women in early modern England by illuminating the knowledge, ability, and agency enjoyed by women of means. Women's historians have established that early modern Englishwomen had a good working knowledge of the legal system.[8] Likewise, this book will show that during the years of the Financial Revolution women had a level of financial knowledge and skill that may strike us as surprising. While today we leave investments to specialists, such as financial planners and stockbrokers, in early modern England women from various ranks did their own investing. And rather than having to consult their male relatives for financial assistance and advice, women were often the financial investors in their families.

This book will not only show that women moved their capital into public investments during the years of the Financial Revolution but how these new investment opportunities were most beneficial to women who had to support themselves, specifically middling and genteel spinsters and widows. Moreover, women's public investments not only aided them, they were also crucial to the British imperial project. This book posits that without the money of thousands of Englishwomen, Britain's trade, wars, and empire would not have been possible or as successful. In making this argument I extend David Green and Alastair Owens's theory on "gentlewomanly capitalism" to a century earlier.

---

[8] Examples include Amy Louise Erickson, *Women and Property in Early Modern England* (London: Routledge, 1993) and "Common Law vs. Common Practice: the use of marriage settlements in early modern England," *Economic History Review* 2nd ser., 43:1 (1990), 21–39; Jennifer Kermode and Garthine Walker, eds., *Women, Crime and the Courts in Early Modern England* (Chapel Hill, NC: University of North Carolina Press, 1994), especially essays by Geoffrey Hudson and Tim Stretton; Tim Stretton, *Women Waging Law in Elizabethan England* (Cambridge: Cambridge University Press, 1998); Margaret Hunt, "Wives and 'Marital Rights' in the Court of Exchequer in the Early Eighteenth Century" in Paul Griffiths and Mark S. R. Jenner, *Londinopolis: Essays in the Social and Cultural History of early modern London* (Manchester: Manchester University Press, 2000), 107–29.

In their 2003 article Green and Owens argued for the national significance of British women's wealth and its contribution to economic development.[9] They posited that in the nineteenth century middle-class single women parlayed their wealth into investments in government securities and that this investment was of "crucial importance" to the British nation state. Green and Owens contended that women's contributions to national economic development had been underestimated and lacking in acknowledgement in preference to a focus on English gentlemen. This book will show that what Green and Owens posited for nineteenth-century Britain was in place much earlier, with women's capital contributing to the colonial and imperial endeavors of early eighteenth-century Britain.

The main sources I use to study women's public investing fall into three categories. The first is the records of the British government and the financial corporations themselves. Some of these documents, especially those of the Bank of England, the East India Company, and South Sea Company have been fruitfully studied by other historians of the Financial Revolution. This book will also focus on some of the lesser-known companies and their investors, such as the Mine Adventurers and the London Orphan's Fund. And I will utilize the records of the national debt to chart the important role of female creditors to the government from the 1690s through the first half of the eighteenth century. The second source base for this book is the periodical literature of the time, especially newspapers, pamphlets, and periodicals. Natasha Glaisyer made use of some of this literature in her study of the period's "culture of commerce." However, these sources have not been integrated with or read alongside the government and corporate records of the Financial Revolution. The third source base for this book is the personal papers, account books, and correspondence of individual women, often found among larger repositories of family papers. These sources allow us to build up a more holistic view of individual female investors, rather than just a name in a subscriber list. Accounts also provide an avenue for investigating the portfolios of individual female investors. There is not yet much research on the individual portfolios of investors from this period, whether male or female. This book will show how such recovery can be done through a thorough cross-referencing of material in family papers and archives. In addition to these main groups of sources, I use other types of records to fill out the picture, including popular literature and court records.

While the source base for this book varies from previous work on women investors another difference is that I take a longitudinal approach to the topic. I examine women's investing experiences over the first seventy-five years of

---

[9] David R. Green and Alastair Owens, "Gentlewomanly capitalism? Spinsters, widows and wealth holding in England and Wales, c. 1800–1860," *Economic History Review* 56:3 (2003): 510–36.

the Financial Revolution, from the late 1680s to the 1750s. Most of the scholarship on women and the Financial Revolution so far has either focused on the 1690s or on the years around the South Sea Bubble of 1720. In contrast, this book examines women's role in the Financial Revolution for two generations, from the earliest years up to the mid-eighteenth century. This longer view allows us to see how women acclimatized and adapted to the Financial Revolution, as well as to chart change over time.

The historiography on women's role as public investors during the Financial Revolution has only emerged in the last decade or so. Up until recently the scholarship on the Financial Revolution largely eschewed questions of women and gender. Nevertheless, even the earliest works noted the presence of women among public investors in joint-stock companies, the Bank of England, and the national debt. P. G. M. Dickson who coined the term "Financial Revolution" was the first scholar to note that numbers of women were public investors. Studying shareholder and subscriber lists, Dickson found that women were present from the start and were "to become increasingly important as the [eighteenth] century went on."[10] Dickson's foundational work appeared in 1967. While the research on the Financial Revolution began to increase in the 1990s, it largely steered clear of questions of gender.[11]

In the last decade scholars have returned to women's involvement in early financial capitalism. Ann Carlos, Larry Neal, Anne Laurence, and Barbara Todd have further charted the numbers of female investors in the Bank of England, the South Sea Company, and other joint-stock ventures. And Laurence and Todd have produced case studies of individual female investors and their investing behaviors.[12] This project builds on these important articles. Instead of looking at aggregate numbers of women investors or providing a case study of a single female investor, this book explores a range of women

---

[10] P. G. M. Dickson, *The Financial Revolution in England: A Study in the Development of Public Credit, 1688–1756* (London: MacMillan, 1967), 256, 269, 298.

[11] Larry Neal, *The Rise of Financial Capitalism* (Cambridge: Cambridge University Press, 1990); Henry Roseveare, *The Financial Revolution 1660–1760* (London: Longman, 1991), Bruce G. Carruthers, *City of Capital: Politics and Markets in the English Financial Revolution* (Princeton: Princeton University Press, 1996), Wennerlind, *Casualties of Credit,* Daniel Carey and Christopher Finlay, *The Empire of Credit: The Financial Revolution in Britain, Ireland, and America, 1688–1815* (Dublin: Irish Academic Press, 2011); Murphy, *The Origins of English Financial Markets.*

[12] Ann Carlos and Larry Neal, "Women investors in early capital markets, 1720–25," *Financial History Review* 11:2 (2004), 197–224; Ann M. Carlos, Karen Maguire and Larry Neal, "Financial Acumen, Women Speculators, and the Royal African Company during the South Sea Bubble," *Accounting, Business & Financial History* 16:2 (July 2006), 219–43; Anne Laurence, "Women Investors, 'That Nasty South Sea Affair' and the Rage to Speculate in Early Eighteenth-Century England," *Accounting, Business & Financial history* 16:2 (July 2006), 245–64, Anne Laurence, "The emergence of a private clientele for banks in the early eighteenth century: Hoare's Bank and some women customers," *Economic History Review* 61:3 (2008), 565–86, Anne Laurence, "Lady Betty Hastings, Her Half-Sisters, and the South Sea Bubble: family fortunes and strategies," *Women's History Review* 15:4 (2006), 533–40.

investors—from London servant maids and criminals, to tradeswomen and distressed gentlewomen, on up to some of the wealthiest Duchesses in the land. It examines women's involvement in a range of investment options, in particular government annuities and lotteries, and mines new sources, such as women's financial correspondence and account books. Significantly, it investigates how women invested not just for themselves but also for their families, friends, and business associates. This book also explains how women learned to invest in order to gauge their financial knowledge. Lastly, it places women investors into their individual and familial contexts, in order to more fully flesh-out women's financial decisions and the repercussions of their investments over their life spans.

This book also provides an important earlier context for the growing literature on British (including Scottish and Welsh) female investors post-1750. This research allows us to examine some of the continuities and differences between female investors in the early stock market and the later period when there was a broader and more established market. For instance, in the late 1700s the options for public investment exploded with the emergence of provincial banks, turnpike and canal trusts, and in the following century, railroads. Women invested in all of these opportunities. Compare this to the period before 1750 when the stock market was still fairly small and focused on London.[13] Scholars have found that women in the 1800s preferred safe and reliable investments; moreover, these types of investments were also specifically "marketed" to women in the nineteenth century.[14] This is very different from the earlier period when there are few instances of gendered marketing and fewer assumptions that women comprised a specific type of investor. Research on women investors in the modern period points to important differences between the early modern and modern era. It opens up the possibility that women investors before 1750 were more open to risk. This book will also suggest that the early, unregulated years of the Financial Revolution provided more freedom to women investors, especially married women, than did the long nineteenth century.

* * *

Englishwomen did not suddenly become creditors in the 1680s and '90s. Before the Financial Revolution opportunities for women to invest money at interest were limited and focused primarily on private loans to individuals. Some of these loans were to family members. As Leonard Davidoff and Catherine Hall

[13] Lucy Newton and Philip Cottrell, "Female investors in the First English and Welsh Joint stock Banks," *Accounting, Business, and Financial History* 16:2 (July 2006), 315–40.
[14] Lucy A. Newton, Philip L. Cottrell, Josephine Maltby, and Janette Rutterford, "Women and Wealth: The Nineteenth Century in Great Britain," in *Women and Their Money 1700–1950: Essays on Women and Finance* edited by Anne Laurence, Josephine Maltby, Janette Rutterford (London: Routledge, 2008), 89–91.

have shown for the later eighteenth century, women's capital was also integral to family businesses.[15] Women's loans to non-kin were sometimes informal but most were secured by formal instruments such as bonds and mortgages. Only unmarried women, or femes soles, could legally sign contracts and make loans. Thus it was primarily single women and widows who were active in the private securities market. From the late medieval period onward women were active participants in local credit markets. While many of these women were of middling to elite status, even working women, and particularly servants, loaned money.[16] What changed with the Financial Revolution is that there were now public institutions in which women could invest capital. These included the Bank of England, joint-stock corporations such as the East India and the South Sea companies, and the newly established national debt.

Various scholars have provided estimates of the number of individuals who put their capital into these new public investments. They have also broken down the numbers of investors by gender. Women's contribution to public investment can be thought of in two ways: the percentage of shareholders in particular stocks and securities that they comprised and the proportion of capital that they loaned. Subscriber and shareholder lists reveal that women were present among investors in joint-stock companies from the Restoration period onward. Their numbers started out low in the seventeenth century and grew more substantial over the first half of the eighteenth century. For instance, K. G. Davies estimates that in 1685 women investors in the East India Company held a mere 2–4 percent of the company's stock. Barbara Todd, however, has found slightly higher numbers for the 1680s; she estimates women held 13 percent of East India Company stock in 1688. Ann Carlos, Erin Fletcher, and Larry Neal found numbers closer to those of Davies for female holders of East India Company stock in the 1690s, when women comprised 7.43 percent of stockholders. They also estimate that the proportion of female EIC shareholders grew in the eighteenth century, with women comprising 13.38 percent of stockholders by the early 1720s.[17] Women's shareholding rose again

[15] Davidoff and Hall, *Family Fortunes: Men and Women of the English Middle Class, 1780–1850* (Chicago: The University of Chicago Press, 1987), see chapter 6: "'The hidden investment': women and the enterprise."

[16] Amy Froide, *Never Married: Singlewomen in Early Modern England* (Oxford, 2005), chapter 5, 128–41; B. A. Holderness, "Widows in Pre-Industrial Society: An Essay Upon their Economic Function," in Richard M. Smith, ed., *Land, Kinship, and Life-Cycle* (Cambridge: Cambridge University Press, 1984), 423–42; Judith Spicksley, "'Fly with a duck in thy mouth': single women as sources of credit in seventeenth century England," *Social History* 32:2 (May 2007), 187–207; Judith Spicksley, "Usury legislation, cash and credit: the development of the female investor in the late Tudor and Stuart periods," *Economic History Review* 61:2 (May 2008), 277–301; Robert Tittler, "Money-lending in the West Midlands: The Activities of Joyce Jeffries, 1638–49," *Historical Research* 67:164 (1994): 249–63.

[17] K. G. Davies, "Joint-Stock Investment in the Later Seventeenth Century," *Economic History Review* n. s., 4:3 (1952), 300; Barbara Todd, "Property and a Woman's Place in Restoration London," *Women's History Review* 19:2 (2010), 188, and notes 65 and 66; Ann Carlos, Erin

by the mid-eighteenth century. Dickson found that in 1748 as many as 485, or 22.5 percent, of EIC shareholders were women, and that they held £527,734, or 16.5 percent, of stock.[18] So women rose from as little as 2 percent of EIC shareholders to almost a fourth between the 1680s and the 1740s.

Another of the joint-stock companies popular with investors during the Financial Revolution was the South Sea Company. It is difficult to reconstruct women's (and men's) holdings of South Sea stock since the ledgers have not survived. Julian Hoppit posits that women were only 6 percent of the investors in the initial South Sea Company subscription of 1720.[19] Anne Laurence points out that many more women ended up holding South Sea stock because their government annuities (of which women were significant holders) were converted into South Sea stock under the debt-for-equity swap engineered by the South Sea Company and the British government. This may help explain why by 1723 women had risen to a much higher 20 percent of the holders of South Sea stock. They also owned 12 percent of the stock's value.[20] Women comprised an even higher percentage of holders of South Sea annuities as compared to stock holders. Carlos, Fletcher, and Neal have recently posited that as many as 30.93 percent of South Sea Annuity holders were women during the period 1719–23.[21] By the mid-eighteenth century, the numbers of women still remained this high. Dickson estimated women comprised 31.8 percent of the holders of South Sea Old Annuities in 1744.[22] In sum, women investors made up nearly a third of annuity holders and at least a fifth of stockholders in the South Sea Company before 1750.

While the proportion of female investors in joint-stock companies was notable, the percentage of female shareholders in the Bank of England was higher from the start. Anne Murphy found that 153 of the 1,268 original subscribers to the Bank of England in 1694 were women. They comprised 12 percent of the subscribers and invested £71,975 out of £1.2 million, or 6 percent, of the initial capital. Women as a group subscribed a bit less money than gentlemen and retailers, but more than professionals, manufacturers, or tradesmen. In the 1690s women rose to 15.36 percent of the Bank's shareholders and by the early 1720s, they made up 17.26 percent.[23] Dickson found

Fletcher, and Larry Neal, "Share Portfolios in the early years of financial capitalism: London, 1690–1730," *Economic History Review* 68:2 (2015), 588, Table 3, 589, Table 5.

[18] Dickson, *Financial Revolution*, 298, Table 43.

[19] Julian Hoppit, "The myths of the South Sea Bubble," *Transactions of the Royal Historical Society* 6th series, 12 (2002), 150; Dickson, *Financial Revolution*, 282.

[20] Anne Laurence, "Women, banks and the securities market in early eighteenth-century England," in her *Women and their Money*, 47; Dickson, *Financial Revolution*, 282, Table 38.

[21] Carlos, Fletcher, and Neal, "Share Portfolios," 589, Table 5.

[22] Dickson, *Financial Revolution*, 298, Table 43.

[23] Anne Murphy, "Dealing with Uncertainty: Managing Personal Investment," 208, Table 1; Carlos, Fletcher, and Neal, "Share Portfolios," 589, Table 5.

that women comprised 20.7 percent of Bank shareholders in 1724 and that the number of women rose again to 25.4 percent by 1753.[24] So between the 1690s and 1750s, women, as a percentage of Bank of England shareholders, consistently rose from 12 to 25 percent.

Women also made up a consistently high percentage of investors in the State lotteries, loans, and annuities established to fund the national debt. Barbara Todd has researched some of the earliest (albeit indirect) female lenders, the holders of the so-called "Bankers Annuities." These were individuals who deposited money with goldsmiths in the 1660s and '70s, which these early bankers in turn loaned out to the government. Charles II stopped payment on these loans in 1671 but an agreement was worked out in 1677. The lenders would receive a 6 percent annuity in perpetuity and thus according to Todd became "holders of the first long-term English government debt." She found that some 300 women were among these "Banker Annuitants." Examining the customers of one banker, Sir Robert Vyner, Todd found that 124 out of 731 (or 17 percent) of those who took these annuities were women.[25] This shows that even before the 1690s, the critical beginning decade of the Financial Revolution, women comprised almost one fifth of the government creditors.

Women investors in government funds continued to make up at least 17 percent of creditors and sometimes rose to over a third, or 34 percent. Dickson found that 34.7 percent of investors in the 5% Annuities of 1717 were women, as were 21.3 percent of investors in the 14% Annuities of 1719. A few decades later, in 1748, 17.2 percent of holders of 4% Government Stock (which had originated as loans to the government) were women as well.[26] A. C. Carter found similar figures for the mid-eighteenth century. For instance, women comprised 17.84 percent of the buyers of Consols (or Consolidated Annuities) in 1755.[27] Thus, women consistently comprised between 17 and 34 percent of government creditors in the first seventy-five years of the Financial Revolution.

This snapshot of the number and percentage of women investors illustrates that female creditors were present in modest numbers from the beginning years of the Financial Revolution. By the turn of the eighteenth century women were regularly comprising 10–20 percent of public investors. And when it came to bonds and annuities the percentage of women was even higher, near one third. This was also true for government funds and lotteries,

---

[24] Dickson, *Financial Revolution*, 282, Table 38; 298, Table 43.

[25] Barbara J. Todd, "Fiscal Citizens: Female Investors in Public Finance before the South Sea Bubble," in Sigrun Haude and Melinda S. Zook, eds., *Challenging Orthodoxies: The Social and Cultural Worlds of Early Modern Women* (Farnham, Surrey: Ashgate, 2014), 60.

[26] Dickson, *Financial Revolution*, 282, Table 38; 298, Table 43.

[27] A. C. Carter, *Getting, Spending, and Investing in early modern Times* (Assen, Netherlands: Van Gorcum, 1975), 68, Table II.

where women regularly formed between a fifth and a third of government creditors. And even the proportion of women investing in corporations gradually grew until by the mid-eighteenth century, a quarter of investors in many companies were female.

1.1. TYPES OF INVESTMENTS AVAILABLE DURING THE FINANCIAL REVOLUTION

The options for women who wanted to invest capital in public securities increased exponentially from the 1690s onward. One way to gauge the opportunities available to a female investor is to examine the list of stocks commonly included in the newspapers of the time. For instance, in 1696 the *Post Boy* listed the following investment options: "Actions of the East-India Company is now sold for 47 l. per share, the Royal African 14 l. The Hudson's Bay 100 l., The Royal [sic] Bank of England 64 l. Blank Million Ticketts 6 l. 5s. Benefit Million tickets of 10 l. per ann. Million Bank 46 l. Orphans Fund 55 l. and Orphans Credit in the C[h]amber of London 57 l. per share."[28] While this entry might be somewhat undecipherable to us today, it is a list of the stocks and securities that were publicly traded in the 1690s, along with their share prices. According to the *Post Boy* a would-be female investor could buy shares (or actions) in the East India, Hudson's Bay, and Royal African companies. These joint-stock companies all engaged in overseas trade. The East India Company was one of the earliest joint-stock companies to receive a charter from the monarch as well as a monopoly on trade. Chartered in 1600 by Queen Elizabeth, by the end of the seventeenth century, the company was focused on profits it could reap in trade with India. The Hudson's Bay Company was incorporated in 1670 and given a monopoly over the fur trade in the Hudson Bay region of present-day Canada. The Royal African Company was chartered in 1672 and received a monopoly over English trade to West Africa. Although its monopoly ended in 1698, the company continued to trade slaves in the eighteenth century.[29] Shares were also available in the newly established Bank of England (mistakenly called "Royal" in this newspaper, but not usually referred to as such). The Bank was founded two years

---

[28] *Post Boy*, August 1, 1696. 17th and 18th Century Burney Collection Newspapers <www.galegroup.com> (accessed October 2005).

[29] For the history of English joint-stock companies, see W. R. Scott, *The Constitution and Finance of English, Scottish, and Irish Joint-Stock Companies to 1720*, vols. 1–3 (Cambridge: Cambridge University Press, 1911). For shareholders in the companies, see K. G. Davies, "Joint-Stock Investment," 300; Ann M. Carlos, Jennifer Key, and Jill L. Dupree, "Learning and the Creation of Stock-Market Institutions: Evidence from the Royal African and Hudson's Bay Companies, 1670–1700," *The Journal of Economic History* 58:2 (1998): 318–44.

earlier, in 1694, as a shareholder (rather than a deposit) bank. Its purpose was to lend money, primarily to the English government. It quickly proved a popular investment. In addition to the Bank, the *Post Boy*'s stock listing mentioned tickets in the Million Adventure. This was the first government or state lottery. Tickets sometimes drew prizes, or "benefits," or came up "blank," meaning the investor would receive back the purchase price plus 10 percent interest over sixteen years.[30] In 1695 the subscribers to this lottery established the Million Bank to handle their money. The last listing was the Orphan's Fund. This was a fund set up in 1694 to pay back the orphaned minors of London freemen whose legacies had been lodged in London's Court of Orphans. The City had raided the orphans' legacies for municipal expenses, so an Act of Parliament established the fund. Shares in the fund were publicly traded as stock throughout the eighteenth century.[31] The seven investments listed in the 1696 issue of the *Post Boy* provide a snapshot of the public investment opportunities available to women with capital to lend out in the late seventeenth century.

In the mid-1690s the *Post Boy* listed the trading prices for a mere seven investments, but the number of options rose considerably over the next twenty-five years. In 1721 the *Post Boy* recorded the previous day's prices for thirteen investments, double the number in the 1690s. Public investments now included South Sea Company, Bank of England, and East India Company stock, East India bonds, South Sea bonds, [Royal] African stock, Insurance on ships, London [Assurance] shares, York Buildings Company stock, Lottery Annuities, Army Debentures, Sword-Blade shares, and State Lottery Tickets.[32] Some of these investments were similar to what was available in 1696, including the East India and Royal African Company stocks, Bank of England shares, and State Lottery tickets. But more options were now available for the woman interested in public investment. There were more corporations publicly trading stock, including the infamous Sword-Blade and South Sea Companies. The former was established as a joint-stock company in 1691 for domestic manufacture of hollow sword blades. Around 1703 a group of London businessmen purchased the company for its corporate charter and tried their hand at other ventures, including land deals, mortgages, and banking. The South Sea Company was established in 1711 with a monopoly to trade in the South Seas (or South America). Due to the War of Spanish Succession there was little hope of making money this way so the company proposed a debt equity swap in which they bought a portion of the government debt. Corruption led to the South Sea Bubble of 1720, but the company's stock continued to trade throughout the eighteenth century. In addition to these companies, in 1721

[30] Scott, *Constitution and Finance*, 275.
[31] Charles Carlton, *The Court of Orphans* (Leicester, 1974), chapter 3.
[32] *The Post Boy*, issue 5031, Oct. 17, 1721. Burney Collection (accessed October 2005).

a female investor could loan her capital to the London Assurance insurance company (incorporated in an Act of 1719), and the York Buildings Company. The latter was established during the Restoration to pump water from the Thames and was incorporated in 1691. Along with these company stocks, the *Post Boy* listed a number of bonds in 1721 (although they had been available in earlier years as well). Company bonds were debt securities that guaranteed an investor a return at a specified rate of interest, and, unlike stock, they had a defined maturity date. Bonds were less risky than stock but could be less profitable. Company bondholders were not shareholders in a corporation, rather they were creditors to it. The *Post Boy* also listed more government-related investments, including Lottery Annuities and Army Debentures. The former were state lotteries in which the government returned the investor's principal in the form of an annuity. The latter were short- and long-term debt instruments issued by the military to borrow money. Debentures could be traded and like bonds were risk free. These were the many options available to would-be female investors in 1721.

By the mid-eighteenth century the public investment opportunities listed in the newspapers had increased by another third. The January 19, 1739 issue of the *Daily Gazetteer* recorded the trading prices of stocks and securities at the bottom of the middle column on the front page. This and the bottom right had emerged as common positions for stock price listings. The 1739 newspaper included prices for twenty-one investments including Bank of England, East India, and South Sea stock, South Sea Old and New Annuities, 3% government annuities, the 7% Loan and 5% [Emperor's] Loan, Royal Assurance, London Assurance, and [Royal] African stock, [East] India Bonds, Prem[ium] South Sea bonds, New Bank Circulation, Salt Tallies, Prem[ium] English Copper and Welsh Copper shares, 3½% Exchequer Orders, 6% Prem., 3% Prem, and Million Bank shares.[33] Although more numerous, these investment options primarily related to new companies (such as the Royal Exchange Assurance, another insurance company established in 1720, and the English and Welsh copper companies, both chartered in the 1690s to smelt copper); new types of investments in those companies (South Sea annuities); further forms of government debt (Salt Tallies, 3½% Exchequer Orders); or foreign loans (the Emperor's Loan, which was a 7 percent loan to the Holy Roman Emperor in 1705 during the War of Spanish Succession; many British people subscribed).[34] Also appearing in this listing were the popular South Sea Annuities, which came in the wake of the Bubble. The Company reconverted half of its equity into perpetual annuities earning a guaranteed interest rate of

---

[33] *Daily Gazetteer*, issue 794, January 19, 1738. Burney Collection (accessed October 2005).
[34] *Remarks on the Preliminary Articles of Peace: As They Were Lately Transmitted to Us from the Hague... To which are Subjoined, Some Observations Concerning the Payment of the Late Emperor's Loan*, vol. 12 (L, 1713).

5 percent. Another option listed in 1739 (although available since the Restoration) were Exchequer-issued tallies, orders, and bills.[35] These government loans were secured by customs and duties, thus the tallies secured by duties on salt in the 1690s. Tallies had been used since the Middle Ages, but being wooden sticks they were not suitable for currency. Orders, which were first issued in 1667, became a state-issued form of paper money. Three and a half percent interest was guaranteed on the Exchequer Orders listed here, but these orders also circulated as currency.

The listings of publicly traded stocks and shares in the English press reveal that an investor during the first fifty years of the Financial Revolution had a growing number of options available to her. These options can be summed up as stock and bonds in joint-stock corporations, shares in the Bank of England, and various forms of investment in the government debt, including lotteries, short- and long-term loans, and annuities. How did a would-be investor choose from among these options and where did they get their information? The remainder of this chapter will outline the skills and knowledge needed by women who wanted to invest in these public options.

1.2. LEARNING TO INVEST

How did women in seventeenth- and early eighteenth-century England learn to invest? As we have seen with the lists of stock prices in newspapers such as the *Post Boy*, one of the primary sources of information for would-be investors was the burgeoning London press. Newspapers provided all sorts of information for investors, including names of stocks and securities, the prices at which they traded, as well as notices on where and when investors could buy or transfer stocks and obtain their dividend and interest payments. For example, in 1723 the directors of the Million Bank put in an announcement "that the Transfer-Books will be shut on Friday the 21st instant, till Thursday the 4th of July next, and a General Meeting of the Proprietors will be held on Wednesday the 3rd of July next, in order for an Election of 14 Directors for the Year ensuing, which will be made at their House in Nag's Head Court in Grace-Church-Street, London..." From this announcement, a female investor would learn that she could not buy or sell Million Bank shares between 21 June and 4 July, and that if she held the requisite minimum of shares that allowed her to vote, when and where she could attend or send her proxy vote to the corporation's general meeting.[36] In March 1720 the *London*

---

[35] Richard Richards, *The Early History of Banking in England* (London: Routledge, reprint 2012), 58–60.

[36] *Daily Courant*, issue 6753, Jun. 13, 1723. Burney Collection (accessed October 2008).

Journal noted "On Monday they began to pay the Interest due at Michaelmas last, on the several Orders in the Lottery for Fourteen Hundred Thousand Pound, for 1714." And "On Tuesday the East-India Company began to pay their Dividend."[37] These announcements let a reader know when they could collect interest and dividends, the profits for which a woman invested. Announcements such as this provided any literate female investor with much of the information she required just by perusing the newspaper.

We know that women investors read these papers. For instance, Elizabeth Freke paid to receive several newspapers at her residence and she recorded current political events taken out of the *London Gazette* and the *Post Boy* in her remembrances.[38] Elizabeth was also related to John Freke, the publisher of *Freke's Prices of Stock, etc.* in the years 1714–22, so she may have had another way to glean financial information. An earlier counterpart to Freke's publication was John Castaing's *Course of the Exchange*, which began publication in the 1690s. It was taken over by his children in the eighteenth century, including his daughter Arabella who was involved with the stock-listing publication until the 1770s.[39] Another paper, *The British Mercury*, was published by the Sun Fire Office insurance company during the years 1710–15. The paper was full of news about "trade and business" including stock prices and exchequer loans. The company delivered free issues to shops, taverns, and coffeehouses, but policyholders also received the paper. Natasha Glaisyer has found that among the 2,450 subscribers to the paper in December 1710, 138 were women; and this number went up to 213 women out of 3,295 policyholders in 1714. This means that about 6 percent of those who had a copy of *The British Mercury* delivered to their homes were female—and this does not account for those women who may have read the paper even though it was delivered to a male family member or acquaintance.[40]

While women could access financial information in print, they could also do so in person. The lace trader turned investor, Hester Pinney, provides an example of how gender did not keep a woman from the sites of financial exchange, such as coffeehouses, the Exchequer, the Bank of England, or South Sea House. In 1701 her brother Nathaniel asked Hester to deliver some papers for him. "I presume you know the coffeehouse about the Exchange wherein the Nevis Captain's use . . . " wrote Nathaniel. Of course, Hester had worked in the nearby Royal Exchange and her family were involved in West Indian ventures, but it is notable that Nathaniel had no compunction about sending a

---

[37] *The London Journal*, issue 84, Mar. 3, 1720. Burney Collection (accessed October 2005).

[38] Raymond A. Anselment, *The Remembrances of Elizabeth Freke, 1671–1714*, Camden Fifth Series vol. 18 (Cambridge University Press/Royal Historical Society, 2001), 207.

[39] James Raven, *Publishing Business in Eighteenth-Century England* (Woodbridge, Suffolk: Boydell and Brewer, 2014), 159–60.

[40] Natasha Glaisyer, *The Culture of Commerce 1660–1720* (Woodbridge, Suffolk: Boydell and Brewer, 2006), 156–61.

woman into the coffeehouse to conduct business. In the 1710s Hester was collecting payments from the Exchequer and the East India Company for her brother. She did so in person, as a 1719 letter from Nathaniel apologized for sending papers separately and causing her "a separate journey to Westminster," where the Exchequer was located.[41] In the throes of South Sea stock mania, Nathaniel wrote to Hester saying he wanted her to sell an annuity to Mr. Colbrooke [the banker] in Threadneedle St. and he begged her "to go into the City and talk with Mr. Colbrooke." In 1730, Hester's agent D. Stanley informed her he had bought £600 Bank stock at the price of £144 1s. 8d. and "it to be delivered to you at the Bank of England on Wednesday next at 11 clock where I would desire you to be at the time in which you will oblige your humble servant." He expected Hester to show up in person to sign off on the transfer in the Bank's books.[42] Hester Pinney personally traversed the majority of the London sites of the Financial Revolution. As we will see in the following chapters she was not alone in her access as a female investor.

In addition to knowing where to go for financial news, women needed other skills to aid them in sound investing. In order to keep track of their portfolios of stocks and shares, compare investments, and make financial decisions a woman needed some level of mathematical proficiency. All that was really needed was basic arithmetic, something in which urban, middling, and elite women gained instruction from the 1680s onward. For instance, we know that in the 1690s women were teaching arithmetic to girls in London. One, Elizabeth Penniston, had a trade card made advertising her "Maidens Writing-School" where both young ladies and gentlemen could learn "fair writing, Arithmetick and True Spelling of English." Elizabeth Beane was another "Mistress in the Art of Writing" who also taught arithmetic.[43] The exercise book for one of Elizabeth Beane's students, Sarah Cole, has survived and is an excellent source for illustrating the mathematical competency of a woman in late seventeenth-century London.[44] Sarah Cole's exercise book is a comprehensive, 121-page tutorial on basic arithmetic. It includes sections on addition, subtraction, multiplication, division, and some algebra. It is significant that the majority of the examples and word problems focused on arithmetic and money and that Cole provided a definition of arithmetic based in accounting. One of her addition problems concerned a loan between a creditor and debtor and a subtraction problem dealt with moneylending. Cole's book also included examples of foreign monetary exchange and how to calculate interest. What is

[41] University of Bristol (hereafter UB), Special Collections, DM 58, Pinney Papers, Box 3, folder II.

[42] UB, DM 58, Pinney Papers, Box 3, folder II, and Box 2, folder XII.

[43] Laura Lunger Knoppers, ed., *The Cambridge Companion to Early Modern Women's Writing* (Cambridge: Cambridge University Press, 2009), 25.

[44] Folger Shakespeare Library, V.b.292, Sarah Cole's Arithmetic Exercise Book, 1685. I would like to thank Georgiana Ziegler for recommending this source to me.

striking about the arithmetic in Sarah Cole's exercise book is that it is presented as an applied discipline for financial purposes.[45] Cole was not alone. Other women's exercise books from the late seventeenth and eighteenth centuries also include exercises in adding, subtracting, and multiplying monetary sums, computing interest rates, and keeping accounts.[46]

Arithmetic instruction extended beyond the London daughters of tradesmen and merchants. For example, in 1702 the Scots gentlewoman Grisell Baillie, who was a proficient accountant and investor herself, recorded payments to a master for instructing her daughters in arithmetic. A decade later she paid a Mr. McGie to teach the girls bookkeeping.[47] In the mid-eighteenth century an elite woman like Mary Wortley Montagu continued to extol the education of young women in arithmetic. In a letter dated 1753, Montagu wrote to her sister that she was "particularly pleased" to hear her sister's eldest daughter "is a good arithmetician." She added, "it is the best proof of understanding: the knowledge of numbers is one of the chief distinctions between us and the brutes." Here we see arithmetic transformed from a vocational skill for women to a signifier of enlightened female education in the mid-eighteenth century.[48]

If a woman was not able to take classes in arithmetic she might also teach herself with some of the handbooks increasingly published in the eighteenth century. For example, the *Female Tatler* advertised Thomas Lydal's, *The Accomptant's Assistant in Vulger and Decimal Arithmetic...Aimed at Revenue, Excise and Customs officers, but also for the recreation of gentlemen, and the use of merchants, bankers and tradesmen and schools.*[49] Although designed for men, the fact that the book was advertised in a female periodical meant that it was also aimed at women.

Another title advocating instruction in arithmetic for women, as well as supplying it, was *The Accomplish'd Housewife: Or, the Gentlewoman's Companion* (1745). The book first began with "Reflections on the Education of the Fair Sex" in which the author told her readers that "they will find in the subsequent Pages such a comprehensive though compendious System of Arithmetick, as will sufficiently answer all the Ends before-mention'd."[50]

[45] Sarah Cole's Arithmetic Exercise Book, 9, 17, 20, 35, 59.

[46] Examples include Nottinghamshire Archives, DD SR 212/38, Madam [Mary] Pratt's exercise book and Henry E. Huntington Library, Box 13, HE 63–70, Agnes Herbert's exercise books.

[47] Robert Scott-Moncrieff, ed., *The Household Book of Grisell Baillie*, Scottish History Society, 2nd series, vol. 1 (Edinburgh: Edinburgh University Press, 1911).

[48] Reginald Brimley Johnson, ed., *Letters from the Right Hon. Lady Mary Wortley Montagu 1709–1762* (London: J. M. Dent & sons, 1906), 412.

[49] *The Female Tatler* no. 6 (1709). Eighteenth Century Journals I, Adam Matthew Digital <www.amdigital.co.uk> (accessed July 2014).

[50] *The Accomplish'd Housewife: Or, the Gentlewoman's Companion* (L, 1745), 8. Eighteenth Century Collections Online (hereafter ECCO) <www.galegroup.com> (accessed October 2013).

Section four included "an easy introduction to the study of practical arithmetic." The author recommended, "After they have been taught as much Arithmetick as may suit their Age and Sex, (and a very moderate Proficiency therein will serve their Turn) that is to say, after they have run through the first four Rules, they then should proceed to the practical Part, and be shewn the Method of Stating an Account." Here we see arithmetic and accounting linked as skills appropriate for young women. Also appearing in the 1740s was *Arithmetic Made Familiar and easy to Gentleman and Ladies*.[51] The author John Newberry recommended arithmetic "to the Youth of both Sexes as an Attainment that will be of extreme Service to them almost in every Station of Life." He went on to address women in particular, "Even the Ladies themselves, who have generally the Care of the domestic Expences of a Family, ought therefore to have a proper Share of this useful Accomplishment." Newberry tied numeracy for women to household budgeting and accounting.

Women's skill in arithmetic is also well evidenced by the content of the *Ladies Diary, or Woman's Almanac*. This publication did not necessarily teach arithmetic but it certainly provided a platform for women to practice it. First appearing in 1704, the *Ladies Diary* began to regularly feature mathematical questions and puzzles in 1707. The editors posed the questions and women wrote in with the answers (although men also answered the questions which is most interesting since this was a publication directed at the ladies).[52]

These examples illustrate that early modern educational treatises and teachers linked arithmetic with accounting; both of which were necessary skills for the would-be investor. In England, accounting was a common skill for women from urban and trade households, as well as mercantile and professional households on up to genteel ones. Women were expected to be able to keep track of profits and losses and tabulate monetary amounts. Bookkeeping and accounting were requisite skills for the financial management of family households, businesses, and estates.[53] The necessity of accounting

---

[51] *Arithmetic Made Familiar and easy to Gentleman and Ladies, Being the Second Volume of the Circle of the sciences, etc.* 2d ed., (L, 1748). ECCO (accessed November 2013).

[52] Geoffrey Howson, *A Historical of Mathematics Education in England* (Cambridge: Cambridge University Press, 1982), 69–71; T. Perl, "The Ladies Diary or Woman's Almanack 1707–1841" *Historia Mathematica* 6 (1979), 36–53; Joe Albree and Scott H. Brown, "A valuable monument of mathematical genius': The Ladies Diary (1704–1840)." *Historia Mathematica* 36:1 (2009): 10–47.

[53] While historians have studied women's trade and household accounts, there is not yet much research on accounts kept by women of their stock investments. Judith Spicksley has produced an edition of the business and household accounts of the single gentlewoman, Joyce Jeffries. The accounts are extant for 1638–48 and include Jeffries's "receipts of rents, annuities and interest moneys" which she obtained by private money lending. As such, the accounts are exceptional for recording the investments of an early seventeenth-century woman. Judith Spicksley, ed., *The Business and Household Accounts of Joyce Jeffreys: Spinster of Hereford, 1638-1648* (The British Academy/Oxford University Press, 2012). Margaret Hunt has also noted early modern Englishwomen's skill in accounting. Hunt writes about the motivations for accounting and sees accounting as part of the Enlightenment project of ordering and

skills for urban women is reflected in the 1678 pamphlet, *Advice to the Women and Maidens of London.*[54] The pamphlet's subtitle continues:

> shewing, that instead of their usual pastime, and education in needlework...it were far more necessary and profitable to apply themselves to the right under-standing and practice of the method of keeping books of account: whereby, Either Single, Or Married, They may know their Estates, Carry on their Trades, and avoid the danger of a Helpless and Farlorn Condition, Incident to Widows...

This illuminating pamphlet was addressed to women by one of their sex. Whether the author was female, as she claimed, or male, it is significant that s/he advocated for female education in accounting.[55]

The author of *Advice to the Women* addressed directly whether accounting was suitable for women: "Methinks now the objection may be this art is too high and mysterious for the weaker sex...it will make them proud: Women had better keep to their Needle-work..." But s/he argues that having herself practiced both accounts and needlework "I never found the *Masculine* Art harder or more difficult than the *effeminate* achievements of Lace-making, gum work, or the like..." After this preamble, the author belies the notion that accounting was a masculine endeavor by addressing the next pages to the rudiments of account keeping for "gentlewomen." As a good way to under-stand bookkeeping, the author urges women to "keep a fair account of receipts and payments of Money, or Cash book" and to enter them into a book daily "fair without blotting." S/he then provides an example of a monthly expense account that includes writing out the items purchased, or paid for, as well as numerically stating the monetary amounts paid. The monetary amounts from the cashbook are then copied into a second book of accounts "wherein I do only set the Sum, and not recite for what" (so what starts out as notes becomes completely numeric). The author says that if parents train up their children in household accounts they will be "handy in Accounts of greater Moment"; in other words, business or estate accounts.

In the early 1700s handbooks for accounting were regularly being pub-lished. Roger North's *The Gentleman Accomptant; or, An Essay to unfold the Mystery of Accompts* (1714) was one of the first manuals to aim itself at a genteel and noble audience, rather than a mercantile one. Section IV of

---

controlling; in this case, the numbers on the page. She acknowledges that women in families of business also promoted accounting. Margaret Hunt, "Time Management, Writing and Account-ing in the Eighteenth-Century English Trading Family: A Bourgeois Enlightenment," *Business and Economic History*, 2d series, vol. 18 (1989), 150–9.

[54] *Advice to the Women and Maidens of London* (L, 1678) Early English Books Online. <eebo.chadwyck.com> (accessed August 2013).

[55] *Advice to the Women and Maidens of London* was sometimes bound with Stephen Monteague's *Debtor and Creditor*, which has led some to conjecture he was the author. Glaisyer, *Culture of Commerce*, 132.

North's manual was particularly useful for investors, since it focused on banks and trading companies and Section V dealt with "Stocks, and Stock Jobbing; the Frauds therein detected." This manual made a direct connection between account keeping and investing.[56] North helpfully included examples of accounts with interest owed on bond (or loan), bills received from Child the banker, and the purchase of new East India Company stock. An Account of "all the Debts and Credits at Interest" follows, featuring loans on bond and mortgages. A balance of the account is also included, which profitably records credits exceeding debts.[57] Such a book would have modeled for the would-be investor how to account for investments in stocks, annuities, and other types of private loans.

Also aimed at the gentry and nobility, but more explicitly at women as well as men, was Alexander Brodie's *A New and Easy Method of Book-keeping, or Instructions for a Methodical keeping of Merchants Accompts* (1722).[58] The Scotsman emphasized that for those unacquainted with bookkeeping he has included both rules and examples and has gone to "the Trouble and Expence of having the Examples engrav'd by good Artists, so that they become a written Pattern to be followed by all Beginners . . ." Brodie distinguished his book from other manuals on accounting by saying his rules were "fewer, plainer, and easier."[59]

Brodie's tutorial on account keeping would have been particularly useful for a female investor looking to learn how to keep accounts to record her investments. He instructed his reader in Rule 6 for Book-Keeping that "when you lend Money at Interest, make the Borrower, viz. Andrew Johnston Debtor to Cash, for Principal at the lending, and you need to Create an Account of Profit and Loss till the Interest is received."[60] Many of his examples explicitly dealt with stocks. Brodie says that he included them "to shew the great Advantages were got by that Way of Dealing, while the South-Sea Company, and other Stocks were on the rising Credit; and the vast Losses many sustained by grasping too eagerly without a thorough Knowledge of such Affairs . . ." Here Brodie linked knowledge of accounting to wise investing. His example highlights someone who did well in the South Sea Bubble, cashing in stock for £2,010 and reinvesting it in other stocks and bonds. Brodie's model of a waste book also includes most of the common investments held by women in the period, including entries for purchases of Royal Exchange Assurance Stock, South Sea stock, lottery tickets, London Assurance stock, and South Sea bonds. Brodie's example of a Journal included the buying

---

[56] *The Gentleman Accomptant: or An Essay to unfold the Mystery of Accompts* (L, 1714). ECCO. Accessed October 2013.

[57] *The Gentleman Accomptant*, 62–4.

[58] Alexander Brodie, *A New and Easy Method of Book-keeping, or Instructions for a Methodical keeping of Merchants Accompts* (L, 1722). ECCO. Accessed October 2013.

[59] Brodie, iv.   [60] Brodie, 8.

and selling of various stocks and Malt Lottery tickets in 1721, as well as noting the payment of brokerage fees for these transactions to a broker. Although aimed at the beginner, Brodie's accounting in Ledger B of his South Sea investments was quite complex (with separate sub-columns for stock purchased in different subscriptions and for bonds). Perhaps he was showing off a bit.[61]

The last few pages of Brodie's book include an address to the nobility and gentry noting how "book-keeping might be useful to Persons of all Ranks." Significantly, Brodie thought that the elite of both sexes might engage in accounting. He says "the Whole is so easy, and entertaining, that I dare recommend the Practice thereof to all Ladies and Gentlewomen, who delight in a good Œconomy in the management of their Household, or Family Affairs... "[62] The few examples that Brodie includes focus on rents and interest, the two mainstays of elite incomes, the latter coming from investments.

Brodie was not the only male instructor who thought accounting suitable for women. For instance, "J. Maddux, Writing-master and Accomptant, at the Golden Hand and Pen" advertised his classes to both "Gentlemen and Ladies [who could be] taught Abroad, Or privately at Home, at any Hour." Maddux was willing to teach male and female pupils writing, arithmetic, merchant's accounts, or "Book-keeping after the Italian Manner."[63] Edward Hatton's *The Merchant Magazine* also included sections on arithmetic, accounting, and bookkeeping. The Folger Shakespeare Library's copy of the 1707 edition has the name of Elizabeth Owen inscribed in it; perhaps a sign of ownership, but certainly a sign of engagement with this financial text.[64] In the 1740s appeared *The universal library of trade and commerce; or, a general magazine for gentlemen, ladies, merchants, tradesmen, and schoolmasters ... or the education of youth of either sex...* [65] The author specifically addressed his book to a mixed gender audience, thinking that ladies as well as young women might need these skills. This lengthy textbook included sections on adding up money, addition, subtraction, multiplication and division, decimal arithmetic, and compound interest.

Other guidebooks were specifically geared to investment, providing an individual with the skills and knowledge to assess and manage their investments. Useful to a woman who invested in stocks to maintain herself were two books by Richard Hayes. The first was *The Money'd Man's Guide: Or, the Purchaser's Pocket Companion. Shewing, at Sight, What Interest is made by Money laid out in Companies Stocks, or any other Publick funds; and*

---

[61] Brodie, part II, 6, 7, 14, Journal B, p. 3, Ledger B.   [62] Brodie.

[63] *General Advertiser* Oct. 25, 1751. Burney Collection. <www.galegroup.com> (accessed February 2011).

[64] Glaisyer, *Culture of Commerce*, 136.

[65] *The universal library of trade and commerce* (L, 1747). ECCO (accessed October 2013).

T H E

BROKER'S BREVIAT,

Whereby to caſt up

Stocks, Bonds, Annuities, any Number of Shares, and Lottery-Tickets, Premiums, Brokerage, Commiſſions, Diſcounts, &c. with Diſpatch.

A L S O

An Annuity upon any ſingle Life is valued, &c. The Profits made by Money laid out on any of the above Securities are there ſhewn at Sight.

To which are added,

Some curious TABLES, ſhewing the Intereſt due upon Bonds for any Number of Months and Days, at 3, 3 ½, and 4 *per Cent.*

By *R. HAYES*, Author of *Intereſt at One View.*

L O N D O N:

Printed for W. MEADOWS, at the *Angel* in *Cornbill*
M.DCC.XXXIV.

Figure 1.1. Richard Hayes *The Broker's Breviat* (L, 1734).

also the present Value of any yearly Income … The Whole being made plain to the meanest Capacity (1726). Whether women counted as those among the "meanest capacity" is not made clear but the book certainly aimed itself at a non-elite audience. Hayes's preface states that this publication is for "the generality of Mankind," in particular the cautious investor, or "those who would willingly lay out their Money to the best advantage, and not precipitately or inadvertently hazard the Loss of it, by a chimerical Notion of an exorbitant Gain." Hayes begins his book explaining what business is transacted in Exchange-Alley. He cautions the reader that he can only teach them arithmetic, but as for "hazard and risque in Securities; that must be left entirely to a Man's own Judgment."

Hayes published his second guide, *The Broker's Breviat*, in 1734.[66] (See Figure 1.1.) The title page boasted instruction in how "to cast up Stocks, Bonds, Annuities, any Number of Shares, and Lottery-Tickets, Premiums, Brokerage, Commissions, Discounts, &c. with Dispatch." In addition, Hayes included information on how to calculate annuities, profits made by investing in securities, as well as tables to calculate interest on bonds (or loans). Hayes's epistle said that his book would be of "great use in dispatching of the other Businesses, belonging to those Things which are usually negotiated in Exchange-Alley…", in other words, stocks, shares, securities. For example, Hayes included an example of how to calculate what £700 of East India stock was worth at 158 and 7/8 percent (the answer was £1112 2s. 6d). Hayes's tables for casting up stocks referenced the most popular investments of the 1730s, such as "Bank, India, South-Sea Stock, and Annuities, Million-Bank, African, Royal and London Assurances, York-Buildings…" He also included addition tables for calculating shares "in the English or Welch Copper, Charitable Corporation &c." as well as the premiums on bonds and the value of lottery tickets. Hayes explained how dividends were declared by companies at half yearly General Courts and how to calculate "what Interest is made by Money laid out in this way [in these companies]." He provided a complicated example calculating profits on Bank of England Stock: "Suppose that the Bank divides for half a Year 2¾ per Cent upon the Capital that is 5½ per Cent. Per Annum, and the Stock is valued, or bought at 153. You [would like to] know what Interest is made by Money laid out in this Stock at the Price?" After some computation the answer of £3 11s. 10½ d. in annual interest is supplied. A modest sum, but the same math would be used for larger amounts.

Another source of information for women who wanted to keep accounts of their finances were the popular and annually issued pocket books (shown in Figure 1.2a.).

[66] Richard Hayes, *The Broker's Breviat* (L, 1734). ECCO. Accessed October 2008.

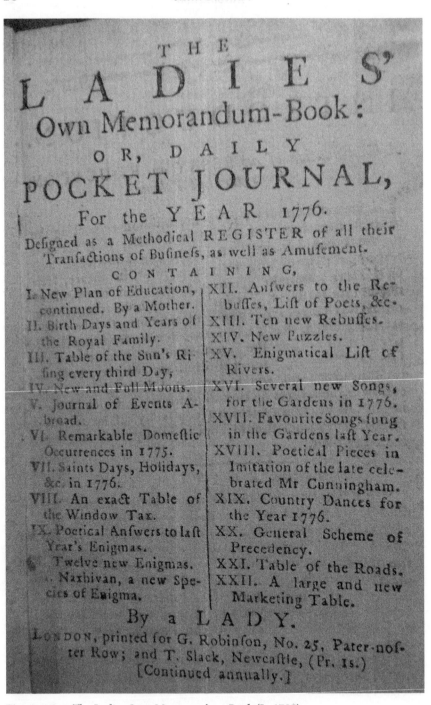

THE

LADIES'

Own Memorandum-Book:

OR, DAILY

POCKET JOURNAL,

For the YEAR 1776.

Defigned as a Methodical REGISTER of all their
Tranfactions of Bufinefs, as well as Amufement.

CONTAINING,

I. New Plan of Education, continued. By a Mother.
II. Birth Days and Years of the Royal Family.
III. Table of the Sun's Rifing every third Day,
IV. New and Full Moons.
V. Journal of Events Abroad.
VI. Remarkable Domeftic Occurrences in 1775.
VII. Saints Days, Holidays, &c. in 1776.
VIII. An exact Table of the Window Tax.
IX. Poetical Anfwers to laft Year's Enigmas.
Twelve new Enigmas.
Nazhivan, a new Species of Enigma.

XII. Anfwers to the Rebuffes, Lift of Poets, &c.
XIII. Ten new Rebuffes.
XIV. New Puzzles.
XV. Enigmatical Lift of Rivers.
XVI. Several new Songs, for the Gardens in 1776.
XVII. Favourite Songs fung in the Gardens laft Year.
XVIII. Poetical Pieces in Imitation of the late celebrated Mr Cunningham.
XIX. Country Dances for the Year 1776.
XX. General Scheme of Precedency.
XXI. Table of the Roads.
XXII. A large and new Marketing Table.

By a LADY.

LONDON, printed for G. Robinfon, No. 25, Pater-nofter Row; and T. Slack, Newcaftle, (Pr. 1s.)
[Continued annually.]

Figure 1.2a. *The Ladies Own Memorandum-Book* (L, 1785).

Photograph by Amy M. Froide, from the Collection of the Folger Shakespeare Library. M.a. 149.

An exact Account of the Days and Hours for buying and accepting or felling and transferring the feveral Stocks, or Government Securities, and receiving the Intereft or Dividends due thereon, at the Bank, India-Houfe, or South S a Houfe.

At the Bank in Threadneedle-ftreet, near the Exchange.

Bank-ftock is transferred, Tuef. Thurf and Friday. Dividends the eon are due at Lady-day and Michaelmas, old ftyle, viz. 5th of April and 10th of October.

Three per cent, reduced, Tuef. Wed. Thurf. and Friday. Dividends are due, 5th of April and 10th of October.

3 per cents. of 1726, Wed. and Sat.	Dividends due
3 per cents. confol. Tu Wed Th. Fr.	
3 1-half 1756, Tu. and Th.	} Jan. 5th, July 5th.
3 1 half 1758, Mon. Wed. and Fr.	
4 p r cent. confol. Tu. Wed. Th. Fri.	April 5th, Oct. 10th
4 per cent. 1777, Mon. Wed. Frid.	April 5th Oct. 10th
Long annuities, Wed. and Sat.	Jan. 5th, July 5th.

Hours of transfer are, from 11 to 1 on the days abovementioned, and for receiving the dividends, from 9 to 11, and 1 to 3, every day in the week, except Saturday afternoon.

South-Sea Houfe, Threadneedle-ftreet. Dvidends due South fea ftock, Mon. Wed and Fri. Jan. 5th, July 1 th Old annuities, Mon. Wed. and Fri. April 5 h, Oct. 10th New annuiti s, Tu. Thurf. and Sat. Jan. 5th, July 5th 3 per cents. 1751, Tuef. and Thurf. Jan. 5th, July 5th The hours for transferring are from 12 to 1 on the days abovementioned, and for receiving the d vidends, from 9 to 12, and 1 to 3, every day, except Saturday afternoon.

Eaft India Houfe, Leadenhall-ftreet. Dividends due. India-bonds, 3 per cent. April 5th. Oct. 10th India-ftock, Tuef. Thurf. and Sat. Jan. 5th, July 5th India-annuities, Mon. Wed. and Fr. April 5th, Oct. 10th Hours of transfer are, from 11 to 1, Tu. and Th. and 9 to 12. Sat. payment of dividends 9 to 12, and 3 to 5, every day.

N. B. No bufinefs done at either of the above places, on Sa-

Figure 1.2b. *The Ladies Own Memorandum-Book* (L, 1785).

Photograph by Amy M. Froide, from the Collection of the Folger Shakespeare Library. M.a. 149.

A January 1750 advertisement in the *London Evening Post* for the *The Lady's Compleat Pocket-Book* suggested that, "if presev'd [the pocket book] will enable any Lady to tell what business she has transacted...every Day during any Period of her Life."[67] In 1748 the *General Advertiser* ran an ad for "A Pocket Companion for the Purchasers of Stock in any of the Public Funds." Priced at 1s., such a portable and handy book included "Tables ready cast up, shewing the Value of any Parcel of Stock, whether above or below Par. Calculated for the Ease of Proprietors of the several Transferrable Stocks, in Buying, Selling, and Casting up Dividends."[68]

Pocket books devoted more space to accounting and investing over the eighteenth century. For example, the 1763 edition of *The Daily Journal, or The Gentleman's and Tradesman's Complete Annual Accompt-Book for the Pocket, or Desk* included fifty-two pages "properly rul'd for keeping an Account, in the easiest Manner, of all Monies Receiv'd, Paid, Lent, or Expended..." It also boasted sections devoted to "Tables of Interest, of Stock, and Transfers, Brokerage India Bonds..." and a "Table of the intrinsic Value per Cent. Of the Public Funds, and the Proportion they bear to each other, and to the Value of Landed Estates."[69] Figure 1.2b. shows similar information to what a would-be investor could read on the third page of the *Daily Journal*: "A Table, shewing the Amount of each Capital in the several transferable Stocks, the Days and Hours of transferring, and the Time of paying the Dividends."

Beginning with the Bank of England, the table listed what type of public investments could be bought and sold at the Bank, particularly noting government funds such as Consolidated Annuities, Reduced Annuities, and Long Annuities. Dates were included for transfer days and interest payment days as well as interest rates on these annuities.[70] For a female investor out and about in the City on financial business, a pocket book provided space for recording memoranda and accounts, as well as useful tables for calculating interest and information on where to go to conduct business. The examples discussed here illustrate that a female investor in eighteenth-century London had a multitude of print sources to consult for help and assistance in how, when, and where to invest her capital and how to collect and account for her profits. What she would do with this knowledge varied by individual as we shall see.

* * *

We know that women were public investors during the Financial Revolution and that they had the knowledge to engage in such investments. The

---

[67] *London Evening Post*, January 11–13, 1750. Burney Collection (accessed October 2005).

[68] *General Advertiser*, issue 4084, Dec. 1, 1747. Burney Collection (accessed October 2005).

[69] *The Daily Journal, or The Gentleman's and Tradesman's Complete Annual Accompt-Book* (L, 1763). ECCO (accessed October 2007).

[70] *The Daily Journal*, iii and iv.

individual chapters of this book will examine various women who illustrate specific investing behaviors and strategies and who put their capital into particular types of investments. Chapter 2 examines women who ventured their money in the private and State lotteries that were so popular and ubiquitous in England from the Restoration period on through the eighteenth century. Contemporaries recognized women's embrace of lotteries and began to characterize lottery players as dowry or husband hunters. In this way, the lottery became figured as a way for a woman to improve her fortune, not only in terms of money but of marriage and social position. Contemporary writers stereotyped female lottery players as young single women, old maids, or widows hoping to win a lottery prize that they could use to obtain the ultimate social prize—a husband. But over time, pamphlets discussing the lottery also came to recognize the lottery as a solution for women who needed to support or maintain themselves.

Chapter 3 examines what I call female "early adopters" of the Financial Revolution's new investment options. These were women who jumped eagerly into the world of public investing in the very first decades of the Financial Revolution, the 1680s and 1690s. This chapter presents three case studies. The first is Sarah Churchill, Duchess of Marlborough, well known for her prominent political role under Queen Anne, but less studied for her financial management. The Duchess managed one of the largest stock portfolios in seventeenth- and eighteenth-century England and thanks to her prudent financial dealings augmented the Marlborough fortune. The second case study focuses on the story of Martha Hutchins, who adapted to public investment as a way to maintain herself after her husband's business failed. Hutchins dipped her toe into the early stock market with the aid of a female broker. The last case study examines the financial accounting of Elizabeth Freke. Freke may be familiar to readers as a diarist but she also loaned money to the English government and invested in stocks during her marriage and widowhood. Due to her early start in investing, by the time she died in the 1710s she had already been a public investor for over four decades.

Chapter 4 explores the role of women as financial advisors and portfolio managers for their families. This chapter also shows how married women, despite their coverture, were able to invest for themselves and for their family members. This was due to a number of factors, including married women's separate property, which enabled women to invest their separate estates and their pin money, a legal system that had to play catch-up to the financial innovations of the time, and familial acceptance of married women investing. Husbands and families sometimes recognized that the women in their families were the most informed and adept investors. Rather than women turning over their money to male relatives to manage, in some families it was the reverse. Husbands, brothers, and nephews turned to their wives, sisters, and aunts for financial assistance and portfolio management. This chapter includes case studies of two women who invested for their families: Cassandra Willoughby, the eventual Duchess of Chandos, and the single gentlewoman, Mary Barwell. Both women augmented the fortunes of their male kin.

Chapter 5 focuses on how women utilized public investments as a way to fund their "retirement" or old age. Many never-married women and widows found shares in the Bank of England, and investments in the government debt, to be a boon for supporting themselves in their later years. Attracted by decent rates of return, security, and liquidity, women of the middling and genteel classes turned their savings over to the government, the Bank of England, and major corporations in return for guaranteed annuities, fixed rate bonds, and reliable stocks that paid out dividends and interest. These new financial investments served an important role in ensuring a comfortable retirement, especially for women without spouses. This chapter includes case studies of the widow Barbara Savile and her spinster daughter Gertrude Savile, as well as of the never-married sisters, Patty and Teresa Blount. These unmarried women enjoyed years of comfortable retirement thanks to their investment returns.

Chapter 6 examines women's relationship to risk during the Financial Revolution. Risk was by no means an entirely new phenomenon for women in the 1690s, rather it predated women's roles as pubic creditors. Moreover, public stocks and securities could be less risky for women than collecting revenue from rents and private loans. This chapter examines some of the risky scenarios the first forty years of the Financial Revolution presented for female investors. While the South Sea Bubble is one of the best-known examples of large-scale financial risk, this chapter explores less studied examples of fraudulent corporations such as the London Orphan's Fund, the Mine Adventurers Company, and the Charitable Corporation. The chapter concludes by showing that women were not always the victims of risk; sometimes they were the ones who committed fraud, forgery, and theft. Some women found agency, however illicit, in the risks of the early stock market.

Chapter 7 examines various types of financial agency exhibited by women who were public investors during the Financial Revolution. Women who inherited public stocks and securities exhibited one type of financial agency. Instead of being passive investors who merely collected dividends, heiresses managed and transformed inherited funds into stock portfolios of their own design. Other types of financial agency are exhibited by Hester Pinney, who began her adult life as a lace trader but then took her profits and invested them in the stock market. A case study of Pinney illustrates the financial agency of a woman who not only made and managed her own fortune, but who provided investment advice and assistance to friends and family, even serving as a financial agent for a man to whom she was unrelated. The chapter concludes by examining how women's participation in public investment translated into political agency. Some individual women used their capital to claim a political voice. Moreover, women investors as a group also engaged in what I term "financial patriotism." By investing in Britain and its commercial ventures, women contributed to the military, economic, and imperial success of the nation. As such, women, as much as men, were implicated in both the pros and cons of financial capitalism.

2

Playing the Lottery for Marriage and Profit

The English were lottery mad in the seventeenth and eighteenth centuries. In the seventeenth century private lotteries were popular among both genders and all classes. At the end of the century the English government hit on the idea of turning the fad for lotteries into a way to raise money to fund its wars. This ushered in over a century of State lotteries that not only offered prizes as did private lotteries, but also returned the adventurer's money with interest like a government bond. This chapter explores the relationship between women and both private and public lotteries. State lotteries appealed to unmarried and older female investors in particular because they were low-risk and offered secure returns, often in the form of annuities. In fiction there was also a clear cultural connection between unmarried women and the lottery. Pamphlets, broadsides, and ballads represented women, especially single ones, as playing the lottery to win a marriage portion or as lottery "prizes" for prospective husbands. Such schemes reveal the satirical association that would grow up between the presence of never-married women in the new investment economy and new concerns about surplus single women. In the later seventeenth century the numbers of women in England who never married were on the rise. Lotteries suggested a solution to the dilemmas of spinsterhood. Financial instruments such as State lottery tickets provided unmarried women, both single and widowed, with an investment by which they could maintain themselves. The Financial Revolution made available new investment options that aided single women and allowed them to survive economically on their own. However, it was this financial independence that seems to have generated the most cultural anxiety, and I posit, led to the fictional stress on marriage as the ultimate goal for women who won the lottery.

This chapter will begin with an overview of the lotteries in seventeenth- and eighteenth-century England. We will then examine the participation of women in both private and public lotteries. Women were common adventurers in private lotteries from the start and they quickly transferred their participation to the more investment-oriented State lotteries. The second part of the chapter will explore the cultural associations between lotteries, single women, and marriage. Fictional accounts represented the lottery as the answer to the unmarried woman's prayers, providing her with a marriage portion and presumably the status of a married woman. We will see that these fictional tropes bled back into reality as early modern women confided in their diaries and letters that they played the lottery in order to win a marriage portion.

*   *   *

Lotteries came to England via the continent as early as the mid-sixteenth century. France and Italy had already run a number of public and state lotteries by the time a woman, Queen Elizabeth I, authorized one in England in 1567. Standing lotteries were held in London while running or ring lotteries traveled amongst the larger towns such as York, Norwich, Exeter, Southampton, Oxford, and Cambridge. Lotteries seem to have been popular with never-married women from the start. Fortunately for historians, in the second half of the sixteenth century the practice of recording one's motivations for subscribing to the lottery was quite common, and it is this evidence that indicates the presence of single female adventurers. Subscribers commonly wrote "posies" (short mottoes or verses) on the counterfoils or receipts of their tickets so that they could be identified if drawn. For example, in 1567 Sibbel Cleyon purchased a lottery ticket for 2s. 1d. and wrote on her stub "I am a poor maiden and faine would marry, And the lacke of goods is the cause that I tarry." While lottery tickets could be relatively expensive for working women, some got around this by pooling their money to purchase a ticket. The ticket stub of Dorothie Hawes of Cheapside had the following words written on it: "We put in one lott, poor maydens we be ten: We pray God send us a good lotte, that all we may say Amen."[1] In the early years of private lotteries young and working single women figured regularly among those who ventured their money, and the intention at least for women like Cleyon was to win a dowry to enable them to marry.

Private lotteries continued across the early modern period, becoming increasingly common in the 1690s. As Anne Murphy notes, a "successful lottery required reasonably priced tickets, the promise of a large cash prize, a diverse network of contacts to facilitate the distribution of tickets, and some element of originality to attract the interest of the skeptical or the sensible." Private lotteries traded on spectacle; they attracted large crowds with drawings held in public spaces. And the more rare and scientific the machine that held the tickets to be drawn the better.[2]

[1] C. L' Estrange Ewen, *Lotteries and Sweepstakes* (London: Heath Cranton Ltd., 1932), 35–7, 42, 56–63, 84.
[2] Anne Murphy, "Lotteries in the 1690s: investment or gamble?" *Financial History Review* 12:2 (2005): 227–46, esp. 237.

Private lotteries were so successful that in the 1690s the English government adopted this model to raise money needed to fight its foreign wars.[3] Women easily transferred their loyalty from private to State lotteries and in the process transformed from gamblers to investors. These schemes proved so popular that there were twenty-eight State Lotteries between 1694 and 1750.[4] The first foray by the State into the lottery business was the Million Adventure. The government hired Thomas Neale, a government official who had successfully organized a private lottery in 1693. He copied a Venetian lottery of the time for the design of the tickets, subscription books, and drawings. Players paid £10 for a lottery ticket and were guaranteed an annuity of £1 for 16 years; in other words they received £16 on a £10 investment. And a few lucky winners received an additional prize, which ranged from £10 to £1,000. Because it combined a guaranteed income with the fun of a prize drawing, this hybrid of government bond and lottery was very popular. Murphy estimates tens of thousands of people invested in the Million Adventure and that this lottery "established an important connection between the investor of limited means and financial knowledge, and the state."[5] Good evidence for the reach of this lottery comes from the fact that even modest women of the middling sort who lived in the provinces invested in it. For instance, Mary Horner, a spinster from Bishops Waltham, a small town in Hampshire, died in 1698 with an estate worth £190 14s. 6d. She had invested £10 (or over 5 percent) of her estate in the Million Lottery.[6] Anne Murphy has also found that a significant percentage of the investors in the Million Lottery were female. Out of 212 players, 133 were men and 79 were women, meaning that 37 percent of lottery participants were women.[7] This is the highest proportion of female participation in a lottery from this time period and shows that women were active participants in lotteries from the very beginning of the Financial Revolution.

After the unsuccessful Malt Lottery of 1697, and a decade-long lull, the government turned to the State Lottery model again to raise money.[8] In 1711 the government ran the first Classis Lottery, a lottery divided into five sections or classes. Each class offered prizes of differing amounts, with the last, or fifth, class drawing the highest prizes. Malcolm Balen says this model in effect

---

[3] Bruce G. Carruthers, *City of Capital: Politics and Markets in the English Financial Revolution* (Princeton University Press, 1996), chapter four, esp. 127–30.

[4] Ewen, *Lotteries and Sweepstakes,* 163.

[5] Ewen, *Lotteries and Sweepstakes,* 127–33; Murphy, "Lotteries in the 1690s," 229–31.

[6] Hampshire Record Office, 1698 P 30/1–2, will of Mary Horner, spinster, 23 May 1698.

[7] Murphy, "Lotteries in the 1690s," 238.

[8] Only 1 per cent of the Malt Lottery tickets were sold, possibly due to that year's bad economic climate, but also perhaps due to relatively low prize amounts, and problems with repaying interest on the Million Adventure tickets. Georges Gallais-Hamonno and Christian Rietsch, "Learning by Doing: The Failure of the 1697 Malt Lottery-Loan," *Financial History Review* 20:3 (2013): 259–77.

created five lotteries instead of only one and helped generate excitement.[9] This government "loan lottery" guaranteed repayment of the principal or cost of the ticket at 6 percent interest. Contributors paid £100 and prizes ranged from £110 to £20,000. Such a high sum meant that only a certain class of women could participate until lottery brokers began to spring up in London. These retailers would buy lottery tickets, which usually started at £10 (although Classis tickets were £100), and divide them up into as much as 64ths (or 4s.) so that a much wider social spectrum could afford to participate. The largest prizewinner in the fourth Classis of the 1712 State Lottery was the single woman Susanna Barnes, of Grace Church St., All Hallows parish, London, who won £3,000. Since a widow, Margaret Williams, won the largest prize of £20,000 in that year's fifth Classis, it is apparent that unmarried female investors were common participants in the early Classis lotteries.[10]

Women remained consistent investors in the State lotteries during the eighteenth century, making up between a fifth and a third of investors. For instance, women comprised 34.7 percent of investors in the 5 percent Annuities lottery of 1717 and also infused 20.1 percent of the funds. Two years later, women made up 21.3 percent of the investors in the 14 percent Annuities lottery of 1719.[11] Women continued to comprise these same proportions of investors into the next two decades of the eighteenth century. They made up 18.4 percent of contributors to the 3 percent Annuities lottery loan of 1726 and 27.85 percent in the 3 percent Annuities lottery of 1731.[12] These lotteries appealed to women looking for a steady and sure income, especially single women and widows. And they were not a gamble. Even if a woman did not win a prize, over time she got her money back with interest.

Women could easily access information about both private and State lotteries in the English press. Lotteries frequently appeared in commercial, business advertisements. The range of private lotteries is apparent from the November 28, 1699 issue of the *Post Boy* which featured news from "the Office of the Wheel of Fortune." The paper provided information about the second or New Wheel of Fortune Lottery, the Leicester Lottery, the Land-Lottery, the 12d. Lottery with 5 Balls, also called the Nonsuch Lottery, and a proposal by Mrs. Peart to sell her husband's collection of paintings by lottery.[13] In the 1720s London newspapers even began to advertise foreign lotteries, evidently

[9] Malcolm Balen, *The Secret History of the South Sea Bubble* (Harper, 2003), 29.

[10] Carruthers, *City of Capital*, chapter eight, esp. 245–9, 140, 160, 162; Ewen, *Lotteries and Sweepstakes*, 140.

[11] P. G. M. Dickson, *The Financial Revolution in England: A Study in the Development of Public Credit, 1688–1756* (London: MacMillan, 1967), 282, Table 38.

[12] Bank of England Archives, AC 27/104, 3% Annuities, 1726, sample of A–C alphabet ledger; AC 27/131, 134, 3% Annuities, 1731, sample of A–C alphabet ledger.

[13] *Post Boy*, no. 725, Nov. 28, 1699. 17th and 18th Century Burney Collection Newspapers <www.galegroup.com> (accessed October 2008).

to satisfy the public's desire for lotteries and also because lottery brokers now abounded. In 1723 a newspaper reader could view advertisements for the Dutch, Utrecht, and Groningen lotteries.[14]

Information about the State lotteries also frequently ran in the newspapers. The *London Evening Post* for August 11, 1741 boasted multiple advertisements for that year's State lottery. These ads provided all sorts of information for the new or inexperienced investor. For instance, Jacob de Paiba, who he noted "in all former Lotteries has been one of the greatest Dealers, takes this publick way to acquaint his Friends, that he gives his Attendance daily at Garraway's Coffee-House in Exchange-Alley, from Nine in the Morning till Five in the Evening." He added that "Exchange-Alley being the known Centre for transacting of Lotteries, Adventurers may the better be inform'd of the true Market Price..." Right next to de Paiba's advertisement was a more visually striking one inserted by Francis Wilson. He advertised shares "such as Halves, Quarters, Eighths, and Sixteenths" which could be bought at his "oldest Lottery-Office, Charing-Cross." But most of Wilson's ad was taken up by a table listing the number of prizes and their amounts as a sort of teaser to whet any potential lottery investor's appetite. If this was not enough, both Wilson and de Paiba warned their customers that this lottery would be drawn sooner than previous ones and there were fewer tickets, so prospective investors needed to act fast.[15]

Obtaining and buying lottery tickets was quite straightforward for women. Some used an agent, like Lady Mary Campbell Coke who got her ticket by writing to her banker. But even Lady Mary sometimes bought lottery tickets herself. She recorded in her diary that when in town to run various errands she "laid out twenty pounds in a lottery ticket & a half: I bought it at a lottery Office where I happen'd to be, & ask'd the Man if he was lucky: he said he must esteem himself to be so, for he had married a Lady with a great fortune."[16] No one better from whom to buy a lottery ticket than a man lucky in the lottery of marriage.

Lottery office keepers accommodated women like Lady Mary who wanted to purchase their lottery tickets themselves. They catered to female venturers by advertising their discreet premises and helpful assistance. In 1743 Lowe and Berry noted that their State-Lottery Office, "is most conveniently situated from the Noise and Interruption of the Publick Streets, in Stationers-Alley, Ludgate-Street." The owners also touted that the "Register-Book will be kept in so Regular and Correct a Manner, that Gentlemen and Ladies who Register

---

[14] *Daily Courant*, issue 6753, June 13, 1723. Burney Collection (accessed October 2008).

[15] *London Evening Post*, August 11, 1741. Burney Collection (accessed October 2008).

[16] *The Letters and Journals of Lady Mary Coke*, vols. 1–4 (Edinburgh: David Douglas, 1889) October 1774, p. 415, *British & Irish Women Writers Online*. <www.galegroup.com> (accessed March 2006).

with him, may be assured, that for 6 d. each Ticket, they shall receive the most early Notice of their Success, either in Town or Country."[17] Similarly, at the Hanover Coffee House in Finch Lane, in Cornhill, Thomas Leekey advertised lottery tickets and chances of prizes for an elite clientele of men and women. "N.B. There not being at this Office any Numerical Book, all Gentlemen and Ladies may be treated with about their Affairs, and their Business dispatch'd, without the Interruption and Crowding they meet with at those Offices where Numerical Books are kept."[18] The popularity of the lottery with both men and women also comes across in this news item from the *Daily Gazetteer*: "Saturday last there was the greatest Concourse of both Sexes at the Original Lottery-Office kept by Mr. Wilson, at Craig's-court Charing Cross, to buy Lottery Tickets and Shares that has been known on the like Occasion; it is judged, that on that and the two preceding Days, he sold upwards of 2,000l. [in] Tickets."[19]

Lotteries provided opportunities for women beyond venturing their money. Women sold, made, brokered, and even stole lottery tickets. The State lottery in particular provided women with jobs. In 1710 the editor of the *Tatler* said he had recently been at Whitehall in "an Apartment contiguous to the *Banqueting-House,* where there were placed at Two long Tables a large Company of young Women, in decent and agreeable Habits, making up Tickets for the Lottery appointed by the Government."[20] Not only did these young women find work stitching lottery tickets, but so did the gentlewoman who supervised their work. Similarly, the Commissioners of the Lottery "appointed Mrs. Franks to be Housekeeper to the Lottery-Office, in the Room of Mrs. Gilbert, lately deceased."[21] Other women sold lottery tickets, including Mrs. Elizabeth Bell, Bookseller at the Cross-Keys and Bible in Cornhill, and Mrs. Oakes, at her Office in Three King Court, Lombard-Street.[22] An item from the *Daily Courant* for Aug. 8, 1717 illustrates how women also served as agents or brokers who handled lottery tickets. The newspaper reported that "...there was deposited several Lottery classes in the Hands of Mrs. Jane Appleyard, who kept a Toy-shop at Westminster-Hall, or in the Hands of her Father, Mr. Jonathan Appleyard...by Daniel Smith of the Fleet prison, for the said Appleyards to receive the Interest and to bring back the said Lottery Classes..." Jane Appleyard failed to return either the interest or the tickets to Smith and, as it turned out, absconded with them. The

[17] *London Daily Post and General Advertiser,* issue 2806, Saturday Nov. 12, 1743. Burney Collection (accessed October 2005).

[18] *Daily Journal,* issue 1788, Oct. 7, 1726. Burney Collection (accessed October 2008).

[19] *Daily Gazetteer,* issue 1395, Dec. 10, 1739. Burney Collection (accessed October 2008).

[20] *Tatler,* issue 170, May 9–10, 1710.

[21] *Daily Gazetteer,* issue 1300, Aug. 21, 1739. Burney Collection (accessed October 2008).

[22] *Daily Courant,* issue 6570, Nov. 10, 1722. Burney Collection (accessed October 2008).

advertisement listed all of the lottery ticket numbers (Smith had a total of twenty-eight tickets) and offered a reward for helping find them.[23] Jane Appleyard was either a professional or informal broker, assigned by Smith to collect his interest payments while he was in jail, but unfortunately for Smith, Appleyard was not an honest one. She was not alone in trying to illegally profit from the lottery. Jane Mower also thought to strike it rich in the lottery by stealing someone else's winnings. In 1715 she was tried at the Old Bailey for stealing twenty-eight tickets from the State lottery of 1710 that were valued at £224.[24] If Mower had succeeded she would definitely have hit the jackpot, since this was the annual income of a prosperous gentlewoman.

Turning back to more respectable female involvement with the lottery, evidence of women investing in the State lottery appears in many places. Women talked about lotteries when they wrote letters, noted lottery ticket purchases when they kept accounts, and even took out advertisements when they lost tickets. For instance, an advertisement from October 1720 announced that a lottery ticket in the name of Sarah Harding, ticket no. 90 in the 127th course, had been lost and if anyone returned it to a Mr. Smith, at Mr. Burton's cheesemonger in Covent Garden, they would receive a two guinea reward, no questions asked.[25] Announcements of lottery winners also reveal that players of the State lotteries were often female. In 1738 the *Daily Gazetteer* announced that the Bank of England had paid the £10,000 prize in the last Lottery to Robert Myre Esq. and he had paid "to the three Persons (to whom his Lady had given the Ticket to) their several Proportions therin;— which was half to Mrs. Olimpia de la Ferrette, Widow to the late Colonel de la Farette; one quarter to Mrs. Elizabeth Torin; and the other Quarter to Mrs. Magdalen Torin."[26] Another source identified the latter two women as "two maiden ladies of Throckmorton Street, Miss Elizabeth and Miss Magdalen Torin." Female winners also featured in one of the advertisements run by Hazard's Lottery Office in the *London Evening Post* for August 9, 1748. Hazard informed readers that Ticket No. 43,537 which drew a prize for "TEN THOUSAND POUNDS" was sold by his State Lottery Office. The ticket was divided in shares with "One Fourth to a Gentlewoman in Princes-Street, St. James's. One Fourth to a Gentlewoman in the Haymarket. One Fourth to a Gentleman's servant in Westminster. One Eighth to a Gentleman's Clerk in

[23] *Daily Courant*, issue 4930, Aug. 8, 1717. Burney Collection (accessed October 2008).
[24] *London Lives, 1690 to 1800—Crime, Poverty, and Social Policy in the Metropolis*, Old Bailey Proceedings, t17151207-40 <www.londonlives.org> (accessed November 2014).
[25] *London Lives*, LMSMPS501890095, Middlesex Sessions—Sessions Papers—Justices Working Documents, Oct. 1720 Advertisements. <www.londonlives.org> (accessed November 2014).
[26] The Torin family were French Huguenots in trade.

Bond-Street. And One Eighth to a Gentlewoman in Norfolk." So three (or four if the servant was female) of the five prizewinners were women, ranging from laboring to gentle status. A decade later, another advert from Hazard boasted he had sold ticket no. 25,990, which had won a £5,000 prize in the last lottery. Again women dominated the winners. Half a share of it went to "a Miss at Boarding-School" as well as a sixteenth each to a cook maid in St. James, a Lady near Golden Square, and a gentlewoman in the country (with the remaining 5/16 going to male winners).[27] Again these female winners were quite diverse in socio-economic status.

So far we have been looking at women's actual participation in both private and public lotteries. But women, especially single and widowed women, were also the main focus of the fictional portrayals of English lotteries in the seventeenth and eighteenth centuries. These fictional lotteries both provide support for women's common participation in lotteries but also suggest some of the motivations for their participation; that winning a lottery prize would allow them to marry or to economically maintain themselves. The association of women and lotteries in print started even before the Financial Revolution, sometime in the 1660s. This can be seen in the pamphlet *Fair Play In the Lottery, or, Mirth for Money. In several witty passages and conceits of Persons that came to the Lottery* (L, 1660) by E[dward] F[ord] Gent. The pamphlet included verses on the men and women who played Edward Ford's lottery at the Crown in Smithfield. Women adventurers figured in equal proportion to the male. They included a blind maid (who after drawing a blank, said fortune was as blind as she), a handsome seamstress, a cook's wife, a whore, an honest woman, several gentlewomen, two Ladies, and an old woman.[28] The verses indicate that this was a lottery in which the prizes were plate, with the gentlewoman winning a silver tankard and the honest woman a flagon. Female lottery players of the 1660s were figured as coming from a range of social positions and age groups. Evidently the lottery appealed to all.

As Anne Murphy has shown, the number of lotteries increased in the 1690s and the fictional accounts of lotteries followed suit. *The Wheel of Fortune: Or, Nothing for a Penny, Being Remarks on the drawing the Penny-Lottery* (L, 1698) noted women's participation as lottery players. The poem remarked that the Penny lottery had attracted all sorts, a "Croud,/Rich, Poor, and Proud,/From her Grace down to Susan and Nancy." High and low, the mob and gentry, come to see the lottery drawn. "Here Sarah and Moll/Sit with Richard and Paul." The winner of the Penny Lottery was also a woman.

[27] *Daily Gazetteer*, issue 794, Jan. 19, 1738; *London Evening Post*, issue 3241, August 9, 1748; *Public Advertiser*, Sept. 8, 1758, Issue 7438. Burney Collection Newspapers (accessed August 2005).
[28] The British Library (hereafter BL), E.1865.(2.) E[dward] F[ord] Gent., *Fair Play In the Lottery, or, Mirth for Money. In several witty passages and conceits of Persons that came to the Lottery* (L, 1660).

"The fair Mrs. Wise, Got the Fortunate prize./If *Post-boys*, and *Post-men* [the London newspapers], are true." Foreshadowing a theme that would be prominent in the lottery literature, the poet assumes that Mrs. Wise will use the prize to marry well. "This I am sure of, that she/May have you, him, or me.../ For a thousand pound Sterlin/Will make any Girl in/The Kingdom, succeed in her prayer..."[29]

This cultural association between women and lotteries continued in satire from the 1690s onward. *Diluvium Lachrymarum [Flood of tears]. A Review of the Fortunate & Unfortunate Adventurers. A Satyr in Burlesque, Upon the Famous Lottery, Set up in Freeman's Yard in Cornhill* appeared in 1694. This pamphlet, although satirical, was commenting on an actual lottery—Thomas Neale's private lottery already mentioned.[30] It was primarily a humorous list of the adventurers in the lottery. The author stresses the inclusive and varied nature of the lottery's participants: "No less than Fifty Thousand Tools, A jolly Crew of gaping Fools; Of all Degrees, and of all Ages, Up from young Fops to grave old Sages..." Most of the piece focuses on the female gender and the sorts of women whose hopes were dashed in the lottery. These include "a young Beauty" longing for a coach and six, a "maiden Dame most Trim, With Oyle in Virgin Lamp full Brim" who wants to wed an "honest Brawny Knight," another woman "in purse and beauty somewhat low, Wants that Sum too, to keep a Beau," a bouncing City Dame who hopes to win the money to "dress her Eldest prentice Boy," a Buxom City Matron who would use her money to help "Her Spark at 'tother end of Town'" become a Captain, and a Phil [fille] de Chambre who "Oh, if the great Prize would but hit her, Lord! What a Husband she should get her." The list of female venturers ends with a country girl who hopes a prize will help her "shine in my dear Dicky's Eyes" but the writer warns: "Without the Pence, alas poor Nan, I fear thou'lt dye, and ne're taste Man." The pamphlet notes that while young, virginal women play the lottery in droves, so too do older single women with "Wrinkles and Furrows, Age and Crutches, Want the great Prize too in their Clutches." One such is a Beldam with "More Shilling than sh' had Teeth, Heav'n knows...A sum will purchase Husbands plenty, And get a Boy of five and Twenty." For all of these women, the goal of winning the lottery is to find a man. As the author put it: "Whether for Husband or for Spark, Still that dear Creature Man's the Mark."

The pamphlet *Diluvium Lachrymarum* also emphasizes the laboring women who venture money in the lottery. These include Two Exchange Fillies, or young women who worked at the Royal Exchange, and "Twelve Damsels of St Dunstans West, The plain Domesticks of the Kitchin,... They club'd their Stocks to buy a Lot; Ten Pence a piece made just ten Shilling."

[29] Early English Books Online (hereafter EEBO) <eebo.chadwyck.com> (accessed December 2013).
[30] EEBO (accessed December 2013).

These twelve kitchen maids who pool their money to buy a ticket are purportedly fictional characters and yet they sound exactly like the real single women mentioned above who wrote posies on their lottery tickets. Female laborers appeared as lottery players in a few other ballads from the period such as "The London Lottery, or, Simple Susan, the Ambitious Damsel of Bishopsgate-Street." Susan pawns "her night-rail and smock" and other clothing to raise money to buy a ticket in the lottery. She hopes to win the prize of £3,000 and if she does says: "I will leave off my Service, and near to Cheapside,/Will go take me a Lodging, and lead a sweet Life,/Such a Portion will make me an Alderman's Wife..." The ballad ends with Susan losing her clothes and her place in service, but not winning the lottery. "Now you Lasses of London, pray never presume,/For the three thousand pounds, Lest her lot be your Doom."[31]

After devoting five pages to female lottery adventurers, the author of *Diluvium Lachrymarum* scurries to include a few male ones: One who wants to fill his "Iron Chest," a young heir and a poet who both need money, a religious man who wants to perform "feats of piety" and a "roring Royster" who wants to spend it all on "Wine and Punk." For the men, winning a lottery prize sets them up in life or allows them to pursue their passions, but is not linked to finding a marital partner and settling down.[32]

An answer to *Diluvium Lachrymarum* appeared the same year. Significantly, it is the only example of a satirical lottery pamphlet written from the female perspective (whether it truly was penned by women, or no). *The Poet Buffoon'd: or, A Vindication of the Unfortunate Ladies, from the Sawcy Reflections in a Late Doggrel Satyr* was supposedly written by "A Club of the Fair Sex for that purpose assembled." Described as the "fair Feminine Vent[u]rers" in the lottery who "the sawcy scribler maulld" in ink, those women who convened included "Th' whole Tribe, Wife, Widow, Virgin, Miss." This indicates the female adventurers included women of all ages and marital states and perhaps honest as well as dishonest ones, since Town Miss was a term for prostitute. They admit that when they first entered the lottery it was for personal financial gain, or "Dreams of Gold," but they insist they are not greedy and selfish so much as they wished to have the money to marry and have children. They emphasize their patriotism by saying: "Altho' we long for Procreation,/'Tis not for the empty Titillation,/But for th' Service to the Nation..." Amidst a lot of sexual innuendo, the poem goes on to say: "And, therefore, 'tis we want the Joys/Of Love, for raising thumping Boys, To make Recruits of young

[31] "The London Lottery" (1693) EBBA ID: 22343, University of California English Broadside Ballad Archive. <http://ebba.english.ucsb.edu> (accessed July 2014).

[32] *Diluvium Lachrymarum. A Review of the Fortunate & Unfortunate Adventurers. A Satyr in Burlesque, Upon the Famous Lottery, Set up in Freeman's Yard in Cornhill* (L, 1694). Google Books (accessed July 2014).

Commanders,/And rear a Nursery for Flanders." These women say they played the lottery only to serve their nation by breeding boys who could fight King William's wars against France. Fiction and reality coincide here since the actual women who invested in State lotteries such as the Million Adventure helped England fight France.

The Million Adventure was even referenced in the pamphlet *A Lottery for Ladies and Gentlemen: Or, A New Million Adventure. Invented for the Benefit of Ladies that want Husbands, and younger brothers that stand in need of rich Wives* (1694).[33] This pamphlet still figured the lottery as a way for a woman to win a husband, but now men (specifically financially needy younger brothers) were also included. The authors note that since all of London, if not the nation, was addicted to lotteries, and since lotteries have been held for all sorts of goods, they decided to create this one so that both sexes could raise their fortunes. Their proposal was for 5,000 bachelors, between twenty and thirty years of age and of good family "or at least can pretend to be so" to pay in £100 each; 5,000 gentlewomen of the same age would pay in the same amount. This optimistic pot of £1,000,000 would be divided among women "prizes" who would come with sums ranging from a top prize of £20,000 down to £500 (although even the latter was better than a blank). Tellingly, although both sexes had to pay to enter the lottery, only women were given away and with monetary amounts, echoing the custom of a dowry. Women would draw first and get the prize allotted to their number and even if a woman did not win a monetary prize she would at least "win" a husband. Belying further who would really benefit from this lottery the managers noted that they would take 5 percent of money paid in "to satisfie for all their Pains, Hazzard, and Trouble, besides the Use of the Women, (as other Goldsmiths have of their Money) 'till the Day of Marriage." Such sexual innuendo played on the idea of women putting out—either their money or their bodies—to "use" (in monetary terms meaning "at interest"). The proposers admitted only those of means would be able to play since they would have to raise £100. They assumed women would not be supplying the sum themselves: "we hope all wise Fathers will rather come to us, with one hundred Pounds, than go to the Devil for twenty thousand Pounds to pay their Daughters Portions." The lottery then was a deal for men, whether fathers or would-be husbands.

Fiction not only represented women as playing lotteries but also organizing them. In 1695 a broadsheet appeared touting *The Ladies Invention, being a thousand pounds for six-pence, to the fortunate, and the Triple Adventure*

---

[33] *A Lottery for Ladies and Gentlemen: Or, A New Million Adventure. Invented for the Benefit of Ladies that want Husbands, and younger brothers that stand in need of rich Wives* (L, 1694). Published in Thomas Brown, *The Works: in Prose and Verse*, 3 vols. (L, 1732), 167–73. Google Books (accessed September 2013).

Made into one Lottery.[34] Beyond the name, however, this lottery seemed to have very little to do with women, for the cashiers and undertakers named were all male. This was also noted by a later pamphlet that stated "tho' Ladies bear the Title of the Invention, Men are the Undertakers, and get the profit of it…" In 1698 both the London newspapers *The Flying Post* and the *Post Man* advertised a lottery called The Lady's Invention. The advertisement announced "A New Lottery called the Lady's Invention. In this lottery 6d. could get "the Adventurer, if fortunate" 1,000l. and 18d. ventured could get one £2,000. "This being an invention of the Female Sex, we hear several Ladies of quality design to venture considerable sums in it. Tickets may be had at most Coffee-Houses in Town." Whether the lottery mentioned in the press was real or whether it was fiction confused with fact is unclear.[35]

It was only a matter of time before a satire on the types of "ingenious designing gentlewomen" who invested in the Ladies Invention lottery appeared.[36] The seventeen female lottery players who are satirized in this pamphlet include both young and old, single women as well as widows. For instance, one was a "relation of a certain worthy merchant" who perhaps used money he "got by wagers on the siege of Namur." Another was a "bonny buxom Widow in the Strand, living at the Sign of the Black Bull with the Golden Cod" who was looking to pick "a second husband's marrowbones." A third was a "young termagent widow of twenty two" and another a "riche Quaker's daughter not many doors from the Golden Hart within Aldgate." The particulars and addresses suggest that perhaps actual individuals were being satirized.

Along with the emphasis on unmarried women as lottery players, this pamphlet also included the depiction of women as playing the lottery in order to marry. Like the buxom widow looking for a second husband, a "kinswoman to a physician turn'd poet" was hoping that a win in the lottery would secure her a marriage. In the latter's case, she "sent eight Shillings to the Lottery, in hopes to draw the same person for a Husband, whom she did last week for a Valentine." The language here shows that the prize that the women literally draw is a husband. A cutler's daughter in Cheapside also "ventur'd full 12s. and 6d. to get her a portion" to marry. A Taylor's carrot-pated daughter and a "greasie squobb Tub of Kitchin-stuff cookmaid at the T[em]ple T[aver]n in Fleet street" also ventured her whole Christmas box, or 12s. 6d., for a

[34] *The Ladies Invention, being a thousand pounds for six-pence, to the fortunate, and the Triple Adventure Made into one Lottery* (L, 1695) EEBO (accessed December 2013).

[35] *Post Man*, issue 475, June 11, 1698. Burney Collection Newspapers (accessed 2008). In 1695 appeared *Characters of Several Ingenious designing Gentlemen, who have lately put in to the Ladies Invention* and in 1697 the similarly titled *Characters of Several Ingenious Designing Gentlemen, Who have lately put in to the Ladies Invention.*

[36] BL, 816.M.19 n. 2, *Characters of Several Ingenious designing Gentlewomen who have lately put in to the Ladies Invention* (L, 1695).

husband. This pamphlet features women of various social statuses putting significant sums in the lottery in the hopes of a husband.

This pamphlet also presents the common trope of women who resort to the lottery because they have been unable to marry. While some lack a good portion, and the Taylor's red-headed daughter suffered from the cultural distrust of red-headed women, in this pamphlet it is the women's lack of virtue that is the issue. For instance, the cook maid's "mistress had like to have turned her away a fortnight ago, for shewing one of the Vinegar Drawers what was the end of Man's creation." Similar sexual innuendo, sometimes distasteful, is aimed at the gentleman's natural daughter, "Tho I believe she was too virtuous to lie with her Father, as the Neighbours maliciously suggested, yet 'tis concluded by all that she has no aversion to her Father's Sex." The sexual jokes continue by playing on the occupations of the women's families: the cutler's daughter will find a sheath for a prospective husband's knife and the tailor's daughter both knows how many inches go into making a yard and if her spark brings "so much stuff with him" she will find a deep place to receive it. This is stock satire, as are the lusty widows and the lonely old maid: that "venerable piece of antiquity, near Guild-hall, aged Sixty Five, but as good a Maid... [who is] weary of lying alone, and loath to divert the Devil with leading of Apes in his Dominions." The author says this spinster "may serve for a warning to the rest of the Sex, for that she might have had Corral enough given her gratis in her younger days to rub her Gumms with, is forced now to go the charge of buying it." In this way, a pamphlet about a purported lottery turns into a satire about sexually frustrated unmarried women whose only remedy is to win the lottery and "buy" a spouse to relieve their sexual tension.

Thomas Brown's pamphlet also focused on female lottery players who had been unable to marry. Significantly, eighteen out of the nineteen female caricatures in this version are single women, a higher proportion of spinsters than in the earlier version. Amongst them were two daughters of a Turkey [Levant] company merchant, a virgin actress, a buxom reputed young virgin, a lame and ugly young lady, an ugly clergyman's daughter, a sergeant's daughter "pretty well stricken in years," a virgin aged thirty-six, and an old druggist's daughter. Brown represented the lottery as the pastime of single women who had been unable to find a husband, due to a lack of beauty, a disability, or advanced age.[37]

A variation on the theme of women venturing money in the lottery to win a husband occurs in *A Continuation of a Catalogue of Ladies, to be set up by Auction, on Monday the 6th of this Instant July* (1691). This is the earliest example I have found of a lottery that offered marriageable women as prizes to marriage-minded men, rather than the usual trope of women winning prize

---

[37] Thomas Brown, *The Characters of several ingenious, designing Gentlewomen, that put in to the Ladies Invention* (L, 1699). EEBO (accessed October 2013).

money to use as their marriage portion.[38] This catalogue listed twenty women up for auction including a "buxom young maid of 19 years," three sisters who are "but 2d hand, and go for Maids," a rich widow with "humpt back, and crooked Legs," a brandy-loving councellor's daughter, a very tall Irish lady, a tayler's daughter "with a carrot head," a barber's wife lately divorced, and a young orphan. Differing from other satirical lotteries, these women actually had marriage portions, which ranged from the fat widow's £200 to the "not streight" (deformed) solicitor's daughter's £4,000. These were quite generous portions in an era when the daughter of a tradesman might receive £50–100 for her portion and the daughter of a clergyman or merchant £100–£500.[39] But the pamphlet suggests that the women were unmarried for other reasons, ranging from physical deformity to drunkenness, as well as undesirable characteristics such as red hair and tallness. It is highly unlikely a woman's hair color would actually detract from her £800 portion, but it made for good satire. More importantly, it inculcated the idea that women must marry at all costs and perhaps settle for an inferior match before they too had to auction themselves off.

The pamphlet *A Continuation of a Catalogue of Ladies, to be set up by Auction* is indicative of the social anxiety England was under at this time over high numbers of never-married women and lower marriage rates.[40] In the late seventeenth century the English began to lament what they perceived as a decline in marriage rates and rising numbers of single people. Contemporaries responded to this "marriage crisis" by presenting a number of options including the need for Protestant nunneries for the growing numbers of single women as well as a marriage tax to encourage recalcitrant bachelors to marry. The former did not rally support, but the government did pass the Marriage Duty tax in the 1690s. It is within this context that we can view popular literature's association of lotteries with marriage as well as proposals for marriage lotteries. Lotteries had proven to be one of the most popular forms of entertainment and financial speculation in the late seventeenth and early eighteenth centuries. Lotteries were used to fund private philanthropic schemes and by the British government to fund foreign wars. It was not a big leap to adapt lotteries to the needs of single women. This helps account for the flurry of pamphlets on the subject at the end of the seventeenth century.

After a lull, pamphlets connecting women, marriage, and the lottery began to appear again in the early eighteenth century. It is probably not a coincidence that these pamphlets reappeared around the same time the actual State lottery also began again in 1710. These pamphlets reference concerns about

[38] BL, 816.m.19.(20.), *A Continuation of a Catalogue of Ladies, to be set up by Auction, on Monday the 6th of this Instant July* (L, 1702).

[39] Amy Erickson, *Women and Property in early modern England* (London: Routledge, 1993), 86–9.

[40] See Amy Froide, *Never Married: Singlewomen in early modern England* (Oxford: Oxford University Press, 2005).

high numbers of single people, the real Marriage Duty tax and similar "projects" for addressing lower marriage rates. For example, the anonymous author of *The Love-Lottery: Or, A Woman the Prize* (1709) stated "Tis something strange, that among the number of wise projectors with which this nation is plentifully stock'd, none of 'em shou'd ever think of a Lottery for Marriages; which seems to be of a much more taking and edifying species, than one lately propos'd for raising 3 Millions." Instead of taxing marriages the author says "they shou'd have propos'd to have help'd 'em to Matches, and then every one, especially the Women, would have been striving which shou'd pay first." In this proposed lottery maids and widows would venture 10s. to win a husband or a £500 portion. While bachelors and widowers could also play if they wished, the author depicted unmarried women as the individuals desperate to marry. He said that 300 names had been sent in already, and 200 of these were widows. This project was purportedly aimed at many types of women including beautiful women without fortunes, daughters of tradesmen, servants, exchange-girls, seamstresses, and others in the clothing trades. But it is the prominence of widows that is something different from the pamphlets of the 1690s; which may well reflect the demographic rise of widows during the eighteenth century.

Differing from earlier fictional accounts, *The Love-Lottery* also emphasized that some women would not be permitted to venture into this lottery. These banned women included those who were unchaste; virgins over twenty-five years of age and widows over thirty-five, unless they had "money enough to supply the defects of age"; maids who chew charcoal or widows who smoke tobacco or drink gin; and women with eyesores or imperfections. In fact, women venturers "must be straight, agreeable, and free from disease (green-sickness excepted), not deformed in body or mind and not hiding deformities under their clothing." According to this author, some women were not suitable for marriage even if it was a game of chance. Nevertheless, "any batchelor [who] shall meet with a leaky vessel, we think he may well venture to continue the voyage of matrimony in her, when she is either freighted, or at least ballasted with a little money: And besides, he has but the common chance of all husbands, for any man may be deceiv'd." According to this author, both the lottery and marriage were a gamble, and a man needed to accept that he could venture into either and lose.

As we have seen in other fiction, the author of *The Love-Lottery* was less concerned with the plight of women without husbands and more interested in satirizing such women. In reality, an Englishwoman over the age of twenty-five (virgin or not) was by no means unmarriageable. The average age at first marriage was actually twenty-five or six, and many women married for the first time well into their thirties. Widows also remarried well past the age of thirty-five. The author's equation of marriage with money was closer to the mark. The prize in the love lottery was a husband or a £500 portion.

Presumably the female winner would use the portion to attract a husband. Although one wonders if a female reader could have perceived the alternative. If she did not want to marry, the unmarried woman could always take the £500 prize and invest it for her own maintenance, rather than "investing" in marriage.

The Love-Lottery was followed in 1710 with *Proposals for a Matrimonial Lottery; From the Record Office.*[41] The need for this project was ascribed to the wars, which were causing damsels to labor "under the torments of an insupportable solitude." Only "maids, widows and single women" were allowed to enter this game. (This lottery promised 10,000 prizes without any blanks.) The drawing would be held after the war was over and the prizes would come from amongst the "officers now bearing commission in her Majesty's service by sea and land" to the number of 10,000. This scheme was purportedly so popular that a few weeks later, in March, an advertisement warned of traffic outside the Record Office due to the "great numbers of Maids, Widows, and Single Women resorting there." A rule had to be initiated limiting each lady to one ticket. It is unlikely that this lottery was real, but the realism of the announcement and the advertisements, and their similarity to actual lotteries is striking.

In the eighteenth century periodicals joined with pamphlets in chronicling marriage lotteries. For instance, in 1710 *The Tatler* ran a "sketch of a lottery for persons" more properly styled "The Amicable Contribution for raising the Fortunes of Ten young Ladies."[42] The author said he was making his proposal public so that the town could comment on and improve it. The scheme was to raise 100,000 crowns "by way of lots" so that each lady would receive £2,500 and the gentleman who drew such a woman for a prize would receive both a wife and her portion. This proposal was more legalistic and perhaps realistic, admitting that if the matched partners did not marry then the individual who refused would receive only £1,000 and the one willing to marry would receive the rest. Even if the two did agree to marry, before the man could collect his money he would be required "to settle 1000 l. of the same in substantial hands, (who shall be trustees for the said ladies), and shall have the whole and sole disposal of it for her use only." This description was quite in keeping with the gentry's use of separate estates and marriage contracts to provide their daughters with some financial security after marriage. Lest we think this proposal was forward-thinking in considering marriage from the woman's perspective, restrictions were only put on the type of women (and not the men) who could enter the marriage lottery. "They shall be ladies that have had a liberal Education, between fifteen and twenty three, all genteel, witty, and of unblameable characters." Such a description reveals a glimpse of what men

---

[41] BL, *The Records of Love: or, Weekly Amusements for the Fair Sex*, v. 1, n. 7 (18 February 1710); n. 9 (4 March 1710).

[42] *The Tatler*, issue 200, July 20, 1710. Google Books (accessed December 2013).

considered the ideal female spouse at this time; she should be young, virtuous, and educated (the last is a bit of a surprise). The scheme also included specifics for how the money paid in by the women would be secured. "The money to be raised shall be kept in an iron box, and when there shall be 2,000 subscriptions, which amounts to 500 l. It shall be taken out and put into a Goldsmith's Hands, and the note made payable to the proper lady, or her assigns . . . and as soon as 100,000 [l.] subscriptions are completed, and 200 crowns more to pay the charges, the lottery shall be drawn at a proper place." In this lottery women had to pay to enter but men got to draw for free. This was a change from the 1694 proposal where both sexes had to pay for the chance to win a spouse. All of the specific and realistic details featured in the *Tatler*'s lottery show that the editors expected their readers to have an intimate knowledge of how lotteries worked.

1710 was a big year for matrimonial lottery schemes. Likewise from the pen of the editors of the *Tatler* came *A Good Husband for five shillings, or Esquire Bickerstaff's Lottery for the London Ladies* (L, 1710).[43] Bickerstaff also cited the wars in which England had been continually embroiled for the decrease in numbers of men as well as the increase in numbers of women kept unmarried against their will. The author warned that if a woman refused to stoop to marry a man below her station "she may wait beyond the years of Female Patience, till her maidenhood grows as mouldy as an old cubboard crust, that has been pass'd upon by the mice, and long, long neglected by the whole Family." Such a striking analogy may have been calculated to put fear into the heart of an as yet unmarried female reader. As a solution for this marital downturn the pamphlet announced that a "society of honest gentlemen" had decided to start a lottery "for the benefit of all single ladies, widows, maids, or thornbacks [single women past marriageable age]" who were willing to venture their money for a chance to win a husband who can "keep her well, and kiss her roundly, but shall also settle such a jointure upon her."[44] These fictional accounts of marriage and the lottery were now changing from laughing at single women to chastising and blaming them for their marital state.

Bickerstaff's lottery was also different from earlier fictional lotteries in that men were the prizes and women the recipients, which was a reversal of the usual scheme. The prizes were men with jobs and money, although this did not prevent Bickerstaff poking fun at them. The highest prize was a "modern Whig, of £2,000 per annum" and an estate. The secondary prizes were a short

---

[43] BL, 117.n.60., *A Good Husband for five shillings, or Esquire Bickerstaff's Lottery for the London Ladies* (L, 1710). Isaac Bickerstaff was first the pseudonym of the satirist Jonathan Swift and then used by the editor of Richard Steele's *The Tatler* (to which Swift, Steele, and Addison contributed).

[44] *A Good Husband for Five Shillings*, 4, 5.

atheist and an "occasional conformist as tall as a country maypole" who were both members of Parliament and worth £1,000 each. The prizes of lesser value were no less interesting: courtiers referred to as "Tom Doubbs, or Notorious Turn-Coats," "devout citizens of the low church," "soul physicians," land surveyors belonging to the customhouse, trading Quakers, "young spruce Beauish nonfighting officers," cursitors and attorneys. The lowest, or tenth, prizes were Irishmen: "strapping Town bullies, alias non-commision[ed] Captains, all of the true Hibernian Breed." Again in a reversal of roles, Bickerstaff provided the names and addresses of those who would sell the tickets in this lottery; they were all women. While these women sold lottery tickets rather than buying them, they were still sexualized. All of the female lottery ticket sellers' names included slang terms for female genitalia. For example, tickets could be had "at the House of Mrs. Bawdycut, a mid-wife, at the Sign of the Cradle near the Mews-Gate," at the lodgings of Mrs. Pintail the Mantuamaker, or at the shop of the widow Hugwell, a "famous cony-woolcutter, at the Sign of the 3 Tuzzy Mussies in Budge Row."

After the 1710s the proposals for marriage lotteries tapered off but they still rematerialized periodically. There was an uptick again in the 1730s. For instance, *A Scheme for a New Lottery for the Ladies: or, a Husband and Coach and Six for Forty Shillings* appeared in 1732. As in the 1710s these pamphlets scolded unmarried women rather than sympathizing with them. The frontispiece included a poem addressed to maidens, urging them to marry and warning them if they did not act fast enough they might miss out on marriage forever:

> Now Maidens all of every Age and Station,
> To Matrimony Turn your Inclination:
> Then haste away, nor mind the Wind or Weather,
> A clever Spouse and Portion's join'd together . . .
> If this propitious Time you chance to miss,
> Perhaps you ne'er may taste of wedded Bliss.[45]

The scheme was to give 50,000 tickets to maids or widows who could pay the 40s. cost and who were "willing to live in the State of Matrimony with moderate good Husbands." Evidently unmarried women did not deserve to marry very good ones.

The author assumed women from a range of social ranks would be among those subscribers so he stipulated "for the conveniency of the middling sort of Gentlewomen, such as Mantua-makers, Clear-starchers, Milliners, Button-makers, etc." that they would be allowed six months to come up with the ticket cost. The pamphlet also advised "all Chamber-maids, young or old

---

[45] BL, 1486.s.14., *A Scheme for a New Lottery for the Ladies: or, a Husband and Coach and Six for Forty Shillings* (L, 1732).

Maid-Servants etc." to enter this lottery. The author said this lottery was the most fair and "whereas in all other Lotteries, they who had the most Money, might have the most Tickets, and by Consequence a much better Chance," in contrast, in this one each person got one chance. This lottery was presented as particularly useful for "any young Milliner, Sempstress, Mantua-maker, Button-maker, Chamber-maid, House-maid, Cook-maid, nay even Scullions." The author suggested that every common servant who made the usual £4 per annum in wages should leave the money in the hands of their master or mistress for six months so that they would have the price to purchase a lottery ticket.[46] And this lottery would reach out to common women across England. The author claimed that, "I shall not confine my Lottery to the town only, but England over, that all the Fair Sex may have an equal Share..." In fact five pages of the proposal were taken up with a list of the market towns in England that would be supplied with lottery proposals and tickets. These towns included Nottingham, Manchester, Canterbury, Exeter, York, and Bristol. With typical English superiority, Wales was excluded because the author said that 40s. was already a good portion there and so the lottery was not needed for women to marry. Scotland was also left out since the people were "infectious to the English Nation."[47] This marital lottery proposal was unique in focusing so much on working single women, servants, and provincial women, for earlier in the century the concern had been gentlewomen.

As in Bickerstaff's lottery for London Ladies from two decades earlier, women were now the ones who drew the prizes—the men. "Ladies who are Adventurers may have a fair Chance, the first-drawn Ticket shall be a Warehouse-keeper, with the Salary of a hundred pounds per Annum." A husband with a salary of £100 p.a. would have been a good prize of course, but the "greatest prize, [was] the Governor, Salary unknown; sufficient to keep a coach and six." All of the prizes were men who held positions in an unnamed joint-stock corporation, such as Directors (with £300 salaries), assistants and clerks (with £100), as well as "forty inferior places, or offices, in the houses and warehouses" (with £40 salaries). The mention of warehouses, pawnbroking, and Scotchmen suggests this lottery was auctioning off men associated with the Charitable Corporation. This venture (discussed in chapter 6) was estab-lished to provide low-interest loans to the working poor, but was caught up in an embezzlement scandal in 1732, the very year *A Scheme for a New Lottery for the Ladies* appeared. The men of the Charitable Corporation were social pariahs and thus the need to auction them off as husbands perhaps. But the author also seems to be saying that single women should be content to marry these men despite their lack of credibility.

---

[46] *A Scheme for a New Lottery for the Ladies*, 22, 25–6, 29.
[47] *A Scheme for a New Lottery for the Ladies*, 31, 33, 37.

More significant was the proposal's innovative idea of providing money prizes to unmarried women in addition to just husbands. *A Scheme for a New Lottery for the Ladies* suggested 142 women would receive the prize of a husband, but the greater number of 250 female venturers would win a different prize. These women would receive an annuity or amount of money with which they could establish a trade and maintain themselves. They could hope to be either one of the 200 female venturers to win an annuity of £20 a piece or one of fifty "placed in Pawn-brokers Shops, with one hundred Pounds each to begin with, which will turn in one hundred and fifty per Annum, in a moderate Way of Trade." The lottery scheme itself would also employ women. The drawing would be overseen by "two maiden Gentlewomen" in their sixties, who could not participate "being above forty years of age." And "All stitchers, provided they are Maidens, may have Employ for a small time to stitch the Tickets." Once again fact and fiction are blurred, for this was also a real job for women at the State lottery office. Most importantly this pamphlet recognized women's need for jobs. For the first time in the fictional lotteries we see women win monetary prizes that allow them to maintain themselves if they stayed unmarried, rather than reflexively using their prize money to marry.

This does not mean that the authors did not think marriage was the ideal outcome for women who ventured in the lottery. The projectors ensured this by assuring their readers that they would vet the male prizes. Anyone who pretended to be a single man but turned out to have a wife would be "used like a scoundrel by our Black-Guards." Irishmen, footmen, liverymen, and militia men were excluded and the numbers of Scotchmen and Dutchmen were limited. Men who could "give a good Account of themselves" and who had not worked for the government or embezzled public money could vie for one of the 50,000 women who entered the lottery. Where this number came from is unclear, but may well have been used to indicate the sheer size of the never-married female population. The projectors proposed to put 500 men into the lottery specifically to match with old maids. The procedure was that men would be given numbers and "join in bond to marry the Lady drawn against the same, if he prove a Prize." If any man "drawn a Prize, should refuse to be married to the Person drawn against, he forfeits his Bond...and the Lady at Liberty to chuse any other Person she can get." But the author cautioned women venturers not to get too choosy. They told women that although they might draw a husband of "a mean Trade or Extraction" such as a farmer, porter, or tinker, they should remember he would be improved by the monetary prize that came with him; moreover, much of the "mushroom gentry" seen about town in coaches came from the same backgrounds. Likewise "no deformed Person of either Sex" was admitted to the lottery, since they could not perform the duties of husband or wife. While deformity might keep one from marriage, a lack of physical attractiveness would not. The projector said that all women "must take their Chance, of either a handsome or indifferent

Husband." Interestingly, it was women and not men who had to be told not to fixate on the physical appearance of a spouse.

In the 1730s some fictional accounts of lotteries begin to figure themselves as charitable schemes providing marital partners for old maids. One such proposal was *A Scheme for Dispensing of (by way of Lottery) a dozen and half of Old Maids Resident in or Near Covent Garden; recommended to the consideration and generosity of such well-disposed Bachelors and others as through a tender regard for the spiritual parts of the same old maids, will risk their own mortal and natural parts to prevent the poor Girls leading apes in Hell.*[48] In this pamphlet spinsters, or single women past marriageable age, are equated to the odd lots and leftover goods that habitually had been disposed of by auction or lottery since the seventeenth century. This lottery represented spinsters as less than desirable marriage partners. "As an incouragement to persons to become adventurers, 'tis proposed that instead of paying for their Tickets ... they shall here be intitled to a portion ... for taking them." In other words, those men who entered the lottery did not have to pay; rather they were rewarded for taking on the burden of one of these "old maids." The male investor received money and the woman received a husband. Both sexes took a risk but both might also improve their condition. The similarity of this scheme to one of the prints in Hogarth's series *A Rake's Progress* is suggestive. The 1735 engraving entitled "A Rake's Progress: Marries an Old Maid" depicts the foppish Rakewell marrying a one-eyed, unattractive old maid, presumably for her money. The picture invites some sympathy for the "old maid," especially because the groom is making eyes at the bridesmaid during the wedding ceremony. But an alternative reading would be that this single woman was playing the lottery, a game of risk. She was willing to pay to shed the title of old maid for that of respectable married matron.[49]

In the 1730s fictional marital lotteries continued to represent these proposals as helpful to the nation and reflective of the pro-natalist stance of the time. In 1734 appeared another proposal entitled *A Bill for a Charitable Lottery for the Relief of the Distressed Virgins in Great Britain.*[50] In this scheme the author represented single women as the objects of charity. In fact, the

---

[48] BL, c. 116 i. 4/11 (n.d.). I am grateful to Aki Beam and Beverly Lemire for bringing this proposal to my attention. There is no date for this scheme but it is similar to a 1727 Charitable Proposal to help Old Maids to Husbands, discussed in *Mist's Journal*. Daniel Defoe, *A collection of miscellany letters: selected out of Mist's Weekly journal, vol. 3* (L, 1727), 30–3. Another "Lottery for Old Maids" appeared in the *Grub Street Journal* no. 267, Feb. 1735; reprinted in the *London Magazine, or Gentleman's Monthly Intelligencer*, Feb.1735, 61.

[49] William Hogarth, "A Rake's Progress: Marries an Old Maid," June 1735.

[50] *A Bill for a Charitable Lottery for the Relief of the Distressed Virgins in Great Britain* in L'Estrange, *Lotteries and Sweepstakes*, Appendix VII; this was reprinted in *Universal Spectator*, May 11, 1734; *General Evening Post*, issue 90, May 14, 1734; *Gentleman's Magazine*, May 1734, 251 and Mar 1739, 149. Internet Library of Early Journals <www.bodley.ox.ac.uk/ilej/> (accessed October 2005).

author orders that the lottery proposal should be read every Sunday in the parish churches throughout Britain "for the consolation of the godly women there assembled, and to the end that the preachers may instruct the men not to fail in this act of Christian charity." Marrying a single woman was evidently now an act of piety or national service. The author also explained that singleness was a threat to the nation that had to be stopped:

> "Whereas by the melancholy disuse of holy matrimony in these kingdoms, an infinite number of his Majesty's female subjects are left upon the hands of their parents, in the un-natural state of virginity, to the prejudice of the common-wealth, the unsupportable burdening of private families, and the unspeakable affliction of the said females; And whereas all ordinary methods to prevent or remedy so great an evil have hitherto proved ineffectual: Be it enacted for the better hindrance thereof in times to come, and for the necessary encouragement of propagation, which we ought particularly to attend to upon the prospect of an approaching war, that all the Virgins in Great Britain from fifteen to forty shall be disposed of by lottery."[51]

Here never-married women are figured as a national concern, a threat to the nation that must be addressed. The proposed Virgin Lottery deftly illustrates the eighteenth-century anxiety over the role and place of single women in British society. Lotteries were needed to dispose of such "superfluous" women, saving both the women and the nation.

Like the earlier scheme for disposing of "old maids," this lottery also made women the objects or prizes. In this scenario men entered for the chance to marry the few single women with money, but most received a less remunerative prize. For instance, two lucky recipients would "win" a single woman with a fortune valued at £100,000. And a number of others would win smaller (but still considerable) fortunes ranging from £80,000 down to £10,000. The second prizes, which were much more numerous, included women referred to as Beauties, Pretty Girls, Agreeables, Wits, Huswifes, Ladies of quality, and Relations of the first minister or his mistress [Robert Walpole and Maria Skerrett]. The most common (or lowest) prizes would be Women of Fashion and Breeding, Card players, "Misses of great accomplishments," "Special breeders, most of them parsons' daughters," and "Good conditioned girls, alias friskies." Whatever prize a man drew he would have to keep.

Fictional lotteries continued to push pro-marriage and pro-natalist debates, even resorting to chastising men who avoided marriage or procreation. In response to the *Bill for a Charitable Lottery, for the Relief of Distressed Virgins* came *Good News to the Distressed; or Proper Amendments to the Bill...* (1734).[52] The unknown author added the Bill to this new pamphlet since

---

[51] *A Bill for a Charitable Lottery.*
[52] BL, C.194.a.1188(1)., *Good News to the Distressed; or Proper Amendments to the Bill...* (L, 1734).

"there was so great a Demand last Year, and whereof none are to be now had." This new pamphlet says that many schemes have been put forward for the "furtherance of Procreation, and putting a Stop to the great and melancholy Disuse, and Contempt, of the comfortable State of Matrimony, in these Kingdoms" and names the Bill for a Charitable Lottery as one of them. But some amendments to that bill were now suggested, among them enlarging the pool of eligible participants. These amendments were all aimed at helping the nation's bachelors. This pamphlet suggested ending the eligibility threshold of an estate worth £100 per annum and argued that all bachelors should receive a ticket in the lottery before any widowers. And to ensure bachelors subscribed to the lottery, and did not shirk or eschew marriage, any bachelor under forty years of age would have to pay a fine if he did not enter the lottery and any over forty "being deem'd useless in his Generation, and an unprofitable Member of the Commonwealth" would have half of his estate forfeited annually for life. But lest we think women escape this pamphlet's purview, the author suggested any man married for a year whose wife had not become pregnant would also have to pay a fine. The fines paid by laggard bachelors and unfertile husbands were to go to bachelors who wanted to play the marriage lottery. Even more surprising, the author recommended that married men who had no children after seven years should "lose the Testimonies of their Virility." This focus on men and their contribution to England's infertility is rare. Usually, women were blamed for instances of personal and national infertility. And the idea that men over the age of forty, like women, might be incapable of generation is without parallel. The author even suggests that women who have husbands who cannot perform their conjugal duty should be allowed to take "helpmates" as a way to avoid "frequent divorces."

The amendments to the bill also turned the focus to widows, noting that those between the ages of fifteen and forty were now to be eligible "to be disposed of by Way of Lottery, after the same Manner as the Virgins." The widows, like the virgins, were ranked. A pretty, young widow with no children "and consequently is little the worse for wearing, shall always be reckon'd a prize of the first Class." Widows of quality and honor with "powerful relations" but small jointure, and those with "tolerable" jointures but over thirty years of age were rated as second prizes. The third and last class of widows included those with pretty good jointures but more than one deceased husband, as well as genteel and well-bred widows who were neither pretty nor agreeable. "In the List of Blanks [those tickets that are not prizes], are to be included, all such as are known by the Name of Termagents, Teazers, Scolds, Curtain-Lecturers, Whitechapel-Fortunes, etc."[53] In other words, scolds and poor women were not lottery prizes.

---

[53] A "curtain lecture" was a private reprimand a wife gave her husband within the curtains of the marital bed. A "Whitechapel fortune" was a term for a woman without means or a

Figure 2.1. William Hogarth *The South Sea Bubble* (L, 1721).
From Collection of the Author.

The connection of unmarried women to the lottery was not only a trope in literature it was also a feature of the visual arts and theater.[54] For example, William Hogarth's engraving *The South Sea Bubble* (1721) provides a rich and dense satire on financial speculation and risk (see Figure 2.1.). One of the lesser-noticed sub-plots in the print is in the top left-hand corner. Here women wait in line on a balcony to enter a building. Above the door to the building are the words: "Raffling for Husbands with Lottery Fortunes.—In Here—."

Once again we see the connection between women, marriage, and the lottery in the midst of a satire on financial speculation. Another illustration of a lottery dating from 1740 includes an image combined with the text from Tom Brown's 1690s pamphlet discussed above (see Figure 2.2.).

On the left-hand side of this image is a crowd of well-dressed women outside a lottery office. On the right-hand side is a crowd of poor people

portion—one who came only with the clothes on her back. Oxford English Dictionary Online <www.oed.com> (accessed December 2013).

[54] The theme of unmarried women as lottery players also made its way into drama, appearing in Henry Fielding's *The Lottery, A Farce* which was also printed in 1732.

Figure 2.2. *The Lottery: Or, The Characters of several ingenious designing Gentle-women that have put into it* (L, 1740).

outside the "bankrupt and pocket-pickt" offices. This is an obvious statement about the ill effects of gambling on the poor. It is also significant that men do not appear in the crowd of lottery venturers; rather the men in the picture are Cox, an actual "noted lottery factor," who holds a pamphlet advertising halves, fourths, eighths, and sixteenths shares of lottery tickets, and a man with a quill who is coming out of the lottery office in which he is an employee. This image figures men as lottery organizers and women as lottery players.[55]

After sixty years of marital lottery proposals and schemes, a new theme of skepticism emerged in the 1750s. A 1755 issue of the *Connoisseur* emphasized the unhappy lot of the non-prize winners, many of whom were women.

> How many poor maidens, of good family but no fortune, must languish all their days without the comforts of an husband and a coach and six! . . . and even Mrs. Betty, the possessor of a single sixteenth [share of a ticket], flies to the Office, pays her penny, and receives the tidings of her ill luck with surprise; goes to another Office, pays her penny, hears the same disagreeable information, and

---

[55] BL, 1851,0308.522, *The Lottery: Or, The Characters of several ingenious designing Gentle-women that have put into it* (L, 1740).

can hardly, very hardly persuade herself, that Fortune should have doomed her still to wash the dishes and scrub down the stairs.[56]

Lotteries and marriage were also slowly being disconnected. We now see wives as well as single and widowed women venturing in the lottery as well as the new idea that unmarried women might use their prize money for something other than marriage.

> "The married ladies have sufficient calls for even double this sum, to supply them with the necessaries of dress, and to answer the expenses of frequently public diversions; and as to the unmarried ladies, they very well know the truth of that maxim in the ballad, that 'in ten thousand pounds, ten thousand charms are center'd.' Some ancient maiden ladies, who could never be brought to think of an husband, or to give into the vanities of the world, were resolved to live retired upon their Prize in the country, and leave proofs of their good dispositions behind them, by swelling out their Wills with a long list of Items to this or that charity or hospital."

According to this pamphlet, depending on her marital status lottery winnings enabled a woman to enjoy domestic consumption, conjugal blessedness, or independent retirement in old age. By the 1750s fiction represented the options for women who won the lottery as extending beyond marriage.

The relationship between marriage and the lottery did not end entirely, however, but continued as a theme into the later decades of the eighteenth century. For example, "The Maid's Hopes in the Lottery" appeared in collections of ballads in the 1760s and '70s.[57] The protagonist of this ballad sang:

> I am a young damsel that flatters myself,
> That I shall grow rich in abundance of wealth,
> I have got but one guinea, 'tis all I am worth,
> And a fortunate girl I have been from my birth,
> So I'll buy a ticket my hopes for to crown,
> With flattery of the lottery of ten thousand pound.

The maiden continues that she knows she will win because "My fortune was told me that I should be rich/'Twas by an old woman, I think she's a witch." This young woman enters the lottery after visiting a fortune teller, a theme that appeared a few decades earlier. 1732's *The Scheme for a New Lottery for the Ladies* had introduced the trope of single women resorting to fortunetellers, or reading the grounds in a coffee dish, to divine their future prospects in the lottery. The projectors had offered to let subscribers have any lucky lottery number they

---

[56] *Connoisseur*, issue XCIII, Nov. 6, 1755, pp. 559–64. Burney Collection Newspapers (accessed October 2008).

[57] BL, 1346.M.7(4), "The Maid's Hopes in the Lottery" (Edinburgh, 1776) and "The Maiden's Hopes in the Lottery" with "The Answer" in *The Glasgow Lasses Garland, composed of some excellent new songs* (Newcastle upon Tyne, 1765).

dreamt of if no one had yet taken it. In other words the lottery had begun to be associated with pure chance and quackery. This play on the concept of "fortune" as well as the gullibility of young women who waste their money on fortunetellers and lotteries, also features in the "The Maid's Hopes in the Lottery."

This late eighteenth-century ballad also presents a more positive tale than in earlier marital lotteries wherein a single woman could not hope to marry without winning the lottery. The maiden of this song says her beau young Roger will marry her whether she has a fortune or not. But in a new twist, the maiden thinks that if she wins she could aim higher: "But if I a lady of fortune should be,/Why should I accept such a fellow as he?" She goes on to dream: "Then many a nobleman should me approach,/And oftentimes take me abroad in his coach,/I'll wed the best bidder my fortune to raise." In the end she determines it is fine if her ticket comes up a blank because she can still have Roger, the bird in her hand. The moral is that as long as she marries she has won the lottery of life. Unfortunately for the maiden, one of the versions of the ballad includes an "Answer" from young Roger. In it Roger presents himself as sensible and frugal and criticizes the maid's (now named Kitty) lottery play. He decides to punish Kitty for playing the lottery by rejecting her as a marriage partner.

> But now I have left you, my Dear, for a new;
> Your Pride and Ambition will ne'er do for me,
> From a Servant to aim a grand Lady to be,
> So Farewel proud Kitty, your Pride will come down...

In the ultimate reversal of the marriage lottery trope the lottery prevents Kitty from marrying. Her venturing is proof of her spendthrift nature and unsuitability as a marriage partner. Like Roger, the English had grown stale on lotteries and were now critiquing them accordingly. After a century of encouraging women to play the lottery for marriage and profit, the tide had turned.

*   *   *

Much of this chapter has detailed how fiction presented single women as the most common adventurers in English lotteries and that their motivation was to win a prize that they could use as a dowry to attract a husband. Marriage and the lottery were linked in significant ways in the period. Not only were lotteries figured as a way to enable women to marry, but the reverse, marriage as a lottery, also became a metaphor. For example, after marrying a French Catholic of whom her family disapproved, and with her marriage slowly crumbling due to his debts, Ann Cole, Baroness D'ongnyes, equated marriage to a lottery. Writing to her mother in 1727 Cole said: "A Woman runs so great a venture of being miserable in Maryage that there daring to trye there luck at that Lottery is as wounderfull as it is comon: I know many wounders at my maryage, tho I had the greatest proof a man can give of love, tht of making me mistress of my Fortune..."[58] Ann Cole was no stranger to risk, she and her female kin were regular investors in the State lottery and other financial investments, but she fared better in her financial risks than in her marital ones.

We can also find numerous examples of real women who got caught up in the fantasy of winning the lottery and attracting a husband with the winnings. For instance, at a relatively advanced age Sarah Cowper noted in her diary on February 14, Valentine's Day:

"My Birth: Day 66 years past. A foolish wish as never before came in my Head enter'd now. It was that I might live another year to know, whither I got any thing in the lottery or No. I had conceiv'd a Jest that if I sho'd gett the 1000£ per An: how suitors wou'd haunt me for it, since never was woman so old or ugly but the man who wants sho[e]s will come barefoot to her shrine. But now I must stiffle my conceit, ffor the *Tattler* has hitt upon the like Ridicule of these Fortune Hunters."[59]

Here Cowper hit on a truism of the times, money could compensate for a marriageable woman's defects—whether physical or temporal. But she also admitted embarrassment that social commentators were aware of this as well. Cowper was not the only woman who dreamed of winning the lottery and marrying. Mrs. Ann Bedingfield, a self-described old maid, also hoped to do so. Writing to her friend Henrietta Howard, the Countess of Suffolk, in 1726, she thanked her for news of the stocks and added: "I have hopes that fortune will turn the wheel in my favour when they do begin to draw the lottery."[60]

The governess Agnes Porter illustrates how the association between playing the lottery and winning in marriage continued into at least the late eighteenth century. Porter kept a journal in which she confided a secret love for one Dr. McQueen, a man she feared might be beyond her socially and financially. Porter was a governess in her forties who had worked to support both herself and her mother since her clergyman father had died some years before. The next year she ruefully reported that Dr McQueen was "on the point of matrimony with [what she termed] a lady of fortune." It is perhaps no coincidence that at the same time Porter decided to invest in the lottery. More than a month later she noted down a story that she had heard from Mr. Nichols the writing master, a tale that resonated with her. A woman's father had died in debt and the woman had decided to go into service. Passing by a lottery office she bought a sixteenth share of a ticket (incidentally, the

---

[58] Nottinghamshire Archives, Savile of Rufford Papers, DD/SR/219/9, Ann Cole to Barbara Savile, October 1727.

[59] Sarah Cowper, *Diary*, vol. 5, Feb. 14, 1710, f. 112. *Perdita Manuscripts* <www.perditamanuscripts.amdigital.co.uk> (accessed August 7, 2013).

[60] John Wilson Croker, ed., *Letters to and from Henrietta, Countess of Suffolk and her Second Husband, the Hon. George Berkeley. From 1712 to 1767*, vol. 1 (London: John Murray, 1824), 257.

same amount Porter had recently bought). The next day the woman found out that she had won a £1,200 prize. She went to board with a merchant's family where she met a man of fortune to whom she was married in a matter of weeks. For Agnes Porter "fortune" was evidently the only means that would allow a woman like herself to marry.[61] Although Porter did not marry she was not without funds, funds that she had grown through public investing no less. When Porter died she was worth £2,000, a sum she had invested in Navy Annuities, known as "Navy 5 per cents," which could have produced £100 a year for her to live on.[62] Porter had amassed this sum through 25 years' of wages from her work as a governess and companion. The sad irony is that a woman worth £2,000 felt she had missed out on marriage because of her lack of money.

Other scholars have remarked on the association between gender and credit and how credit was gendered. Catherine Ingrassia and others have noted the cultural anxiety about gender and credit that was stimulated by the South Sea Bubble. Ingrassia posits that credit itself became gendered when speculative investment became associated with hysteria and disorder, two feminized forces. Contemporaries also feminized the concept of credit. Thomas Gordon complained that stock jobbing (or trading) had turned Great Britain into a nation of "old women," while Daniel Defoe and Joseph Addison represented credit as a young, virginal female. And of course fortune, or Fortuna, was figured as a woman.[63] This chapter makes a slightly different argument however. Not only did contemporaries perceive credit as gendered, they were also cognizant that real women participated in financial speculation. We have not fully explored this link between gendered metaphor and gendered reality. Contemporaries represented credit as female at the same time that women were becoming participants in the new financial economy. Credit was literally and not just figuratively gendered. Not only was subscribing to the lottery gendered, contemporaries also associated it with women of a certain marital status. The relationship between lotteries and single women reveals contemporary anxiety about both of these new phenomena—money divorced from work and women divorced from marriage. If a woman could support herself through investments, then she might not need to marry. What better way to remind her of her duty to marry than to create an integral relationship between the lottery and marriage?

---

[61] Jeanna Martin, ed., *A Governess in the Age of Jane Austen: The Journals and Letters of Agnes Porter* (London: Hambledon Press, 1998), 109.

[62] Martin, *Governess*, 38–9. Porter died in 1814. For more on the popular and high return 5 per cent Navy Annuities of 1810–21, see The Annuity Museum <www.immediateannuities.com/annuitymuseum> (accessed June 1, 2015).

[63] Catherine Ingrassia, *Authorship, Commerce, and Gender in Early Eighteenth-Century England* (Cambridge: Cambridge University Press, 1998), p. 11, and chapter one.

But the cultural trope of the marriage lottery did not translate into reality. In the following chapters we will see how a variety of women—single, married, and widowed—entered the new stock market and engaged in financial speculation. They did so not just or even necessarily to marry, but for a variety of other reasons. Women invested in the new financial instruments made available by the Financial Revolution to maintain themselves, to assist their families, and to serve as agents of kin. It is to some of the earliest adopters of these public investments that we now turn.

3

Early Adopters

Women Investors in the Early Years
of the Financial Revolution

In the spring months of 1697 a number of women, primarily single and widowed, appeared at Mercers' Hall, the home of the new Bank of England, to become shareholders in the national bank. Among them were Dame Jane Smith of Isleworth, Middlesex, a Huguenot widow Marie Prevereau, who resided at Monsieur Dergue's in Church St., St Anns, Westminster, and Susan Lands, who lived at Mr. Ferns' of the Exchequer. Dame Smith signed her own name in the Bank's books and noted that she subscribed £375 in the Bank. The widow Prevereau, while not able to sign her name, was able to purchase a £125 share in the Bank. Susan Lands, whose marital status was not recorded, had her money paid in by Israel Pallgate. Lands, a lodger or servant at Mr. Ferns', subscribed one of the smallest amounts to the Bank that year, £35.[1] What did Smith, Prevereau, and Lands have in common? Not only were all three women subscribers to the Bank of England (see Figure 3.1.) but they were also all early adopters of the financial instruments made available by England's Financial Revolution.

Much of the research on public investors so far has focused on the years surrounding the South Sea Bubble of 1720. While not the intention, this can give the impression that women came late to public investing. This could not be farther from the truth, however. Women were among those who adapted quickly to new public forms of investment. For instance, in her research on the 1690s, the first decade of the Financial Revolution, Anne Murphy has noted the presence of women among public creditors.[2] Barbara Todd's research on

---

[1] Bank of England Archives (hereafter BOE), M1/6–9, Original Subscription Books, 1697, Book A.

[2] Anne Murphy, *The Origins of English Financial Markets: Investment and Speculation before the South Sea Bubble* (Cambridge: Cambridge University Press, 2009); P. G. M. Dickson, *The Financial Revolution in England: A Study in the Development of Pubic Credit, 1688–1756* (London, 1967).

Figure 3.1. *The Bank of England in ye Poultry* (c. 1730).
Reproduced by permission of London Metropolitan Archives, City of London.

short-term funding of government debt during the Restoration period has also pushed back the timeline for women's involvement in public investing.[3]

This chapter will explore some of the early adopters of public investments. "Early adopter" is a term used in the entrepreneurship and innovation field for individuals who are the first to take advantage of new companies, products, and technologies.[4] It is an apt term for those female investors who quickly availed themselves of the new financial instruments made available by the Financial Revolution, such as stocks and bonds in joint-stock companies as well as long-term government loans. First we take a look at the numbers of women who subscribed capital to the new public stocks and securities that began to be openly traded in the 1690s. Samples of the proportion of female investors in a number of seventeenth-century stocks and securities are highlighted, including the Bank of England, the Royal African Company, the Land Bank, the Mine Adventurers Company, and the East India Company. While these aggregate numbers of female investors are telling, so are the details of some of the individual women who quickly adapted to the Financial

---

[3] Barbara Todd, "Fiscal Citizens: Female Investors in Public Finance before the South Sea Bubble," in Sigrun Haude and Melinda S. Zook, eds., *Challenging Orthodoxies: The Social and Cultural Worlds of Early Modern Women* (Farnham, 2014), 53–74, esp. 56–60.

[4] Everett Rogers coined the term in his *Diffusion of Innovations* (Glencoe, 1962). Early adopters embrace an innovation right after the innovators, but before the majority of adopters.

Revolution. This chapter also includes case studies of three early adopters who invested in public stocks and securities. The first example is Sarah Churchill, Duchess of Marlborough, one of the most politically and economically power-ful women in England; second is Martha Hutchins, the wife of a tradesman but sister to a government minister; and third is Elizabeth Freke, a provincial gentlewoman. All three women invested in the new market in stocks and securities in the 1690s or even earlier, illustrating that women were present as investors from the very beginnings of the Financial Revolution. What is striking is how eagerly these women pursued new and untested avenues for investment. They exhibited few concerns about these new options and instead dwelled on how pleased they were to profit from these financial opportunities.

* * *

The 1690s were the opening decade of the Financial Revolution when a number of new options for public investing emerged and the market in publicly traded stocks heated up. One of the most significant opportunities was the Bank of England. A joint-stock, national Bank, it was established to lend money to the government and it issued bank notes. Those who subscribed money then held shares in the Bank of England and received 8 percent interest. The Bank's initial subscription filled up in a matter of days. Anne Murphy has found that women made up 153 of the 1,268 original subscribers to the Bank in 1694. Women comprised 12 percent of the subscribers and invested £71,975 out of £1.2 million, or 6 percent of the initial capital. Women's participation can also be charted in 1697 when the capital was enlarged. In this year 1,099 people subscribed their money to the Bank of England between the months of April and June. Of these "original subscribers to capital," ninty-six were women, meaning 8.7 percent of those investing money were female. Twenty-two of these women appeared in person and signed for their subscriptions them-selves. The remaining seventy-four utilized an agent (two of whom were female) to subscribe.[5] These female subscribers were different from women who held or inherited Bank stock. This group of women chose to subscribe to Bank of England stock in their own names and often subscribed in person. They did not inherit this stock from someone else nor were others holding it for them, under another, perhaps male, family member's name.

The female subscribers to the Bank of England invested amounts ranging from the relatively modest sum of £35 up to a noteworthy £2,940 (although this latter amount was a bit of an outlier). The majority of women subscribed somewhere between £100 and £700 in the Bank (see Table 3.1.).

Only four women invested less than £100, presumably because such small amounts did not merit public investment. A quarter of the female investors

---

[5] Bank of England Archives (hereafter BA), M1/6–9.

Table 3.1. Female Subscribers to the Bank of England, 1697

Amount Subscribed (£)	Number of Female Subscribers = 96	Percentage of Female Subscribers = 100%
Under 100	4	4
100–199	24	25
200–299	16	16.6
300–399	13	13.6
400–499	2	2
500–599	11	11.6
600–699	15	15.6
Over 1,000	11	11.6

Source: Bank of England Archives, M1/6–9.

subscribed £100–199, an amount that only a middling or genteel woman would likely have saved in the 1690s.[6] Although very few women invested amounts between £400 and £500, a sizable number, fifteen, invested £600–699. Investors, both male and female, tended to subscribe rounded sums, especially the amounts £125, £250, £375, £500, and £625. The jump between the two latter sums accounts for the gap in the number of investors between £500 and £600. There was another gap at the higher end. If a woman invested more than £675, she usually invested £1,000 or more. In all, eleven women, or 11 percent of female investors in the Bank, subscribed sums over £1,000. This is an amount that Peter Earle associates with the total capital of shopkeepers and tavern keepers in London.[7] When compared to Anne Murphy's figures for Bank of England subscribers in December 1697 we can see that female subscribers invested neither the lowest nor the highest amounts, but clustered somewhere in the middle.[8] For instance, 226 out of a total of 2,175 investors (both men and women), or 10.4 percent, subscribed £100 or less, compared to 4 percent of women who subscribed this same amount. This means more men than women invested at the lowest amounts. And while 12.6 percent of overall investors subscribed between £500 and £999, 27.2 percent of women subscribed this amount, showing that higher percentages of women than men invested sums in this range. Nevertheless, 29.5 percent of all investors subscribed more than £1,000 compared to 11.6 percent of women who invested this much in Bank stock. Women were significantly outnumbered at the highest levels of investment in the Bank of England.

Not all women who subscribed to the Bank of England were wealthy though. Many were urban tradespeople and some even laborers. And almost

[6] Peter Earle, *The Making of the English Middle Class: Business, Society and Family Life in London, 1660–1730* (Berkeley, 1989), 332–3.
[7] Earle, *Making of the English Middle Class*, 45, 270.
[8] I base my figures on Table 6.8 in Murphy, *Origins of English Financial Markets*, 154.

all of the women were commoners. The women who invested ranged in social status from a few noblewomen down to servants and lodgers. For example, among the earliest Bank of England stockholders was Elizabeth Green, a servant in a household in Covent Garden, who subscribed £125 along with another servant.[9]

The Bank of England was not the only option of interest to these early female investors. Prior to the public trading and open subscriptions initiated by the Financial Revolution of the 1690s, joint-stock companies were notoriously nepotistic and it was difficult for an individual without connections to invest in them. Despite these difficulties, women in the know did hold stock in some companies from the Restoration period onward. For example, a list of the "Names of the Adventurers of the Royal African Company" for 1678 included five women out of a total of 195 adventurers. (The list merely included names of adventurers and not the monetary amounts they held.) These five women, Mrs. Elizabeth Ashby, the Right Honorable Katherine, Lady Gray, Mrs. Delitia Nelson (who also appeared among the first subscribers to the Bank of England in 1697), the Lady Priscilla Rider, and Dame Jane Smith, represented the nobility and gentry; the very status groups who had founded and continued to manage the Royal African company. For example, both Rider and Smith were widows of former London aldermen, Sir William Ryder and Sir John Smith.[10] This seems to indicate that it was only elite women with connections who held Royal African Company stock early on. The proportion of women investors in the Royal African Company did slowly rise to 3.93 percent by the 1690s. Women were also more significant as bondholders, holding one fifth of all Royal African Company bonds issued between 1675 and 1681.[11] The number of women investing in another Atlantic world trade company, the Hudson's Bay Company, were also small in the 1690s, but greater than those investing in the Royal African Company. Ann Carlos, Erin Fletcher, and Larry Neal have found that women comprised 4.09 percent of shareholders in the Hudson's Bay Company in the 1690s, two decades after it was chartered in 1670.[12]

Women also invested in less successful ventures. For example, Tories circulated various proposals for a Land Bank as an alternative to the Bank of England; the idea was to issue notes secured on land rather than bullion. In 1696 subscriptions opened for John Briscoe's Land Bank. The subscription list

---

[9] BA, M1/6–9.

[10] "A List of the Names of the Adventurers of the Royal African Company of England" (L, 1681). *The Making of the Modern World* <gdc.gale.com> (accessed September 2013).

[11] Ann Carlos, Erin Fletcher, and Larry Neal, "Share Portfolios in the early years of financial capitalism: London, 1690–1730," *Economic History Review* 68:2 (2015), 588, Table 3; K. G. Davies, "Joint-Stock Investment in the Later Seventeenth Century," *Economic History Review*, n. s., 4:3 (1952), 300.

[12] Carlos, Fletcher, and Neal, "Share Portfolios," 588, Table 3.

included the names of eighty-three women out of 1,511 total subscribers.[13] Women thus comprised 5.49 percent of subscribers to the Land Bank. These female subscribers included two Ladies, four Dames, and two Honourables, but the majority of the women were listed with the title "Mrs." Those whose names appeared had subscribed either land or money, with £1,500 in cash equaling £2,000 subscribed in land. If a person's name had a cross in front of it this indicated the individual had subscribed at least £3,000 and was eligible to be a Director of the Land Bank. Crosses appear before the names of the Honourable Dame Frances D'Averkirque, Dame Elizabeth Archer, Elizabeth Ancher, and seventeen more women, meaning that theoretically these women were eligible to manage the company (although in reality women were never elected to do so in any early modern corporation). Twenty women, or almost a quarter of the female subscribers, invested at least £3,000 in the Land Bank. While such women were enthusiastic about this early venture, unfortunately it was not a success. The Land Bank was only partially subscribed and so it folded.[14]

On the other end of the spectrum of financial success, was the English East India Company. K. G. Davies estimated that in 1685 women held between 2 and 4 percent of East India Company stock. Women were more prominent as East India Company bondholders, holding 20 percent of the company's bonds as early as 1685. (Bonds, or "non-speculative, fixed yield, redeemable securities," were less risky than stock.)[15] Barbara Todd has found that women held 13 percent of East India Company stock in 1688. Like Davies, she discovered women held bonds in higher numbers, comprising 23.3 percent of holders in 1676.[16] Carlos, Fletcher, and Neal found numbers closer to those of Davies for female holders of East India Company stock in the 1690s, with women comprising 7.43 percent of stockholders.[17] So in the last decades of the seventeenth century, we can say women held 2–13 percent of East India stock and 20–23 percent of EIC bonds. The latter was a very high percentage of female involvement in a public investment in the early years of the Financial Revolution.

There were times that women investors comprised a larger proportion of a company's shareholders from the start. One example was the Company of Mine Adventurers. Created in 1700 and incorporated in 1704, the company numbered between 650 and 750 subscribers. A list of the Mine Adventurers

---

[13] *A List of the Names of the Subscribers of Land and Money towards a Fund for the National Land-Bank* (L, 1695) Early English Books Online (hereafter EEBO) <eebo.chadwyck.com> (accessed June 2015).

[14] W. R. Scott, *The Constitution and Finance of English, Scotch and Irish Joint-Stock Companies to 1720*, vol. 3, (Cambridge: Cambridge University Press, 1911), 246–52.

[15] K. G. Davies, "Joint-Stock Investment," 300.

[16] Barbara Todd, "Property and a Woman's Place in Restoration London," *Women's History Review*, 19:2 (2010), 188, and notes 65 and 66.

[17] Carlos, Fletcher, and Neal, "Share Portfolios," 588, Table 3.

dated May 1700 included 731 names, of which 211, or 28.8 percent, were women.[18] This was a comparatively high rate of female subscription for a joint-stock company, only equaled by women's investment in certain government loans. In 1704, another list of subscribers in the Mine Adventurers was printed.[19] This allows a comparison of female subscribers over time. In the second list women comprised 200 out of the 676 subscribers. Both women and overall numbers of subscribers had declined since 1700, but the proportion of female subscribers had increased a bit to 29.58 percent, again a high percentage. Most of the women who appeared in the first list still held their Mine Adventurers stock four years later, but some women had sold out and a few new women had bought in.

Female subscribers to the Mine Adventurers in 1700 included some twenty-eight peers, but the majority of women's names began with the title "Mrs." This means we can conclude that most women who invested in the company were from the gentry or middling ranks. Many of the women who subscribed to this company also appeared in the subscription lists of other investments. For instance, Diana Allington also held shares in the Bank of England. One of the notable names to appear among the subscribers in 1704 was "Mrs. Mary Astell." The author of *A Series Proposal to the Ladies* and *Some Reflections on Marriage,* Astell argued that it was better for women to remain single than to make a bad or venal marriage. Astell herself never married, so it is likely her Mine Adventurers stock was intended to help fund her old age. As we shall see in chapter 6, unfortunately for Astell and others like her, this investment did not come without risk.

Along with joint-stock company and Bank of England shares, women eagerly invested money in government debt in the 1690s. Opportunities for long-term investment in the national debt grew in this decade. Women were regular investors in the Exchequer orders whereby they loaned the government money at interest. Examining the receipts from the Pell's office of the Exchequer reveals that women comprised a notable proportion of these government creditors. A sampling of lenders in 1692/93 reveals that out of 230 lenders, thirty-seven, or 16.08 percent, were women.[20] In 1693 the numbers of female lenders increased. Out of 705 lenders, 136, or 19.29 percent, were women.[21] These numbers are significant; until recently, scholars depicted

---

[18] *A List of all the Adventurers in the Mine-Adventure. May the first, 1700* (L, 1700). EEBO (accessed October 2013).

[19] *A list of the names of the governour and Company of the Mine-Adventurers of England. Nov the twenty third, 1704.* (L, 1704). ECCO. <gdc.gale.com> (accessed October 2013).

[20] The National Archives (hereafter TNA), E 401/1991, Pells Receipts for October 1692–February 1693. Sample of alphabetical lists for surnames beginning with the letters R, S, and T. R= 4 women, 27 men, S= 19 women, 105 men, T = 14 women, 61 men.

[21] TNA, E 401/1992, Pells Receipt Books, April–September 1693. Sample of names appearing on pp. 1–100. Sample = 136 women, 569 men, for total of 705 names.

early short-term lenders to the government as bankers, goldsmiths, and London businessmen. As discussed above, Barbara Todd has found that women figured among these lenders in the 1670s onward. The percentages of female lenders to the government were as high or even higher in the 1690s (19 percent of lenders were female) when compared to the proportion of women lenders Todd found in earlier decades (17 percent). This shows us that from the very beginning of government borrowing women were present as creditors and their numbers only grew with more long-term investment options.

What does this perusal of early investment opportunities reveal about female involvement? As Table 3.2. illustrates, women were early adoptors of the various stocks and securities associated with the Financial Revolution. But the proportion of women involved varied by type of investment. In the 1690s and early 1700s women made up low percentages of investors in private companies. Some of this may have been because they had difficulty gaining access to these popular investments. But there were outliers to this general rule. For instance, women formed a substantial 29 percent of investors in the Company of Mine Adventurers at the turn of the eighteenth century. As we will see in chapter 6, some of this may have to do with the company reaching out to female investors. Women also formed a significant portion of investors, about one fifth, in both short- and long-term loans to the government from the 1670s onward. Who were these early adopters? And how and why did they choose the new public investments made available by England's Financial Revolution? We will now turn to the stories of three women investors to gain a more detailed picture of some of these early adopters.

Table 3.2. Female Investors in the first decades of the Financial Revolution

Investment	Year	Women Investors (%)
Bank of England	1697 and 1690s	8.7 and 13.45
Land Bank	1695	5.49
Company of Mine Adventurers	1700 and 1704	28.8 and 29.58
Exchequer Government Loans	1692/93	16.08 and 19.29
Hudson's Bay Company	1690s	4.09
Royal African Company	1678 and 1690s	0.025 and 3.93
East India Company—stock	1688 and 1690s	13 and 7.43
East India Company—bonds	1676 and 1685	23.3 and 20

Source: Bank of England: Bank of England Archives, M1/6–9 and Ann Carlos, Erin Fletcher, and Larry Neal, "Share Portfolios in the early years of financial capitalism: London, 1690–1730," *Economic History Review* 68:2 (2015), 588, Table 3; Land Bank: *A List of the Names of the Subscribers of Land and Money towards a Fund for the National Land-Bank*; Company of Mine Adventurers: *A List of all the Adventurers in the Mine-Adventure* (L, 1700) and *A list of the names of the governour and Company of the Mine-Adventurers of England.* (L, 1704); Exchequer Government Loans: The National Archives, E 401/1991–2; Hudson's Bay Company: Carlos, Fletcher, and Neal, "Share Portfolios," 588, Table 3; Royal African Company: K. G. Davies, "Joint Stock Investment," 300, and Carlos, Fletcher, and Neal, "Share Portfolios," 588, Table 3; East India Company: Davies, "Joint Stock Investment," 300; Barbara Todd, "Property and a Woman's Place in Restoration London," *Women's History Review*, 19:2 (2010), 188, notes 65 and 66; Carlos, Fletcher, and Neal, "Share Portfolios," 588, Table 3.

3.1. CASE STUDY: SARAH CHURCHILL, DUCHESS
OF MARLBOROUGH (1660–1744)

One of the earliest adopters of public investments, in fact an innovator in the field, was Sarah Churchill, Duchess of Marlborough. Sarah Jenyns was born into a Hertfordshire gentry family, who, like many, were saddled with financial difficulties. She began to make her own way in the world at the age of thirteen, when she followed her elder sister Frances's example and went to Court as a Maid of Honor. At Court, Sarah met her future husband, the courtier and soldier John Churchill. The two fell in love and married secretly when Sarah was only seventeen. Sarah later said she was lucky to find a husband who was kind and careful with money. It was in the early years of her marriage that Sarah Churchill became friends with Princess Anne, the daughter of the Duke of York. When Anne married, Sarah became her Lady of the Bedchamber. Sarah would remain by Anne's side and would benefit financially when Anne eventually became Queen in 1702. During Anne's reign Sarah was the Queen's closest confidant and held the highest position for a woman at court, the Mistress of the Robes, before eventually falling from favor and being displaced by her Tory cousin, Abigail Masham. But even then the Churchills' wealth meant Sarah remained a powerful player in English politics.[22]

Sarah Churchill was undeniably one of the most influential public investors, male or female, in the first twenty-five years of the Financial Revolution. While her husband, John Churchill, Duke of Marlborough, was famous for his deeds on the battlefield, Sarah Churchill is better known for being the power behind Queen Anne's throne. Less discussed, is her financial prowess and influence. In fact, sometimes her political influence was due to her financial knowledge. For instance, in 1710 Sarah Churchill wrote to Queen Anne warning her that if she removed the Lord Treasurer from his office "all the considerable men in the City... would not lend a farthing of money, that all their stocks would fall to nothing; and that if there were any money to be had, nobody could be found to remit it, so that your army must starve, and you must be glad of any peace that the French would give you. And this is not my notion, but what all the substantial men declare of their own accord."[23] Admittedly, Churchill had an interest in keeping her ally and son-in-law Lord Sunderland in the Treasury, but her letter illustrates that she certainly understood the financial consequences of political events.

Sarah Churchill's public financial knowledge translated to her domestic affairs as well. The Duke of Marlborough left all matters financial to his

---

[22] For this section I have relied on Frances Harris, *A Passion for Government: The Life of Sarah, Duchess of Marlborough* (Oxford: Oxford University Press, 1991), esp. chapters 1–6.

[23] *Private Correspondence of Sarah Duchess of Marlborough: Illustrative of the Court and Times of Queen Anne*, 2d. ed., (New York, 1972), vol. I, 344–5.

wife, and despite her coverture Sarah Churchill acted as a feme sole. When the Duke was on campaign, correspondence between the spouses reveals that Sarah handled financial matters for both of them and for their family. For example, in 1702 she wrote to their banker Mr. Coggs, saying "I desire you will make my accounts ready against I come to town which will be in three or four days and I will come to you and settle that matter."[24] Sarah stipulated that she wanted to see both Lord Marlborough's accounts as well as her own separate accounts and mentioned that she would be depositing money with Coggs. This reckoning and balancing with male agents and servants was something Sarah Churchill performed regularly, with an eye to keeping the considerable sums she managed in order.

Sarah Churchill also handled the family's investments, noting when stocks should be bought and sold. In March 1702 she instructed Mr. Coggs, "It was Lord Marlborough's desire that the stock in the East India Company should be sold as soon as it could and therefore...I desire you will goe this morning with Mr. Craggs and transfer what he has made a bargain for."[25] That day, Mr. Craggs punctually transferred £1,166 of the stock. She also directed Mr. Coggs to buy government tallies, telling him to take "6,000 l. out of the money you have in your hands and take tallys in my lord M[arlborough]s name for it tomorrow morning at the Exchequer." Here we see Sarah Churchill directing her agents to cash out East India stock and to re-invest the sum in government loans. She shows her knowledge of new investment opportunities and her ability to direct her banker in financial affairs.

Contemporaries and historians have accused the Marlboroughs of financial shenanigans. There is no doubt that they enjoyed what we would today call "insider trading" information, but in a patronage society like early modern England this was the norm. What has been less recognized is that Sarah Churchill (and perhaps her husband too) understood the new investment opportunities ushered in by the Financial Revolution and used them to their economic benefit. Some of the anger directed against the couple may have been sour grapes, or it may have looked like they were crooked since they did so well in the market. But it is worth noting that some of their material success was due to Sarah Churchill's financial acumen and bravado rather than illegal transactions.

Although she employed agents and brokers, Sarah Churchill also chose to keep her own financial records. She did not think her own financial and accounting abilities were extraordinary for a woman; she expected a certain

---

[24] John Coggs (1664–1710), goldsmith and banker, King's Head over against St Clements' church in the Strand. According to Agnes Strickland he was also Queen Anne's banker and Sarah Churchill ran the privy-purse accounts through him. Arthur Grimwade, *London Goldsmiths, 1697–1837: Their Marks and Lives* (London, 1976), 83. British Library (hereafter BL), Add. MS 61472, Blenheim Papers, f 25, 24 Oct 1702.

[25] BL, Add. MS 61472, Blenheim Papers, f 29, 9 Mar 1702.

level of financial aptitude from women of her station. When her daughter Anne died and her son-in-law Charles Spencer, the Earl of Sunderland, decided to marry again, Sarah Churchill critiqued the prospective bride for her lack of financial ability. Criticizing Sunderland's choice of the Irish heiress Judith Tichborne, Sarah said the prospective bride was too young (around fifteen years) and had "no experience as to family keeping or accounts."[26] It is significant that skills in financial accounting were one of two primary characteristics Sarah Churchill identified as desirable in a wife. One wonders if she would have been mollified to learn that Judith Tichborne turned out to be a more than competent financial investor.[27]

Sarah Churchill had high expectations of her financial agents. She wrote again to Mr. Coggs asking him to "do me the favour to get it put in writing what the last dividend came to out of the Bank for 2,000 l. stock, interest and all, from Michaelmas last 1702, to this Lady Day, 1703."[28] She later asked him for what price he had sold some stock, and another time wrote complaining that he had not sent her "any of the tallys, or orders for the money charged to Lord M[arlborough]s and my accounts, but if you have them from the Exchequer" she would get them when she came to town.[29] This last quote is significant because it clarifies that in 1703 Sarah Churchill, although a married woman, had her own separate account with Coggs. She also mentioned this separate account in later years.

A sense of Sarah Churchill's investment portfolio at the beginning of the eighteenth century can be gleaned from a document dated March 1704/5. Included among her personal financial papers, it is entitled: "The Moneys & Securitys & Annuitys which are the Dutchess of Marlborough's & are to be at her own seperate dispose." The list included an Exchequer annuity for ninety-nine years for £500 per annum, £9,000 loaned out on the land tax, £4,100 in Bank of England stock, and several private securities including £2,000 in Lord Godolphin's hands, £2,000 loaned on mortgage to the Earl of Shaftesbury, and £1,500 in Mr. Chudleigh's hands. In all, Sarah Churchill's separate estate amounted to an impressive £19,100 (or £36.6 million in present-day value).[30]

In addition to illustrating Sarah Churchill's investments, this document also reveals that she controlled these investments as if she were a feme sole and not a married woman. At the bottom of this document the Duke of Marlborough had signed the statement "I do agree yt the moneys above mentioned & ye

---

[26] G. E. Cockayne, *The Complete Peerage of England, Scotland, Ireland, Great Britain and the United Kingdom, Extant, Extinct or Dormant*, reprint (Gloucester, 2000), vol. 12, 488.

[27] Judith Tichborne did in fact marry the Earl of Sunderland. After his death she went on to marry Sir Robert Sutton, who was a Director of both the South Sea Company and the Charitable Corporation.

[28] BL, Add. MS 61472, Blenheim Papers, f 34, Apr. 22, 1703.

[29] BL, Add. MS 61472, Blenheim Papers, f 43, f 46, f 51.

[30] Present-day value calculated on <www.measuringworth.com> (accessed Jan. 22, 2014).

securitys for ye same shall be the Dutchess of Marlboroughs & shall be disposed of as she shall by any writing under her hand from time to time direct." Some three years later, in 1708, the Duke signed an indenture wherein he empowered the Duchess to hold a separate estate and to make a will, despite her coverture.[31] As we shall see in chapter 4, many wives less prominent than Sarah Churchill invested in and held stocks despite their coverture, so while she was a prominent married female investor, Sarah Churchill was not unique.

Without these personal financial papers the extent of Sarah Churchill's personal investing would be unknown (and is perhaps the reason historians have neglected it). This is because Churchill's investments were usually held in the names of male agents and political cronies. For instance, out of the investments named above, her exchequer annuity was under the name of Hugh Chidley [Chudleigh], and her loan on the land tax was funneled through Lord Godolphin, as was £2,100 in Bank stock. Another £2,000 in Bank stock was under Mr. Chudleigh's name. In all, at least £13,100 out of £19,100 of Sarah Churchill's investments were put in other men's names and her name did not publicly show up on them. This was common for both male and female elite investors; so Churchill's actions were not exceptional, nor was her gender the reason for the use of proxy investors. In 1711, when Sarah ventured into the State lottery, she once again did so under others' names. She purchased £1,000 of orders in the 1711 Lottery under the names of five separate men and she ordered her banker to make the purchase.[32] She may well have taken such actions to avoid public scrutiny, but unfortunately for the history of women's investing, her strategy worked too well.

Sarah Churchill's investing acumen is best illustrated by her performance in the South Sea frenzy. In May 1720 she cashed out her family's stock in the South Sea Company, making approximately £100,000 for them. This was right before the stock hit its height in the month of June and then began to decline until September when the inflated stock "bubble" burst. The Duchess foresaw that the inflated prices could not last. "Every mortal that has common sense or that knows anything of figures sees that 'tis not possible by all the arts and tricks upon earth long to carry £400,000,000 of paper credit with £15,000,000 of specie. This makes me think this project must burst in a little while and fall to nothing."[33] Sarah Churchill was correct, the project did "burst," but luckily for her she did know something of "figures" and had taken her own advice and sold out while she was ahead.

Sarah Churchill was interested in many different types of investment, and she was not averse to engaging in some risk. In 1711 her investment portfolio

---

[31] BL, Add. MS 61472, Blenheim Papers, ff. 176–7.
[32] BL, Add. MS 61472, Blenheim Papers, f 182. Her lottery ticket numbers were 139, 127, 126, 103, 2, 6, 13.
[33] Winston Churchill, *Marlborough His Life and Times*, 6 vols. (New York, 1933–8), vol. 6, 643.

included exchequer annuities, government loans, Bank of England stock, mortgages, and State lottery tickets. A few years earlier, in 1708, Lord Godolphin wrote to her saying he knew she had entertained some of the managers of the Royal African Company. He warned her that he had very little "faith" in their project, and that adventurers in the past had been cheated by the "pack of knaves" running the company.[34] It is not clear if Sarah invested in the Royal African Company, but her flirtation with South Sea stock shows she was not above making money on risky ventures. Nevertheless, Churchill chose to invest most of her money in the government, a more reliable investment.

Much of the Duchess's financial influence came from her control of the Marlborough trust (which made her one of the richest women in Britain), and her investment of the trust in the government. Her political enemy Sir Robert Walpole had to come to her (Sarah, not her husband) hat in hand to ask if she would loan the government the trust money. As she put it "I heard him very patiently, though I had been ill treated upon many occasions. I found that it was the old business, to lend money, two hundred thousand pounds immediately, which he had the goodness to own would be a service to him." Walpole implied he was helping her family out by paying an advantageous interest rate (above 3 percent). Sarah Churchill was not naïve about financial matters though. She thought his intimation "a little provoking to one that knew how much Lord Godolphin had lost by lending at such low interest, and how impossible it was for Sir Robert Walpole to have made so much as an appearance of sinking the public debt, if I had not consented to lend the trust money."[35] While many women loaned funds to the government, no individual lender (except for perhaps Lady Betty Germaine) was as significant as Sarah Churchill.[36]

Sarah Churchill not only invested her own, and her family's money, she also gave financial advice and assistance, acting as an informal broker for other women. Churchill managed her mother's estate as executrix, and she also handled the financial affairs of her exiled Jacobite sister, Frances Talbot, Countess of Tyrconnel. These financial activities proved quite fraught for Sarah Churchill, as did her investing for other women. In October 1715, in the midst of the Jacobite rising and with invasion of England seeming imminent, an astute Sarah Churchill weighed the effects of such a rising on investments she had made for Mary Clavering, Countess Cowper. Writing to Cowper, Churchill told her:

> I have sent this Morning Hodges to get Mr. Wymondesold to advise what
> is to be done with the Bonds; for that of the South Sea, which is for

---

[34] *Private Correspondence of Duchess of Marlborough*, vol. I., p. 169. Also see Ophelia Field, *The Favourite: Sarah, Duchess of Marlborough* (Sceptre: London, 2002).

[35] *Private Correspondence of Duchess of Marlborough*, vol. II, 436, 447.

[36] Dickson, *Financial Revolution*, 294.

2,100l., is not worth so much by 2 or 300l. at this Time, and upon the
Duke of Ormond's Landing, or any Disorder, all Stocks will fall very much,
and, though I am not so much frighted as to part with my own, I think I
should not run the Hazard of other People's for 5 per Cent. Interest,
which I agreed with Mr. Wymondesold to take upon the first Money he paid
me at 6, though I did not change the Security.[37]

Churchill understood how military and political news affected the price of
stocks. She characterized herself as unafraid to run a risk but she did not wish
to do so with money belonging to friends.

Thanks to her early and continued embrace of public investments, Sarah
Churchill built up vast personal wealth. She not only managed her husband's
estate during his lifetime and in her widowhood, but "she amassed a huge
fortune of her own in land and investments" and bequeathed it to a younger
grandson, "establishing a second, independent branch of the family."[38] In
December 1743 the Prime Minister Henry Pelham approached her about
loaning money to the government. She loaned not only £300,000 from the
Marlborough Trust but also £123,000 from her own account. Her loans would
amount to somewhere between £58 million and £7.4 billion today.[39] When
Sarah Churchill died in 1744 she held twenty-seven estates in England with a
value of £400,000 and had over £250,000 in public investments, primarily in
Bank of England stock and loans to the Exchequer. Her biographer Frances
Harris says this must have made her one of the richest women in England, and
this certainly was the case.[40] Much of Sarah Churchill's fortune was due to her
early and able adoption of new financial instruments.

3.2. CASE STUDY: MARTHA (HARLEY) HUTCHINS (c. 1657–1719)

On the opposite side of the political spectrum from the Whig Churchills were
the Tory Harleys. Despite political party differences, the Harleys boasted some
equally financially astute women in their family. They included Martha Harley
Hutchins, another early adopter of the public investment options made
possible by the Financial Revolution. Martha was the daughter of Sir Edward
Harley of Brampton Castle, Herefordshire, and his first wife. She was also the

---

[37] Letter from Sarah Churchill, Duchess of Marlborough to Mary Clavering Cowper, Countess, Oct. 1, 1715, in Charles Spence Cowper, ed., *Diary of Mary, Countess Cowper, Lady of the
Bedchamber to the Princess of Wales, 1714–1720* (London, 1864), 207.

[38] Harris, *A Passion for Government*, 4.

[39] www.measuringworth.com (accessed September 2015).

[40] Harris, *A Passion for Government*, 346, 349.

half-sister of Robert Harley, 1st Earl of Oxford, Speaker of the House and Secretary of State under Queen Anne, and of Edward Harley, Auditor under Queen Anne. Her relationship to such politically powerful men meant that she enjoyed access and perhaps insider knowledge of financial investments. In addition to his political position, Robert Harley was also involved in the 1696 Land Bank scheme and in establishing the South Sea Company. In her access, Martha Hutchins was similar to Sarah Churchill, but she differed in that she was of much more modest economic and social standing. Hutchins married quite late (in her late forties), and when she did so, it was to the trader Samuel Hutchins, who did not fare so well economically.[41] In 1712, her brother Nathaniel told their brother Edward Harley that their sister had mentioned how kind Edward was to her and that he thought he should also do his part; "nor would I have her live as a broken merchant's wife, but as our sister." Nathaniel Harley was a merchant in Aleppo, and in 1716 he was planning to return to England when he broached the idea of living together with his sister Martha. He asked her if she preferred "the dirt or smoke of London or the pure country air," but balked at living in Wapping or Stepney, the less elite area where she currently resided.[42] So we know that in the mid-1710s Martha Hutchins was living in an East London area that housed immigrants and dockworkers, certainly not an area for a member of the elite or even for a gentlewoman.

Martha Hutchins's accounts reveal that she tried to assist her husband through investing money. In 1708 she wrote up a list of her assets, which included both domestic and foreign gold coins totaling £60 4s. 6d. To this, she added a ring with five diamonds valued at £6 7s. 6d. She then wrote "The gold and this ring I lent Mr. H to cary to Mr. Garet the goldsmith to take up money upon Wednesday June 17, 1708. Lord give me favor in his eyes that he may now lend it and after enable me to redeem them again if it may be . . . " It seems that Martha Hutchins pawned her gold and jewels, worth a modest £66, so that she and her husband could loan out the sum and make some money from the interest.[43]

Like other women in the Harley family, Martha kept accounts. Her sister-in-law, Elizabeth, Robert Harley's wife, kept meticulous accounts of payments in the late 1680s. Martha's accounts, by contrast, had less to do with expenses and more to do with investments and personal finances. In 1703–4 Martha Harley recorded receiving quarterly interest payments of £10–12 for money she had lodged in the Exchequer, or loaned to the government. Her father,

[41] Family papers reveal earlier marriage negotiations in 1687, when Martha Harley was about 30, and in 1691 with a wholesale grocer; but she did not marry Samuel Hutchins until 1705, in her late forties.
[42] HMC Report, Portland Papers (1893), vol. II, pp. 251, 254–5, 257, 260; vol. III, 399, 479.
[43] BL, Add. MS. 70349, Portland Papers, Accounts of Martha Hutchins (nee Harley), c. 1691–1717.

Edward Harley's 1701 will reveals that he bequeathed large sums to his two unmarried daughters, Martha and Abigail. Martha received £1,200 and his Exchequer annuities.[44] So the money she mentioned in the Exchequer could well have been the annuities she had inherited a few years previously.

A decade later Martha Hutchins had changed her investments, creating a stock portfolio based on her own preferences. In 1713 she wrote "An Account of what Mrs. M. Bailey has laid out for me of the money" Hutchins had entrusted to her. This included £100 stock in the South Sea Company and a State lottery ticket that was a blank (not a prize winner but one that would pay her principal back with interest). In mid-1713 Hutchins bought more South Sea stock, for £127 10s. She recorded that she paid for this stock with four blank lottery tickets, bank notes to the value of £10, £15, and £20 respectively, and "ye rest in money."[45]

Martha Hutchins's accounts also reveal that by 1713 she was speculating or trading in the stock market. She recorded buying £100 of South Sea stock for £83 15s. and selling it out at £91 10s. for a profit of £7 15s. Then she took £100 10s. of this money and "bought a [Lottery] class ticket cept it about a month and sould it for £101—so I gained by it 10s." Admittedly these were modest profits, but the majority of female investors at this time held on to stocks and securities for much longer than a few months. And it was rare for a woman to record and proclaim her profits so explicitly in her accounts. Evidence of Hutchins's trades also appears in the accounts of her female broker, Mary Bailey. Bailey wrote to Hutchins in March 1716/17 saying she had received her orders [to purchase stock] and that an unnamed stock had been trading at 98½ yesterday but since she was not sure she could get the money from her she sold out for 97½ and then "bought in for ye same price for a week longer but this morning I have sold again for 98 so yt I have gained one pound five [shilling]. If it falls any time this week I will buy in again so that by this management I hope when we fix our stock it will make it come to an easy price yn [than] I bought at . . . " These examples indicate that Bailey was playing the market, buying and selling stock on a weekly, if not daily, basis, to make a small profit.[46] Along with her trading profits, Hutchins collected £3 16s. 6d. for six months' interest on her South Sea stock and a £20 prize on a ticket from the 1712 State lottery.

Martha Hutchins employed several agents and brokers in her investing. She mentioned Mr. Terry, who handled payments and receipts for her lottery tickets, Mr. Owen, who paid interest money to her maid, and Mr. Blunt, who paid her money from her brother. But most significant, was Hutchins's use of a

---

[44] Nottinghamshire Archives, DD/4P/37/10, 2 Nov. 1700, will of Edward Harley.
[45] BL, Add. MS. 70348, Portland Papers, Account books of Elizabeth Harley (1687–8) and Martha Hutchins (nee Harley) (1687–1715).
[46] BL, Add. MS. 70349.

woman, Mrs. Mary Bailey, as her broker. Bailey bought and sold her South Sea stock for her in 1713, an early date for a woman to hold this company stock. Hutchins paid 2s. 6d. in brokerage fees for purchasing £100 in stock, and it may be that Bailey also received this fee for her work. Mary Bailey also performed other duties for Hutchins, remitting her interest payments on the stock and holding her money. For example, in 1714 Martha Hutchins wrote that Bailey "had then of mine in her hands [£] 170/16/6½."[47]

By luck, some of the financial correspondence between Martha Hutchins, investor, and Mary Bailey, financial agent and broker, survives. These letters provide a rare window on the investment strategies employed by women. In an undated letter written by Mary Bailey and addressed to "Mrs. Hutchings at ye Black and Whit[e] Ball in Holburn Row in Linkon [Lincoln's] Inn Fields" Bailey provides information on purchasing South Sea stock. She tells her that the Sword Blade office will not lend money so that if Martha cannot borrow £120 to help pay for her £250 of stock "we must sell." Bailey helpfully adds "I can lend you an order of a hundred and twenty pounds to borrow money on." She notes that she has not sold the stock "cause you seemd inclined it should be kept" but unfortunately the stock price was falling and "I believe it will still fall so yt I believe you will be looser by keeping itt so long as now. Pray Madam let me know tonight or tomorrow morning wt you will ples [please] to do I am very sorry my own money is so intangled yt I cannot help you." She concludes by saying stock is now [trading] at 99 and "it was at neer a 100. Yr Humble Servant Mary Bayley. This Day morning 10 a'clock."[48] Mary Bailey both provided investing information and advice to Hutchins but she also acknowledged Martha Hutchins's own decisions; for instance, saying she did not sell the stock since it seemed Hutchins was inclined to keep it.

This letter is revealing of several important facets of women's investing. It shows that women such as Mary Bailey were literate, financially knowledge-able, and connected to the news networks of the financial market. It also reveals that women like Mary Bailey traversed the locations of London's early financial market. For instance, she mentions going to the Sword Blade office (the banker for the South Sea company in these early years) and going out in search of current stock prices. And it shows women were active as financial agents and brokers in the early decades of the Financial Revolution.

Mary Bailey was a cautious broker; she kept detailed financial records and showed concern about her decisions and actions at times. In 1712 when Bailey bought £100 of South Sea stock for Martha Hutchins she noted that she had put the stock in her own name, but she also sent a receipt for it to Hutchins which was witnessed by Joshua Gomez Serra (a member of a prominent Sephardic banking and broking family) as an extra caution. Mary Bailey also

---

[47] BL, Add. MS. 70349.   [48] BL, Add. MS. 70349.

alternated between being defensive and apologetic about her brokering abilities. In an undated letter from sometime around the Jacobite rising of 1715, Bailey explained that yes she had sold the stock on Monday for less than it was worth on Saturday "as you observe," but she did because she feared it would fall lower. She admitted that "it proves very unhappy for us but I must blame my own timorousness for I gave him [Bailey's uncle] orders if it rises never so little to sell before any news from Scotland was publish[ed]." She concluded "we must wait for the next fall and hope for better success, as we get but little so we fall short of many others in our losses." After this she noted "Madam yr gain by buying & selling" was £6 15s.[49] It is telling that Mary Bailey ended her missive with the good financial news.

In this letter Bailey comes across as somewhat unsure of her abilities as a broker on the one hand, but knowledgeable about investment strategies on the other. We learn more about where Bailey's broking knowledge came from as well. She mentions an uncle who was involved in trading in Exchange Alley. And she shows her knowledge of what moved the price of stocks, explaining she was worried that news of the rebellion from Scotland would lower prices. Although Mary Bailey's accounts with Hutchins were fairly clear, she apologizes saying she "is sorry the account [in this letter] is not more particular but she is hindered from writing." She also regrets not waiting on Hutchins in her new lodgings [at an apothecary's near Red Lyon Street, Holborn], but explains that she has been "constantly sick." Thus we learn that Bailey made house calls as a broker.

In 1715 Mary Bailey delivered an account of Martha Hutchins's investments to her. It showed Bailey had about £170 of Hutchins's money in her hands. It also revealed Hutchins's profits: £4 18s. from lottery tickets, £5 8s. by dividends, and £11 10s. gained by stock. In all, Martha Hutchins had £199 7s. 6½d. with her broker. Bailey charged Hutchins 13s. 6d. brokerage for buying fourteen lottery tickets and selling thirteen of the same, as well as 4s. 6½ d. brokerage for buying £180 stock. So in all Bailey made some 18s. (or just less than a pound) on a client who had almost £200 invested with her that year.[50] Hopefully Mary Bailey had other clients with more money, or she was just doing a broking business on the side, for 18s. was not an amount that she could live on.

Mary Bailey made another undated accounting of Martha Hutchins's investments, this time for the three-year period she had served as Hutchins's broker. According to this account she had invested Hutchins's money in stocks, as well as in two State lotteries and the Dutch Lottery. And she wrote, "by this account (which I think is exact) it appears you have gained six per cent and £35 od[d] money more." Bailey's document is analogous to a present-day brokerage or investment statement reporting an investor's rate of

---

[49] BL, Add. MS. 70349.   [50] BL, Add. MS. 70349.

return. In this case, it was 6 percent, which was a very good rate, since the government was paying about 4 percent on its loans.[51] This emphasis on profitability was common in Bailey's accounts for Hutchins. For the period June 1713 to September 1714 she also wrote up an "Account of Profits" for Hutchins. She noted £4 9s. 3d. profit from selling South Sea stock, £1 9s. from selling lottery tickets "the night before the drawing" (when expectations were high), and 9s. 2d. in interest on Exchequer notes. The "Account of Profits" then starts to include more explanations. This is perhaps another sign of Mary Bailey's defensiveness, or maybe just her meticulous accounting. She notes she bought four lottery tickets "as you desired" and that two were blanks and sold for £2 13s. 6d., but two more each came up a £20 prize, and were sold for a profit of £4 12s.

Bailey then provided Martha Hutchins with an apologetic discussion of profits and losses in the State lottery. "Ye £74 laid out by your consent in blanks before the cours[es] were drawn you might a got £30 if they had been bought at ye best advantage and com up well but by my [?] management were bought dear and t[hen] unhappily came in bad courses, if th[ey] had been sold before ye Queen's death ye loss had been £5 but [they] were kept till ye rise of stocks and sold of us" for £8 15s. profit. Bailey's mea culpa attitude is surprising since she bought what Hutchins had asked her to and a broker could not control whether a person won a lottery prize. Lastly, although Hutchins did not get the £30 Bailey had predicted if the timing of the selling of the tickets had been just right, she did make over £8 profit. Perhaps this tone was a ploy by Bailey. Hutchins earned more profits when Mary Bailey traded more lottery tickets and "hired money to buy some South Sea stock [because] all your money being engaged but £20 profit you got by this." Bailey also admitted losses were incurred in the purchase of thirteen Dutch lottery tickets and South Sea stock which had been bought by Martha Hutchins's orders. In all, Mary Bailey calculated that Hutchins had gained or profited by £26 12s. 6½d. since their last accounting. It is not clear over what time period she had earned this profit, but other accounts were made every six months. If this was a profit of £26 for half or even a whole year, this was an impressive rate of return for the amounts Hutchins was investing, which were in the low £100s.[52]

As a broker, Mary Bailey was open about doubting her investing abilities at times and was at pains to prove herself honest to her client Martha Hutchins. It is worth asking if a male broker would have been as honest, cautious, and humble about his abilities in the market. Bailey also worked in concert with male brokers, one a relative and one a more formal broker, in investing for Hutchins. At one point Bailey sent Hutchins a receipt for money she had paid "cause I think it absolutely necessary you shood have convincing proof yt so

[51] BL, Add. MS. 70349.   [52] BL, Add. MS. 70349.

Figure 3.2. *The South Sea House in Bishopsgate St.* (*c.* 1750).
Source: Reproduced by permission of © Trustees of the British Museum.

much is paied. Madm I'm ashamed to tell you yt through mistake I tolde you ye stock was to coste but 83 pounds." She went on to say that because of her mistake "I spent the whole morning in Chang[e] Alley in order to inform myself whether he [her cousin] used me ill or nott." Bailey found that he had not and that the stock had sold on the Monday last for the price he had quoted. She added that the broker who had helped her cousin even "went with me to ye South Sea House [See Figure 3.2.] to get it transferred" and so half was now set down to Hutchins's account and half to Bailey's.[53] Despite her worrying, Bailey was able to deliver as an agent.

Mary Bailey also was concerned about her handling of Martha Hutchins's lottery tickets. She noted that she had sold two tickets for as much as they would have yielded the week before, or at least within 12d. a piece "which is too much to loose by mismanagement and what I'm extremely consearned at, ye reason I speak of ye tickets now is sense I've been so unhappy by my over fear... I woud not willingly appear to be more faulty yn I really am." To confirm these prices, Bailey urged Hutchins to send Mr. Terry to Exchange Alley to ask about the selling price of lottery tickets the week before, since she

---

[53] BL, Add. MS. 70349.

knew that a number of gentlemen had told her to expect £9 for a lottery ticket in the nineteenth course (or drawing). To further prove her honesty, Bailey informed Hutchins that she had overpaid her 6d. when she saw her last but that she also owed her 17s. more. Bailey would wait on her the following week she said, "If I'fe the courage enough to see you after so many blunders as I'fe committed in this afaire."[54] Phrases like "my over fear," "more faulty," and "so many blunders" indicate Mary Bailey's lack of confidence about her performance as a broker. But it is unclear if such uncertainty was indicative of her gender or the nascent financial field in which she was engaged, or both.

Mary Bailey's correspondence with Martha Hutchins also provides some insight into male brokers, revealing that just because a broker was male did not mean he was any more successful. Writing to the peripatetic Martha Hutchins at yet another address (at an apothecary's near Red Lyon St., Holborn) Bailey informed her that her stock had sold last night. She said that a new broker had handled the transaction, since "I had so much trouble with my old one." The new broker did not sound any more promising since Bailey had to hope he would be honest even "though very unsuccessful." She noted that the last time the two women were together "we" had agreed to take "our" money out of his hands, but the broker had put her off and never transferred their stock to Mrs. Hiron either. This failure had put Mrs. Hiron "in a fright" so she "sent word to him he should come to an account or she would give him trouble."[55] While Bailey was Hutchins's broker, it appears she utilized other brokers, both male and female, forming a tangled financial web.

The male broker was evidently frightened enough of his female clients that "in tears he told Bailey's father he had left a good place at the Sword Blade office to broker and had lost a lot of money, but told her father [that Mary Bailey] would not lose any if she kept it a secret." He had promised to pay her some each night, but he had reneged, and Bailey was now the one in tears. In fact, Mary Bailey blamed her late illness on the "dread" she had been experiencing over the possible loss of the money. She even brought in the support of her father who had been to see this broker "everyday" and Bailey herself had "been at severall coffee houses after him" and sent him threatening letters. Bailey's concern made her a dogged agent for Hutchins, or that is how she portrayed herself.

Mary Bailey now shifted her burden from her own shoulders, and, as she had done before, used the language of "we" instead of "you" when discussing Martha Hutchins's investments. She confided to Hutchins that the broker had paid nearly £350 to her but still owed £140 more. He begged "them" to take his bond and he would pay the sum with interest in three payments over the next three months. Bailey asked Hutchins, "I beg your opinion whether we shall

---

[54] BL, Add. MS. 70349.   [55] BL, Add. MS. 70349.

take his bond which is rather more security than a note." And she said if they kept it secret she hoped to see the money sooner. Mary Bailey admitted she had not told Martha Hutchins sooner because she did not want to be "Job's messenger" by adding to the latter's troubles, but told her now since she did not want her to think she was rude by keeping her money too long. As she often did, Bailey added some good news at the end, saying she would pay £140 of Martha's share by breaking into her own stock but would still owe her £55. Bailey tellingly concluded "I am very sorry yt after so much caushon as I have used in contenting myself with small gains for fear of large losses I shod now give up my accounts so very imperfect..." If there were two things Mary Bailey prided herself on as a financial agent, it was caution and clear accounting. What had seemed a cautious approach, aiming for "small gains" rather than "large losses" was even risky when one was an early adopter in the early years of the Financial Revolution.

So much of the correspondence between Martha Hutchins and Mary Bailey is undated and seems to be out of order. This means it is not clear how the two female investors did in the long run. But they do not seem to have gained or lost more than modest amounts. The position or role of Mary Bailey is also uncertain; was she informally broking for a female friend or acquaintance? Or was she an investor herself, willing to help out another woman? She employed other male brokers and male kin to help her. And she herself appears to have been a single woman living with her father. Was she learning the family trade from these male kin?

The end result of Martha Hutchins's investing is also unclear. She appears to have invested more after her husband died. In January 1716/17 she had Mary Bailey pay the remainder of the expenses for her husband's funeral. The ne'er do well, as her natal family thought of him, was gone. There was no mention of children, which is no surprise since Hutchins was in her late forties when she married. What her fortune would be in widowhood was up to Hutchins herself. At age sixty or so, her position may have been aided by the bulse (purse) of diamonds she took possession of in 1718.[56] They were probably sent from Aleppo, Syria, via her brother Nathaniel Harley who had mentioned diamonds in an earlier letter. Whether she traded these herself or turned to an agent or broker like Mary Bailey, is unknown. But by exercising caution, demanding clear accounting, and availing herself of financial agents, Hutchins would have continued the track record of modest yearly profits which she had enjoyed for the past fifteen years. Hutchins wrote a will in 1709, and it was proved in July 1719. She made her single sister, Abigail Harley, her residual legatee and executrix. The wealth Abigail inherited included her sister's "money silver or gold in my own hands or the hands of

---

[56] BL, Add. MS. 70349.

anyone else at interest or otherwise or any right to an annuity…"[57] Martha Hutchins's early adaptation to the market in stocks and securities meant that she was able to transform herself from the wife of a "broken merchant" to an independent widow. And when she died she had amassed enough wealth to be able to pass it on to another female member of the Harley family.

3.3. CASE STUDY: ELIZABETH FREKE (c. 1641/42–1714)

The third early adopter of public stocks and securities profiled in this chapter is Elizabeth Freke. As a married woman she invested both with her husband and on her own, but he ultimately controlled her investments. Elizabeth, however, viewed her investing and securities as her own, whether or not the law, or her husband, did. Elizabeth Freke was born in the 1640s, to Ralph Freke, a landed gentleman with an estate at Hannington, Wiltshire, and Cicely Culpepper (a relation of the herbalist Nicholas Culpepper).[58] In her "Remembrances" Elizabeth provides no information about her childhood, but this source does allow us to track her investments, beginning with her marriage. She recorded that after "six or seven years being engaged to my deer cosin Mr Percy Frek" they married without her father's consent on 14 November 1671. She noted that their marriage took place on a rainy day, which was "a presager of all my sorrows and misfortunes."[59] Freke admitted her marital choice was guided by her "affections," and although her father later relented and accepted the marriage, she regretted her obstinacy, since her marriage produced neither emotional nor financial success.

Elizabeth's "fortune" or marriage portion is a central feature throughout her remembrances, as is her husband's control of it. Financial insecurity is Freke's major theme. As Raymond Anselmont puts it "the brief entries recalling the Frekes' first married years in London underscore an insecurity measured in lost sums of money."[60] Elizabeth's marriage portion was in the form of a mortgage for £500 per annum, but her husband sold it to Sir Josiah Child for £5,664 without her father or her knowing. This was the downside of coverture for women, although without a wife's permission such alienation of her property was technically illegal and it certainly circumvented the notion of a

---

[57] TNA, PROB 11/569/392, will of Martha Hutchins wife of Samuel Hutchins, late of Hackney, Middlesex, 27 July 1719.

[58] Three possible birth dates exist for Elizabeth Freke: 1641/42, 1645, and 1647. I use the date accepted by Freke's biographer Raymond A. Anselmont—January 1641/42—which comes from the registers of St Margaret's Church, Westminster. Anselment, *The Remembrances of Elizabeth Freke, 1671–1714*, Camden Fifth Series, vol. 18 (Cambridge: Cambridge University Press, 2001), 4.

[59] *Remembrances of Elizabeth Freke*, 211.   [60] *Remembrances of Elizabeth Freke*, 9.

cooperative marriage. Elizabeth Freke writes that all of her fortune that remained, about £1,500, was in a "banker's hands" and she worried that her husband would spend it or the banker would lose it.[61] Her husband then tried to take money from her portion and buy a landed estate in Hampshire, but they were cheated. This is a perennial lament in Freke's memoirs, the lack of money or being cheated out of it. She complains that during her first few years of married life she "never had...the command of five pounds of my fortune."[62] Freke brought the money to the marriage and seems to have expected to enjoy a certain status and respect from it, and some control over it. Her attitude is similar to what Alexandra Shepard has found in the answers married women gave to church courts officials when asked what they were worth and how they maintained themselves.[63] Elizabeth Freke may also have been alluding to her lack of "pin money" or an allowance, which rankled the more since it was she who had brought the money to her marriage.

In June 1674 Elizabeth Freke gave birth to the couple's only child, a son named Ralph. Two years later, Elizabeth's husband bought an estate at West Bilney in Norfolk, which he gave to her and settled on their son. Anselmont notes this estate would be the only financial transaction of the marriage that provided some security for Elizabeth, although the Exchequer annuities the couple purchased also provided some security.[64] In order to make the land purchase, Percy Freke had to borrow nearly £1,000 from Elizabeth's father, who loaned it to him on bond. A year or so later Elizabeth's father cancelled the bond as a gift to her. Percy Freke continued to buy landed property and to draw on his father-in-law for loans to do so. He always promised to settle the property on his wife and her son, but only sometimes followed through.[65] Percy Freke then moved the family to Ireland where he had purchased his estate of Rathbary. He continually showed a preference for real estate although he was not above investing in stocks and securities.

Elizabeth Freke's father was the individual in her life who repeatedly ameliorated the financial insecurity that she felt. For instance, in 1682 Elizabeth and her son returned to England for a visit. Her father noted her "melancholy" and attributed it to Elizabeth's "want of mony." He went to his closet and returned with two bags of £100 each, "which 200li. Hee charged me to keep privatt from my husband's knowledge and buy needles and pins with itt. This was very kind of my father." Elizabeth's father provided the pin money both he and she believed she deserved due to her status, but which her husband denied her. For whatever reason, Elizabeth wrote and informed

---

[61] *Remembrances of Elizabeth Freke*, 37–9.   [62] *Remembrances of Elizabeth Freke*, 39.
[63] Alexandra Shepard, *Accounting for Oneself: Worth, Status, and Social Order in Early Modern England* (Oxford: Oxford University Press, 2015).
[64] *Remembrances of Elizabeth Freke*, 10.
[65] *Remembrances of Elizabeth Freke*, 41, 43, 48.

her husband of her father's gift and he suggested a use for the money. But she kept it for herself since as she said, she had not had "two and twenty shillings from my husband in the last two and twenty months I were in Ireland."[66]

Elizabeth Freke chose to take the monetary gift from her father and invest it. As we will see in the next chapter, married women frequently invested pin money or other sums at their own disposal. Evidently Elizabeth was very successful, or her father gave her more money, for she says the original sum of £200 grew to £800. But she also notes her husband took it from her the year after her son married. Legally, Percy Freke was within his rights since she was a feme covert, but it hurt nonetheless. In early 1683/84 Elizabeth's father sent her a New Year's gift of £100 "and ordered mee that iff Mr Frek meddled with itt itt should be lost or he to answer itt with the Irish intrest to my son. But Mr Frek took itt from me."[67] Whenever Elizabeth Freke made money through investing invariably it was her husband, and not herself, who reaped the profits.

Elizabeth Freke lost her protector when her father died in 1684. Having no son, his estate went to a brother's grandson and Elizabeth mentions no bequest to herself (although she obviously had received many sums *inter vivos*). After her father died, Percy Freke deserted Elizabeth and her son and returned to Ireland alone. Elizabeth stayed with a cousin Clayton in London, and then with her married sister Judith Austen. But feeling herself a burden, she decided "to try for a subsistance in Norfolk" and in 1685 went to live on the family's estate at Bilney. Percy Freke turned up after nine months of separation and tried to convince her to settle Bilney on their son (instead of herself). Evidently this time he thought he needed her agreement, but Elizabeth stood firm.[68] She said, "Butt I being left the only trusty [trustee] for my self and my son, God gave me the courage to keep whatt I had rather then part with itt...[69] Because Elizabeth stood her ground, her husband left very angry and this time stayed away for almost two years. When he was separated from his wife and son, he did not monetarily support them, but expected Elizabeth to shift for herself. Such was the conundrum for married women like Elizabeth Freke; their husbands could expect them to maintain themselves financially and yet also claim any profits their wives made.

Some of Percy and Elizabeth Freke's forays into investing in public stocks and securities in the 1690s were a joint venture. Percy Freke would make the

---

[66] *Remembrances of Elizabeth Freke*, 49. Amy Erickson interprets Freke's father differently, asking why he failed to make adequate arrangements for her jointure or to protect it. Amy Erickson, "Possession—and the other one-tenth of the law: assessing women's ownership and economic roles in early modern England," *Women's History Review* 16:3 (2007), 375.

[67] *Remembrances of Elizabeth Freke*, 49–50.

[68] Erickson notes that because Bilney was a freehold Percy Freke could not sell or alienate it without his wife's explicit consent. Erickson, "Possession," 375.

[69] *Remembrances of Elizabeth Freke*, 55.

decision and Elizabeth would (voluntarily or not) provide the money. In August 1698 her husband and son Ralph came to England on a matchmaking trip for Ralph. Visiting her at Bilney, Elizabeth Freke records that her husband "haveing before he left me took from mee my thousand pounds given me by my deer father and putt itt in his own name in the East Indy Company in order to remove itt for Ireland, which he did in August 18, 1702 with the intrest." Percy Freke had taken his wife's money and invested it in East India Company stock, in his own name, which legally he could do. Evidently he did this for liquidity purposes, so he could sell the stock and use the money to purchase land in Ireland.

Nevertheless, Elizabeth Freke also seems to have been investing on her own in the early years of the Financial Revolution. Between 1698 and 1702 Freke's husband and son were in Ireland more often than not, leaving Elizabeth alone. Her son married and began having children and her husband continued to make land purchases in Ireland, calling on her for further funds, which she sent him from England. In May 1703 her husband wrote to her to meet him at Bath where he seems to have wanted to attempt some reconciliation, saying he would live with her at Bilney. Evidently this did not go well, since Elizabeth reported: "I went to Bath of a fools errant to meett Mr Frek." She only stayed ten days and returned home alone. It all may have been a ruse to get more money out of her since on the way to Bath she had stopped in London to "make up all accounts with my cosin John Freke." In doing so, Elizabeth found out that of £2,000 and interest that was in Bank of England stock, her husband had "taken up of itt" all but £500 and wanted more. So "I sold itt quite outt of the Bank of England, itt then bearing a great price, I thought I could nott doe better, the banking runing high." Freke records this money had started out as her "own": £1,500 given to her by her father, which had increased to over £2,000, due to "my imporvementt of itt for 18 years." Her husband got all of it but £113 9s., which she took for her "own use."[70] It is unclear whose name the Bank stock was in, but Percy Freke was able to withdraw it and Elizabeth Freke was able to sell it, so it may have been in both their names. It also is possible that cousin John Freke controlled the money and answered to both Percy and Elizabeth's orders. In any case, Elizabeth maintained the money was hers; her father had given her three-quarters of it and she had "improved" the sum by another 30 percent by investing it. Percy Freke was so angry with his wife's independent actions that when he came to England six months later he refused to see her "for moveing that little remaine of my mony outt of the Bank of England."[71]

Even though her husband had mixed feelings about it, Elizabeth Freke was an able manager of money and she was able to find other sums to invest. In

[70] *Remembrances of Elizabeth Freke*, 78, 242.   [71] *Remembrances of Elizabeth Freke*, 243.

1704 she bought "an estate in the parliamentt funds of the exchecker of above a hundred pounds a yeare for ninety nine years" beginning from Lady Day of that year. This was the government loan of 1704 that raised money through the sale of ninety-nine-year annuities that paid 6.6 percent interest. Elizabeth records that this cost her £1,500 and that she bought this annuity not for herself, but for her grandson Ralph Freke, who had been born the previous summer.[72]

In 1705 Elizabeth Freke's husband became ill, which brought an end to their personal and financial quarrels, and ultimately increased Elizabeth's economic authority. Once sick, Percy Freke went to Bilney to live with his wife and have her care for him. The two seem to have reconciled (perhaps due to the accidental death of a grandson or Percy Freke's impending death) and he proceeded to build his vault in Bilney's church in March 1706. When Percy Freke died in June 1706, Elizabeth spent a goodly sum to give her husband what she termed "a gentleman's burial" and funeral. She may have done so to keep up family honor and appearances, but Elizabeth may have been so inclined because her husband had named her as one of his executors and had left his estates to her for life. This was at least some recompense and acknowledgment for all the financial help Elizabeth Freke had brought to her husband during their marriage.[73]

Now a widow, Elizabeth Freke ventured into independent financial territory. A month after she buried her husband, she went to London to meet with cousin John Freke, her co-executor, to prove her husband's will. Percy Freke had revised his will just a few months before his death and one wonders if writing it as his wife nursed him led the document to reflect a more congenial attitude toward her.[74] Elizabeth recorded that her husband generously "left me all his estate unsettled for my life in England, and in Ireland, and in the bank [Bank of England and] excheker [Exchequer] and gave me att my own disposal all his personall estate. And with itt twelve hundred pounds fell to me undisposed of in London." She estimated her annual income to be £850 from the Irish estates, £500 from the English estates of West Bilney and Pentney, and £200 in the Exchequer. In addition to this £1,550 she also received her husband's personal estate and rent arrears owed him.[75] The rents would prove a disappointment. She sent John Freke to Ireland to prove the will there, but he returned after three months with "a most sad account of all my affairs in Ireland... and [how] I am cheated of above fowre thousand pounds" by her husband's steward, and how her tenants were not

[72] *Remembrances of Elizabeth Freke*, 78. Dickson, *Financial Revolution*, 60.
[73] *Remembrances of Elizabeth Freke*, 251, 289–303.
[74] *Remembrances of Elizabeth Freke*, 290.
[75] *Remembrances of Elizabeth Freke*, 87, 252.

paying their rents. Elizabeth blamed John Freke for resolving nothing and merely informing her of these disordered affairs.[76]

The lands Elizabeth Freke inherited were a continual financial disappointment to her. As a widow Freke now controlled her own property, but ironically she had more trouble doing so than when she was married (or at least she claimed she did). In 1708–9 her Norfolk tenants brought legal suits against her, illegally cut down her timber, and skipped out on paying rents.[77] She noted one male tenant named Towers had "thus roged mee by his tricks since my deer husband dyed" three or four different times.[78] Elizabeth implied that Towers took advantage of her once her husband was no longer present. On one level this explanation seems odd, since Freke had usually been on her own at Bilney even when her husband was alive. But perhaps it had been the implied threat of her husband that had been enough to keep her tenants in line, rather than his actual presence. Things only got worse when Elizabeth Freke reported that her tenant Thomas Garrett broke into her house and with several ruffians physically threatened her. In spring 1709 Freke totaled up how much she had lost through unpaid rents, legal cases, and other problems with her tenants, as well as her inability to directly manage her affairs because she could not "goe outt of my chamber" due to ill health. She reckoned a loss of £758 from her landed property. For Elizabeth Freke, depending on rents and landed property for income put her in a precarious situation.[79]

Elizabeth Freke also reveals how a woman's lack of legal knowledge could leave her financially vulnerable. Elizabeth blamed her loss of rents on "my cosin John Freks nott letting me know I ought to have made new leases att my deer husbands death and my ignorance." In other words, if Elizabeth Freke wanted to take a tenant to court for not paying rent, the validity of her leases were in question because they retained the name of her husband rather than her own as a widow. These were not the only losses she blamed on her cousin John Freke. She had given her letter (or power) of attorney to cousin John Freke when he went to Ireland to prove her husband's will there. Taking advantage of his legal authority, John Freke—"my pretended truste" as she called him—"gave away from me to my son my deer husbands estate in Ireland hee gave me of 750 pounds a year." She asked rhetorically whether this was "kind or faire" for cousin Freke, her trustee, to give away her Irish estate to her son who had £800 a year settled on him.[80] Once again, Elizabeth found herself legally vulnerable, with her cousin taking advantage of his position and

[76] *Remembrances of Elizabeth Freke*, 91–4.
[77] *Remembrances of Elizabeth Freke*, 96–7, 100–1.
[78] *Remembrances of Elizabeth Freke*, 96–7, 100–1.
[79] *Remembrances of Elizabeth Freke*, 105.
[80] *Remembrances of Elizabeth Freke*, 106, 257.

rewarding her son over her.[81] The toll Elizabeth Freke's landed property had taken on her was immense. Constant repairs, tenants who would not pay their rents, or worse physically threatened her and stole from her, as well as legal disputes, wasted her time and energy.

After these experiences, perhaps it is no surprise that in her widowhood Elizabeth Freke chose to put her money into stocks and securities and not into land. Like other women we will see in later chapters, she altered the stock portfolio she inherited from her late husband. Along with the East India Company stock in her husband's name, and some possible Bank of England stock, by the early 1700s Elizabeth Freke also invested in Parliamentary or government annuities. After her husband's death, Elizabeth took £1,200 undisposed by her husband's will, and adding some more to it, put it in another ninety-nine-year Exchequer annuity for her third grandson. In 1707 Freke also mentioned putting "out in the tax of England a thousand pounds for my grandchild." The following year she was collecting interest on £1,000 invested in the Land tax. Overall, Freke chose to alter her portfolio in the direction of government funds and annuities. This was a move many older women made.

Freke's example also illustrates that widows, even though femes soles, could, like femes coverts, sometimes experience difficulties in claiming investments as their own. Cousin John Freke served as Elizabeth's financial agent and purchased her investment instruments for her. In late 1707 or early 1708 Elizabeth began to get angry with Freke's management of her affairs. She accused cousin Freke of denying her her exchequer orders even though they were bought with "my own money."[82] Perhaps cousin Freke was treating them as part of the deceased Percy Freke's estate, of which he, along with Elizabeth, was an executor. Fed up, in 1711 Elizabeth went to London to take control of the £3,000 in cousin John's hands and "to place [it] outt" since she said there was "nothing to show for itt." This was an indication that she did not believe he had invested or improved the capital. She instructed her cousin John to take her money out of the East India Company and "to place itt in the Bank of England for me in hundred pound tickets [that] I might command itt, [it] being 3,100li."[83] Elizabeth Freke recorded that her cousin "came very early in the morning very angry with me and brought with him the three thousand pounds tickets, which hee said was as secure in his hand. I told him my reputation was all I had to live on, and I had nothing to show for this my mony butt his memorandum, and that hee had refused me his bond . . . Twould be beyond all discretion for me to have three thousand two hundred pound in his hand thatt had not a foot of land for the security of, Eliza Frek." He went away

---

[81] *Remembrances of Elizabeth Freke*, 21–2, 24, 28.
[82] *Remembrances of Elizabeth Freke*, 91, 95.
[83] *Remembrances of Elizabeth Freke*, 164, 276–7.

angrily, of which she said she took no notice.[84] Elizabeth Freke stood firm against what she saw as a mismanaging, if not cheating, male financial agent; a situation made worse by the fact that he was kin. She wanted "security" for her investments and felt that John Freke's word was not secure enough. If he would not formally document their financial arrangements, she wanted the investments in her own name and in her own hands. Elizabeth Freke may have been an early adopter of public investments but she had also learned quickly from her experiences in the market.

While in London in 1711 Elizabeth Freke also made a foray into the new State lottery. She does not record if she invested in the lottery for herself, but she did buy a lottery ticket for her cousin Mary Lackendane, so she could "try her luck." The ticket did not win a prize for Lackendane, "by which she gott nothing butt lost my mony," said Freke. This statement indicates Freke may not have understood that her money would be paid back over a series of years with interest. Freke did not avail herself of other public securities, rather, she made private loans of £1,300 to George Norton on bond at a rate of 6 percent annual interest, and another £1,200 on mortgage. And she left about £1,000 in cousin John Freke's hands for which she got his note.[85] These were securities, but were personal rather than public investments.

Elizabeth Freke was a reckoner or accountant by character. Anselmont posits that "measuring or accounting may have provided both diversion and reassurance amidst the tedium and fear of pain and age" for Elizabeth. He adds that over time "money had become for her, quite simply, a measure of self-definition amidst isolation, sickness, and loneliness."[86] Certainly the listing of property and money allowed Elizabeth Freke a way to define herself and her life, but it was also a way for her to control and bring order to what had been a disorderly and fraught financial history. Among her papers was "a true account of the rents of West Billney" dating from 1672, the year when her father first bought the estate, and extending forty years up to 1712, through the years the property was under her management. The accounts show that Elizabeth was able to increase the rents to £518 a year after the profits had fallen under her brother-in-law's management to a low of £414. Elizabeth also recorded the ownership of West Bilney from the year 1547 up to 1712. She proudly recorded that the estates had been "in me, his daughter Elizabeth Freke, viz., for thirty eightt years and upward, and in my deer father's possession neer fifty three yeares, iff right recknd by me, EF." It is significant that Elizabeth's lineage of ownership extends from her father to herself to her

---

[84] *Remembrances of Elizabeth Freke*, 277.
[85] *Remembrances of Elizabeth Freke*, 189.
[86] *Remembrances of Elizabeth Freke*, 17, 30–1.

son, something she downplayed when confronting legal officials, but emphasized in this more private document.[87]

Elizabeth Freke created another financial record in 1712, which she entitled
"Account of Money E. Freke Lent and Brought to Her Husband." Elizabeth
again figures herself as the actor and the subject in this document. In a
prefatory note, Elizabeth says she showed this account to her husband in
1705 "who after reading of itt said I was true and that he could deney noe part
of itt..." According to this document Elizabeth Freke began giving money to
her husband as early as 1672, right after their marriage, when "I lent him of my
own savings" £320 to pay Aunt Freke his parent's bond to her. The following
year she covered a significant £350 in drinking debts that her husband had run
up. In all she gave Percy £920 in the first three years of their marriage. The fact
that Elizabeth viewed these sums as "loans" is also significant, since legally her
property was now her husband's, and could thus be used by her husband
without any expectation of repayment. Elizabeth Freke saw things differently.
For the years 1674–81 she listed her marriage portion and the amounts she
and her husband had borrowed from her father, usually on bond, totaling
£11,852 14s. Almost half of this was her marriage portion, which under
English common law was not a loan. Elizabeth next listed monies her father
had given her since she was married, including £200 pin money, a £100 New
Year's gift, and a sizable legacy of £11,232 14s. This list then segued into sums
her husband had "borrowed of me" or "took up of mine," including her "own
proper mony and savings, unknown to me," sums "removed from my stock
into mony," and sums "of my own savings and improvemtt." In all, Elizabeth
subtotaled this account recording £11,232 14s. from her father, plus £12,713
from her "own industry and savings att Billney," for a total of £23,945 14s. By
recording the sums in this way Elizabeth showed she had more than doubled
the inheritance her father had given her.[88]

Elizabeth Freke also totaled up what money she had to bequeath. She listed
her important papers in an "account of whatt parchments and papers I have
laid in my upper closett in a black trunk sowed up to be kept by my executors."
Among them was an "Account of Freke's Personal Estate" dated Sept. 29, 1712.
She labeled this personal estate as "in my power to dispose of in my will and
given me by my deere husband att his death in his will made Feb. 21, 1705."
Her estate consisted of five Exchequer annuities totaling £203 a year, two
mortgages, money in cousin Freke's hands, including interest on her Exchequer funds, and £400 in ready money "in my closet in my great haire trunke,"
all totaling £4,148, and which was readily disposable by her. Below this
amount she listed money that she was owed but not in possession of and
which could probably be written off as "desperate debts." This included the

[87] *Remembrances of Elizabeth Freke*, 304–13.
[88] *Remembrances of Elizabeth Freke*, 316–19.

£1,200 in Irish rent arrears never received after her husband's death, £1,920 still unpaid by her son, as well as five years of rents her son owed her totaling £3,200, for a grand total of £7,268.[89] This is a stark account. As Elizabeth shows, her personal estate should have consisted of over £11,000 and yet she held only a little over a third of that. In effect, her son had taken a huge chunk of his intended inheritance in advance.

Once widowed, Elizabeth Freke had promptly made her will. Despite ill health, she traveled to London in April 1707 to draw up the document. After so many years of having no control over her finances, Freke could now manage her financial affairs without concerns that a husband would override them or seize her assets. The importance of the document to her is attested to in an entry for November 1710 when she recorded that she was sitting in her chamber one evening "reading some part of my will."[90] Freke also altered her will over the years. In 1712 Elizabeth's son and daughter-in-law made a show of reconciliation and contrition; they wrote proposing a visit and asked her to name their new child. Elizabeth named her granddaughter Grace, and wrote her into her will with a bequest of £500. She had settled a £2,000 estate on her eldest grandson Percy Freke, and for her second grandson Ralph Freke, she had provided a £203 annuity from the Exchequer and a £2,000 mortgage on Sir George Norton's estate at 6 percent. Elizabeth Freke proudly recorded her provision for the Freke lineage and how she had made this possible "of my own industry."[91] As for her prodigal son, Elizabeth left him a modest inheritance of a picture of himself and the right to live at West Bilney until his son Ralph came of age and took over. This was because Elizabeth had already given her son much more. A year earlier she had bought "a pattentt of a baronet...to present my son and daughter with, hee being by my Gods blessing on my industrious endeavours now entitled to after my death full two thousand pounds a yeare in England and Ireland and his two eldest sons provided for by me, Eliz Frek, who when I maryed Mr Freke in the yeare 1671 had but two hundred pound a year."[92] At her death, Elizabeth Freke took pains to remind her kin that it was through her blood, sweat, and tears, as well as her sharp financial management and investment, that they received these monetary gifts. Her early adoption of public investment in the government funds, Bank of England, and East India Company, had made much of this possible.

We get a hint of how Elizabeth Freke assessed the success of a woman in her record of the death of her cousin Hamilton. In February 1709/10 Freke noted that Hamilton "dyed vastly rich and handsomely provided for twelve of

---

[89] *Remembrances of Elizabeth Freke*, 319–26.
[90] *Remembrances of Elizabeth Freke*, 91, 270.
[91] *Remembrances of Elizabeth Freke*, 192–3, 199.
[92] TNA, PROB 11/539 15 April 1714, will of Elizabeth Freke.

her grandchildren and her two sons. Eliz Freke."[93] The fact that Elizabeth appended her name, which she did as added emphasis after solemn or significant notations, affirms the importance of this entry to her. As she contemplated her last years and made her will, a similar goal of dying with a prosperous estate that she could pass on to her grandchildren was of the utmost importance to her. Thanks to Elizabeth Freke's investments and "improvement" this was possible for her.

Elizabeth Freke requested to be buried in Westminster Abbey and her natal family saw this wish fulfilled. Freke was buried in the nave of the Abbey in an unmarked grave with her two sisters who had stood by her throughout her life. Elizabeth's sister Norton, the last of the three to die, put up a memorial on the wall. Dedicated to her sisters Elizabeth Freke and Judith Austen, she had it inscribed with the words "frugal to be Munificent," a phrase that echoed their father's monument, and one that certainly sums up Elizabeth Freke's financial and investing history, as well as her definition of self.[94]

*   *   *

This chapter has shown how women were early adopters of the financial instruments and investing opportunities made available by England's Financial Revolution. In the 1690s women appear in the subscriber lists of various types of public investments—the Bank of England, the Land Bank, the Royal African Company, and the East India Company—in small but growing numbers. This chapter has also looked beyond the aggregate number of women to explore in detail some of these female early adopters. They ranged from courtiers and noblewomen, such as Sarah Churchill, Duchess of Marlborough, to merchant's wives such as Martha Hutchins, and country gentlewomen such as Elizabeth Freke. These women were early investors in both the government, via Exchequer annuities, land tax loans, and State lottery tickets, as well as joint-stock companies, notably the South Sea and East India companies. All three women were able to pass on vastly improved personal estates or wealth to their family members due to their adaptation to the new stock market. It is to women's investing for their families that we will now turn in the next chapter to examine the role of women as familial financial agents in more detail.

---

[93] *Remembrances of Elizabeth Freke*, 128.
[94] *Remembrances of Elizabeth Freke*, 21.

4

Women as Investors for their Families

Sarah Osborne, the daughter of Admiral George Byng and the wife of a gentleman, found herself widowed at the young age of twenty-four. She was left with two minor sons and her husband's ill-managed affairs and debts. With the death of her father-in-law a year later, her eldest son became the heir. As guardian for little "Sir Danvers" Sarah Osborne managed his estate. When she turned it over to him sixteen years later the trust was in a "greatly improved condition." One of the reasons for this was Sarah Osborne's investment in public stocks and securities. In 1722 she wrote to her brother Robin for some assistance in persuading the family lawyers to her investment plan. She remarked that the rents from the family estate had been paid into a Chancery [court held] account but she wanted to obtain an order "to permit it to be put out on [East] India bonds, etc. that I might have intrest, and not let it lye dead—for there is above £600 paid in there wch lyes dead without interest."[1] Sarah Osborne wanted to take money from rents on the family estate and invest it in public securities. Her strategy was to transfer rents, one form of personal estate, into public securities, another form of personal estate. She argued that putting the inheritance in East India bonds would improve the interest or profits on her son's inheritance. Following Sarah Osborne's plan this £600 invested at the average rate of 5 percent would have grown to £1,139 39 s. when her son achieved his majority thirteen years later. Despite Sarah Osborne's preference for public securities, and the fact that his inheritance benefited from being invested in them, Sir Danvers did not opt for these investments when he came of age. In 1739, Sarah Osborne again wrote to her brother, asking for almanacs, rulers, pencils, red ink, and ruled paper so that she could keep her accounts. She also remarked disparagingly that: "My son ... is frightened at borrowing mony and mortgaging, and therefore is most inclynd to what is a certainty; tho in ye end not so profitable."[2] In this family, the widow Sarah Osborne was the innovator and the investor in new

---

[1] Emily F. D. Osborn, ed., *Political and Social Letters of a Lady of the Eighteenth Century 1721–1771* (London: Dodd, Mead and Co., 1891), 26–7.
[2] Osborn, *Political and Social Letters*, 60.

forms of property such as stocks and securities, and her son Sir Danvers was the one who embraced tradition and certainty in the form of land.

This chapter examines how women's familial roles both affected and inspired their investment in public stocks and securities on behalf of their families. The women discussed in this chapter included wives, who despite their coverture invested for themselves and their families. Others were women who invested for kin for whom they were financial guardians, or sisters who invested for their siblings. In all of these cases, a family recognized that a female member was the most competent and suitable person to entrust with funds to invest for a profit. These women became financial agents for their families, and more often than not, as we shall see, they were successful in their investment choices. The investing capability of numerous women in eighteenth-century England helped make many a family fortune.

Femes soles, both adult spinsters and widows, enjoyed a legal status in England that allowed them to invest independent of a male guardian. Common law did not allow married women, or femes coverts, to buy or sell or make contracts on their own. But women frequently ignored the strictures of coverture or circumvented them through separate property arrangements. Amy Erickson recently has posited that the particularities of the common law, most significantly coverture, may actually have facilitated England's transition to a capitalist economy in two ways. First, since English wives could not own property this led to "complex legal manoeuvres which produced complex financial instruments and a populace accustomed to them." And second, Englishwomen who were not married, including both single women and widows, were able to fully and independently participate in the investment opportunities of the Financial Revolution, thereby increasing the number of possible public investors in England.[3] While Erickson speculated about the relationship of coverture and capitalism in England, this chapter provides the evidence. We will see specific examples of both married and unmarried women circumventing coverture or utilizing their feme sole status to engage in public investments. We will begin by exploring the new forms of property available to women that enabled them to invest on their own. Then we move on to examining women who invested despite their coverture, as well as women who invested for their families, whether as mothers, aunts, or sisters. The chapter concludes with a case study of Mary Barwell, who served as her brother Richard's financial agent while he was in India and who managed a portfolio of as much as £50,000 for him in the 1760s and '70s. Barwell is an example of a woman who functioned as a financial agent par excellence for her family.

The Financial Revolution created new forms of property for Englishmen and women to purchase and hold, most notably government lotteries and

---

[3] Amy Louise Erickson, "Coverture and Capitalism," *History Workshop Journal* Issue 59 (2005), 3, 5.

annuities as well as company stocks and bonds. The legal status of these new forms of property was undergoing clarification in the late seventeenth and early eighteenth centuries. Charles Sweet asserted that the government funds (lotteries and annuities) of the 1690s were authorized and made assignable by statute law. Exchequer bills were also considered assignable and the common law courts recognized the transfer of any such funds. The charters or letters patent that created the Bank of England and joint-stock companies ensured the stock in such ventures was also assignable. By at least the beginning of the eighteenth century, if not earlier, stock in the government funds and in joint-stock companies was classified as personal estate, in particular what were called choses in action (things not yet in possession).[4] Barbara Todd notes that in 1704 the legal status of government annuities was further spelled out in a statute passed under Queen Anne. Annuities were to be considered personal estate, like cash or other movables, rather than real estate, or land. And if a wife held these annuities, under coverture they were considered the property of her spouse. A wife could hold annuities as part of a separate estate, however. And even if trustees held the wife's annuity, Todd says "a simple letter of attorney registered with the Exchequer allowed her to have full control of that asset, free of her husband's interference."[5] As personal estate, investments were more liquid and more likely to be held by women than real estate.

Single women and widows, as femes soles, were allowed to manage their own personal property, and as such could own, buy, and sell government funds and company stocks and shares. Married women, or femes coverts, could not hold or control their own property according to England's common law. Coverture, however, was always more of an ideal than a reality and this only became even more so with the rise of what Susan Staves has termed "new forms" of women's property, such as married women's separate property and pin money.[6] Married women's separate property, detailed in pre-nuptial contracts, vested in the hands of trustees, and legally upheld in courts of equity became common by the seventeenth century.[7] Amy Erickson has shown

[4] Charles Sweet, "Choses in Action," *Law Quarterly Review* No. XL (1894), 311–14.

[5] Barbara Todd, "Fiscal Citizens: Female Investors in Public Finance before the South Sea Bubble," in Sigrun Haude and Melinda S. Zook, eds., *Challenging Orthodoxies: The Social and Cultural Worlds of Early Modern Women* (Farnham: Ashgate, 2014), 62–3, 55.

[6] Susan Staves, "Pin Money," *Studies in Eighteenth-Century Culture* 14 (1985): 47–74; Susan Staves, *Married Women's Separate Property in England, 1660–1833* (Cambridge, MA: Harvard University Press, 1990).

[7] For married women's separate property see Tim Stretton and Krista J. Kesselring, eds., *Married Women and the Law: Coverture in England and the Common Law World* (Montreal: McGill-Queen's University Press, 2013); Amy Erickson, "Common law versus common practice: the use of marriage settlements in Early Modern England," *Economic History Review* 43 (1990): 21–39; Janelle Greenberg, "The Legal Status of the English Woman in Early Eighteenth-Century Common Law and Equity," *Studies in Eighteenth-Century Culture* 4 (1975): 171–81; Susan Moller Okin, "Patriarchy and Married Women's Property in England: Questions on Some Current Views," *Eighteenth-Century Studies* 17:2 (1983–84): 121–38.

that marriage settlements were not only employed by the nobility and gentry, but also by "ordinary" people to protect property not only for the wife, but for her children. Janelle Greenberg posits a connection between "the doctrine of the wife's separate estate" and the fact that over the early modern period fortunes of daughters were increasingly comprised of personal rather than landed property. Personal property was perhaps more easily "appropriated by their husbands" and thus fathers may have protected property from being alienated by sons-in-law by utilizing marriage contracts and vesting daughters' portions in the hands of trustees.[8] Another type of women's separate property, pin money, was an annual allowance a husband paid to a wife for her "necessaries," a category that included clothes and minor purchases for personal items, entertainment, and charity.

The emergence of all of these new forms of legal property coincided with and perhaps encouraged women's investment in stocks and securities, themselves new forms of financial property. Women's marriage portions and jointures—the two major forms of inheritance received by women during their lifespans—were increasingly invested in public funds and securities. In the sixteenth century, jointure had replaced the common law tradition of widow's dower in England. Instead of a widow's right to a third of her husband's estate, most prosperous families stipulated in writing exactly what family property would make up a widow's inheritance and this inheritance was often in the form of a rent charge on property.[9] The composition of jointures and marriage portions altered with the Financial Revolution. There were some key benefits to putting women's inheritances in the new public securities; they were more liquid and more easily divisible than a jointure or portion based on land. An example of this can be seen in the case of Mrs. Antonia Keck who died sometime around 1739 right on the verge of marriage. Her personal estate included a £4,000 portion in the hands of Francis Keck, Esq. and £800 for four years' interest on it. It seems Antonia's family had chosen to invest her portion in securities, for there were £5,000 in South Sea annuities "to answer [for] the £4,000 portion" at a 5 percent rate of interest.[10] Likewise, in 1754 when Lady Hester Grenville married William Pitt (the future Prime Minister), her portion consisted of £12,000 in 3½ percent Consolidated Bank annuities.[11] Public stocks and securities provided a neutral and safe place to lodge a child's inheritance in the event of a parent's early

---

[8] Greenberg, "The Legal Status of the English Woman," 125–6.

[9] For jointure see Eileen Spring, *Law, Land and Family: Aristocratic Inheritance in England, 1300–1600* (Chapel Hill, NC: University of North Carolina Press, 1993), esp. chapter 2, and Amy Louise Erickson, *Women and Property in Early Modern England* (London: Routledge, 2002), 25–6.

[10] The Huntington Library (hereafter HEH), Stowe Temple Brydges Papers, STBF Box 11/4, 32.

[11] HEH, Stowe Temple Grenville Papers, STG Personal Box 6/22.

demise, a wastrel heir, or a predatory step-parent. For example, when the orphaned heiress Anna Chambers married Richard Grenville, the 2nd Earl Temple, in 1737, the marriage contract stated that her estate consisted of the impressive sum of £42,212—all held in stocks and annuities in the East India Company, the Bank of England, and the South Sea Company.[12]

The category of pin money led to much consternation over married women's access to new forms of property. The concept of pin money originated in the late seventeenth century as a legal device by which parents could assure their daughters' standard of living after marriage. Stipulating an allowance in a marriage contract assuaged concern about a married daughter being able to maintain a life style to which she was accustomed. Once a husband granted his wife an allowance, however, it was not entirely clear what a wife would choose to spend it on. Pin money was supposed to be for necessaries and small purchases, but some enterprising female spouses went much further than this. Susan Staves, who has examined the emergence of legal theory on pin money from the 1690s to the early 1800s, notes that the legal system had to respond to the problem of women taking "property intended for maintenance and [using] it as capital."[13]

A common trope in eighteenth-century literature was the woman who used her pin money to gamble. For example, the author of the *Female Tatler* wrote: "Gaming is what I always detested, the Consequences of it having been the Ruine of several Families . . . and at the same time Mr. Cogdie is drawing away Sir George's Thousands, Mrs. Cogdie Shall be throwing at my poor Lady's Pin-Money."[14] Here the author draws attention to women using their pin money as gambling stakes, although this could be considered a permissible use since it was acceptable to use pin money for entertainment. Married women, however, did not just gamble with their pin money; they also invested it and profited by it.

Throughout the eighteenth century the equity courts heard cases resulting from wives using their pin money to buy real estate, to secure loans, and to invest in stocks and securities. The question for jurists (and interested husbands) was did property purchased with pin money belong to the wife, or to the husband, since the woman was a feme covert? Susan Staves has found that at the turn of the eighteenth century the courts upheld a wife's right "over savings or other proceeds of her pin money." The case of *Milles v. Wikes* (1694) determined that a wife could bequeath savings from her pin money, the equity case of *Gore v. Knight* (1705) established that a wife could dispose of the produce or interest of her separate estate, and *Wilson v. Pack* (1710)

---

[12] HEH, Stowe Temple Grenville Papers, STG Personal Box 5/2.
[13] Staves, "Pin Money," 50.
[14] *The Female Tatler* no. 9 (1709). Eighteenth Century Collections Online <www.galegroup. com> (accessed October 2007).

found that if a wife purchased items from her separate allowance the items were hers.[15] What this meant for women who invested money from their separate estate was that it and any interest or profits belonged to the wife.

Guides to the law also recognized a wife's right to the proceeds from her separate estate. For instance, *The Laws Respecting Women* (1777) stated "And if the wife has any pin-money, or separate maintenance, it has been asserted that the savings which she may make therefrom, she may dispose of by testament without the control of her husband." The legal guide also included another case of a husband and wife who were separated and living apart and had agreed between them that the wife should have £150 per annum separate maintenance, "from which she having saved certain sums of money put them out to interest, and took bonds in a friend's name, which money she disposed of by will; and this was established in chancery to be a good disposition."[16] Thus, by the 1770s the law recognized that women were able to claim and bequeath proceeds (including interest and dividends) from their separate property.

One of the cases to most directly address the issue of whether a woman could invest her separate property was the 1789 Chancery suit *Fettiplace v. Gorges*. In this case the Chancery court upheld the precedent of a wife using savings from her pin money to purchase public securities in her own name. Sophie Charlotte Fettiplace, who received £200 annually for pin money, had purchased £1,900 in Consolidated Annuities (or Consols) for her separate estate, although she was married. She employed a female trustee to hold and secure this separate estate for her. This was not problematic, but Sophie Fettiplace's decision to bequeath her separate estate to a niece evidently was. Her husband sued, saying he had never agreed to his wife having a separate estate, and that since Sophie was a feme covert she could not bequeath the Consols because they belonged to him. The Lord Chancellor did not side with the husband, instead stating that a wife could bequeath personal property when it was enjoyed separately by her.[17]

While Sophie Fettiplace's case did not appear until 1789, married women were using their pin money to purchase property much earlier in the century. For instance, when her husband died, Mary Dowager Countess Ferrars specifically wrote out what property she had purchased during his lifetime with her pin money, so that her husband's executors would not include it in her husband's estate. She mentioned a strong box, a sedan chair, and other things specifically bought with "her own pin money." And a scribe noted an "Indian Japan tea table and china and dishes bought out of her Ladyships pin money."[18]

[15] Staves, "Pin Money," 60–1.

[16] Foreward by Shirley Bysciewicz, *The Laws Respecting Women* (1777; reprint Oceana Publications, 1974), 179–80.

[17] Staves, "Pin Money," 64. My discussion of *Fettiplace v. Gorges* relies heavily on Staves.

[18] HEH, Hastings Papers, HA Inventories Box 2/24.

Countess Ferrars counted such movable or household goods purchased with her pin money as part of her personal estate. Likewise, in 1720, Sir Theodore Janssen, one of the Directors of the South Sea Company, noted that "my wife had £3,520 South Sea stock in her name, wch she had from Time to Time bought with the money she sav'd in the Course of 23 Years, and, with the dividends, she sold the said £3,520 stock, the 21st of Dec. last, for £6,018, and hath the money by her."[19] It seems that Lady Janssen had been saving money out of her annual allowance and using these savings to purchase stock in the South Sea Company, thereby almost doubling her investment. When she earned dividends on the company stock, she used them to buy more stock, thereby reinvesting her profits.

Gentry and noble wives increasingly had sums at their disposal that they could use to invest in public securities. The separate estates families negotiated for their daughters were what provided married women with their own money to invest. For example, when Anna Grenville died in 1741, she was married to Richard, 2nd Earl Temple. Despite being a wife, she made a will stating that she was "seized of real estate and personal estate in several stocks to a considerable value notwithstanding her coverture."[20] Not only did the feme covert Anna Grenville hold separate property, she also chose to bequeath it in a will. In this case, her husband may not have minded because she bequeathed the property to him. Nevertheless, her married sister Mary Vere contested the will, perhaps dubious that her sister would have alienated her separate estate to her husband's patrimony. And it was not just noble wives like Grenville who owned stocks as part of their own separate estate. Thomasin Surman, whose husband was the deputy cashier of the South Sea Company, also had a marriage contract that stipulated she would enjoy a separate estate from her husband. In 1720 Surman "claimed in her own name as separate estate" £1,000 South Sea stock listed under her name in the Company's books. Her husband also deemed his wife's stock, as well as her jewels and her plate as her separate estate.[21]

Married women often had their separate property vested in male (and to a lesser extent unmarried female) trustees. We have had a tendency to view women with securities held in trust as passive investors, but as Maxine Berg has argued, women frequently made use of trusts to proactively protect their property, and thus we should not assume women who had property held in trust were dependent or passive.[22] The example of Hester Grenville Pitt also casts doubt on the assumption that the presence of trustees implies that

[19] HEH, Rare Book 261661, *The Particulars and Inventories of the Estates of the late South Sea Company Directors*, 3 vols. (L, 1721), vol. II, 71. Inventory of Sir Theodore Janssen.
[20] HEH, Stowe Temple Grenville Papers, STG Personal Box 5/13.
[21] HEH, *The Inventories of the South Sea Directors*, vol. II, 40. Inventory of Robert Surman.
[22] Maxine Berg, "Women's property and the industrial revolution," *Journal of Interdisciplinary History* 24 (1993): 233–50.

women investors were passive. Hester's marriage portion was comprised of securities, in particular Consols. Although her family vested her property in male trustees, her marriage contract stipulated that "notwithstanding her coverture" Hester Pitt had the right to direct the trustees and receive interest and dividends "for her own proper use."[23] Hester Pitt definitely took advantage of these provisions, making her own financial decisions and directing her trustees to follow them. Her husband, William Pitt, was a busy man and a poor financial administrator who seems to have deferred to his wife in arranging their affairs. In 1757 Hester Pitt wrote to her brother (who was one of her trustees): "to mention to you my desire of being empowered to receive the dividend of the money due" instead of keeping it in their banker's power. A year later, she wrote him again, asking to put £5,000 of the trust money into the purchase of what would become the Pitt family estate at Hayes, in Kent. Tellingly, she assured her brother "I am now speaking for myself and impatient to assure you that I have weighed the matter..." Her letter conveys reassurance that her husband was not pressuring her to alienate her own and her children's money into a patrimonial estate, but that she was the one making this financial decision.[24]

The legal concept of a wife's separate estate could also protect a married woman's investments. Realizing this, husbands seem to have taken advantage of separate estates to hide or transfer their assets to their wives so that they could not be seized. For example, the Lady Elizabeth Masters, the wife of Sir Harcourt Masters, one of the Directors of the South Sea Company, pled her case to the House of Commons, arguing that the interest from her stocks should be considered her own separate estate. Elizabeth Masters (née Sidney) explained that when she married Sir Harcourt in 1720 "she was possess'd in her own Right of Three Thousand Five Hundred Pounds Capital Stock of the South-Sea Company."[25] She transferred this stock to her brother, Philip Sidney, the Earl of Leicester, and to Lord Viscount Cheney, to hold in trust for her. But due to his involvement in the South Sea Bubble the government was holding Harcourt Masters and the other South Sea Directors personally liable for the Company's losses. Elizabeth Masters said "that by reason of her Husband's Misfortunes...She is in the space of Six months become destitute of a Support" and that due to her husband's financial losses he was "incapable of maintaining her in any Condition or State of Life..." She asked that the government "exempt...the Interest of her own Fortune" from her husband's seized estate. Masters had a separate estate vested in trustees but she was also asking that the profits or interest from her separate estate be treated as her own

---

[23] HEH, Stowe Temple Grenville Papers, STG Personal Box 6/22.

[24] HEH, HM Letters, from Hester Pitt to George Grenville, 31559 & 31561.

[25] *The Case of Lady Elizabeth Master* (L, 1721). ECCO <www.galegroup.com> (accessed October 2014). Their surname is also recorded as Masters.

separate property so that she would be able to maintain herself despite her husband's financial woes. It is not clear if Lady Elizabeth Masters succeeded with her petition, but the Commons did allow her husband to keep almost half of his estimated wealth.[26]

At times, wives invested money on their own even when there is no evidence of formal or legalized separate property arrangements. These instances are further examples of the flexibility of coverture in actual practice. As we saw in the chapter on early adopters, Sarah Churchill, Duchess of Marlborough, Martha Hutchins, and Elizabeth Freke all invested money on their own despite being married women. The Scots gentlewoman, Grisell Baillie, is another example of a woman who bought and sold public investments despite her coverture. Lady Grisell's investing directly aided her family's fortunes. Her business acumen was so much better than her husband's that he deferred to her in most financial matters. Grisell Baillie's investments are chronicled in her household and financial accounts, which date from 1692 to her death over fifty years later in 1746. She acquired her financial expertise and business skills early in life. Baillie put her father's accounts in order and when her brother was abroad she managed his affairs, so her financial abilities were apparent while she was still young and single. Once married, Baillie's husband, a career politician, entrusted her with the "entire administration of his finances."[27] Grisell Baillie's account books also reveal a reversal of the gendered norms of early modern marital couples, for she paid her husband pocket money instead of he paying her an allowance, or pin money.

In addition to handling the family finances, Grisell Baillie was also the family investor. In this way, she wielded considerable financial authority as a wife. As early as 1693 Baillie bought 10 shares in a linen manufactory and she continued to purchase shares worth hundreds of pounds through 1696. In 1715 she bought her daughter Rachel a lottery ticket and in 1717 Grisell recorded receiving interest personally at the Bank of England and tipping the servants while she was there. The family also held debentures in Mr. Baillie's name, although it is not clear if George or Grisell Baillie handled this investment.[28] In sum, Baillie's investments included joint-stock companies, State lotteries, the Bank of England, and government funds. Her investing occurred while she was married and was condoned, if not encouraged, by her husband.

Another married woman who invested, but who did so without her husband's knowledge, was Lady Mary Wortley Montagu. Montagu was struck by

---

[26] Rapin de Thoyras (Paul, M.) and Nicolas Tindal, *The History of England*, vol. 19 (L, 1763), 414.

[27] Robert Scott-Moncrieff, ed., *The Household Book of Grisell Baillie*, Scottish History Society, 2nd series, vol. 1 (Edinburgh, 1911), xxxi.

[28] *Household Book of Grisell Baillie*, 1, 3, 4, 6, 31, 44, 56, 58.

South Sea fever in the 1720s. She invested for herself, but also on behalf of a man not related to her, her French admirer Monsieur Rémond. Montagu was very worried about her husband finding out, but it does not seem the investing was the problem; rather it was her losses and the exposing of her relationship with Rémond that worried her. In early summer 1721, Montagu wrote to her sister, the Countess of Mar, explaining how her investing had gone awry the year before. It seems her sister knew of Rémond and Montagu told her that when he came to visit her in England she could not give him what he wanted (presumably a romantic relationship) so she chose to help him out financially with a stock tip. She told him to "sell out of the subscription"—in South Sea stock. On planning his return to France, Rémond "said he would put into my hands the money that I had won for him, and desired me to improve it."

Mary Wortley Montagu did not want to invest Rémond's money, not because she was married, but because she did not want to be responsible for it. She reluctantly took Rémond's profits "and my first care was to employ his money to the best advantage. I laid it all out in stock, the general discourse and private intelligence then scattered about being of a great rise" [in the value of South Sea stock]. Montagu wrote to her sister, "you may remember it was two or three days before the fourth subscription and you were with me when I paid away the money to Mr Binfield." Montagu continued, "I thought I had managed prodigious well in selling out the said stock the day after the shutting the books (for a small profit), to Cox and Cleeve, goldsmiths of very good reputation." But Montagu soon found out that at the opening of the books the stock was still "upon my hands" and its price had sunk from "near nine hundred pounds to four hundred." She immediately wrote to Rémond asking what he would like her to do, and refusing to make any more moves without his direct orders, since she had lost over half of his money. When he did write back, Rémond accused Montagu of tricking him and of stealing his money. Montagu also heard via the rumor mill that he had told people she had borrowed money from him to invest, but she assured her sister that "I have a note under his hand, by which he desire[d] me to employ it in the funds." Though she also had a paper trail of any stock "bargains" she had made, she was very concerned about what Rémond would say about both her personal and financial affairs and to whom.[29]

Mary Wortley Montagu's story, while quite dramatic, is revealing of the investing engaged in by married women in a number of other ways. Her letter shows us that she knew how to invest, that she did so on her own as well as on behalf of a male friend, that she kept apprised of investing news, and that she knew how to trade stocks to turn a quick profit. She thought she was doing so prudently and profitably, only to find out that a mistake left her holding the stock she had wanted to sell before it declined in price. Mary Wortley Montagu was not

---

[29] Isobel Grundy, ed., *Letters from the Right Honourable Lady Mary Wortley Montagu 1709 to 1762* (London: J. M. Dent & Co., 1906), 203–5.

necessarily a successful investor but that she invested at all is significant since she was a feme covert. And the fact that as a married woman she also invested for a third party adds an additional level to women's skirting of coverture. Wives invested not only for themselves but also as financial brokers for others.

Some women began investing for others while they were single and then continued to do so after marriage. A good example of this is the gentlewoman Cassandra Willoughby, who helped manage affairs for her brothers and nephews before she married for the first time in her forties. After she married, Cassandra continued to invest for family members. In fact, her financial acumen may have been one of the things that made her cousin James Brydges consider her as a prospective spouse. Cassandra Willoughby dedicated herself to assisting the men in her family from a young age. In 1687, seventeen-year-old Cassandra began to keep house at Wollaton Hall, Notts. for her eldest brother Francis, and when he died, her younger brother Thomas. She stayed on after Thomas married and assumed a maternal role with her nephews as well. By middle age it seemed that Cassandra was destined to remain a lifelong single woman, but she in fact married at the late age of forty-three.[30] This marriage was to her first cousin, James Brydges, who was a widower with two young sons, and in line to be the next Lord Chandos. The two cousins had been friends since childhood and Brydges thought highly of Cassandra's character and intellect. He also needed a mother for his sons and a manager for his household, and Cassandra had already proven herself more than competent in both of these roles. (see Figure 4.1.) Her impressive portion of £23,000 probably did not hurt either. Cassandra Willoughby had invested the portion she had received from her father's will in stocks, and had improved it to this impressive sum herself.

Cassandra Willoughby may have learned how to invest from her mother and stepfather. In 1676, when Cassandra was six, her mother Emma married Sir Josiah Child. Child was a successful merchant and Director of the East India Company. As a widow, Emma Child invested money in a number of public stocks and securities. In 1699 she started out with East India Company bonds, but around 1712 she cashed these in and re-invested her profits in Bank of England stock and tickets in the government's Classis Lottery.[31] Cassandra's familial exposure to investing in public stocks and securities may well explain her own interest in public securities and how she learned to invest.

Around the same time as her marriage in 1713 Cassandra began to invest legacies belonging to her nephews, Thomas and Rothwell Willoughby. In a

[30] Rosemary O'Day, ed., *Cassandra Brydges, First Duchess of Chandos, 1670–1735: Life and Letters* (Woodbridge, Suffolk: The Boydell Press, 2007), introduction, 1–7.

[31] University of Nottingham, Manuscripts and Special Collections, Middleton Collection, Mi Av 143/6/31, Mi AV 143/15/1–7, Mi AV 143/19/37/1–2. I am grateful to Rosemary O'Day for sharing her notes on Emma Child's investment accounts with me.

Figure 4.1. James Brydges (later 1st Duke of Chandos) and his family (1713) by Sir Godfrey Kneller.

https://commons.wikimedia.org/wiki/File:Chandos-family-by-kneller-1713.jpg. Available under Creative Commons Attribution-ShareAlike License.

letter to her brother Thomas, Lord Middleton, Cassandra mentions "the little sume of money wch I have had to manage for him [his son Thomas]." In 1719 Cassandra wrote about "The money I have had to manage for my nephew Thos wch my Aunt [Lettice] Wendy left him." This legacy had lately increased after losing nearly half of its worth when it was initially let out; but Cassandra predicted that by the following March it would be up to £1,560. Her letter belies the comment that she was managing only a "little sum" but also indicates that her nephew's inheritance had originally been much larger. "Near half" was lost, although it is unclear if this was due to Aunt Wendy's mismanagement or her own. In any case, Cassandra had made up some of the loss with further investments. She also had "begged a little sum for [her nephew] Rothwell" from her Aunt Wendy and added some money from her mother to it, "which I have now brought up to £540."[32] In other words, Cassandra had cobbled together an inheritance for her second nephew and added to it by investing the sum at interest. Thanks to Cassandra, her

---

[32] HEH, STB Box 2 Stowe Collection, Brydges Correspondence, Cassandra Brydges, Duchess of Chandos, copy letter book and misc. papers, letter 38, 9 Dec 1718.

nephews received £2,100 in total, which she gave to her brother Middleton, requiring him to pay it to them or to give security for future payment of the money. Cassandra continued to financially advise her nephew Thomas Willoughby into his adulthood. In 1719/20 she wrote to say she believed he now had his inheritance from her brother Middleton and she thought he might like some investing advice for the large sum he now controlled. She counseled him:

> " ... that South Sea stock is at present rising very fast, & tis my Lord's [the Duke of Chandos's] opinion yt it will still be higher, this I am writing to l[e]t you know, tho I will not advise you what to doe because of ye Hazard yt attends all stocks but as a proof ye Brokers expect ye rise of yt they offer to give 6 guineas per cent for ye refusal of South Sea Stock at 150 at any time within six months if you buy you must not lose time, & if it proves as fortunate to you as I wish, it will be worth your trouble."[33]

In this letter Cassandra gave advice on investing in South Sea stock—its rising value, current price, and the timing for a purchase—but she was also cautious in her assessment of the risk inherent to investing.

In 1725 Cassandra boasted of her management of her three nephews' financial affairs. She wrote that her mother had given her nephew Thomas Willoughby £100 in June 1715. This money "I returned to my mother again in two South Sea Bonds wch with interest upon them [was £200/2/6] ... & in money wth those bonds I paid her [£]18 11[s.] by wch it apper'd yt during y time wch my mother had put yt money in my hands to Trafick wth for my 3 youngest nephew Willoughbys, I had increased this 100li to be then [£]218 13[s.]."[34] In other words, under Cassandra's management, she had more than doubled her nephews' money by "trafficking," or investing it, in South Sea stock. She was able to return the money to her mother in an improved state.

The investing Cassandra Willoughby did for her family members was similar to that done by the widow Sarah Osborne, who we met at the outset of this chapter. Like a widowed mother, Cassandra protected and improved the inheritance of her charges (in this case her nephews and not her own children), turning to investment in public stocks and securities as a way to do so. But unlike Sarah Osborne, Cassandra Willoughby Brydges was not a widow with the right to invest on her own. She did much of her investing for her nephews once she was married to James Brydges and was legally a feme covert. But Brydges was comfortable with his wife engaging in financial matters. He established this at the very start of their marriage, with Cassandra remarking, "the settlements made upon me are much greater than what are

---

[33] STB, Box 2, Cassandra Brydges, letter 60, Jan. 1719/20.
[34] STB, Box 2, Cassandra Brydges, letter 211, 4 Dec. 1725.

usuall, and more is left in my power than I could have asked."[35] The phrase "more is left in my power" is significant. Even though under coverture, Cassandra (now Brydges) retained much of her own financial independence and authority thanks to her marriage settlement. Rosemary O'Day has defined the Brydges' marriage as a companionate one and this is certainly borne out in their finances.[36] Brydges allowed his wife to keep her own investments and their agent Mr. Zollicoffre kept separate accounts for the spouses. For example, Zollicoffre accounted for £1,342 10s. in "bonds and monies received upon annuities under Your Grace's name" as well as £1,121 5s. in bonds and annuities received "under my Lady Dutchess her name." Zollicoffre's separate investment accounts for the spouses show that Cassandra received only £200 less in dividends than her husband (although it is not clear if these are their total dividends). In 1720 Zollicoffre also referred to South Sea stock and annuities subscribed in my Duchess Cassandra's name. And he recorded that the Duke had £500 in the 14 percent annuities, while the Duchess had £1,190 in the Long Annuities under her name.[37] Although married, this couple kept their investments separate and distinct.

James Brydges also expected his wife to aid him in his business and financial correspondence. He was involved in the management of two of the major stock companies of the day—the Royal African and the York Buildings Companies—and he was heavily invested in both the East India and South Sea Companies. As such, he received a multitude of requests for stock advice and for help obtaining subscriptions. He passed on many of these letters, especially those written by women, to his wife, for her to handle. Cassandra's responses show that she was herself knowledgeable about financial issues and investing. For instance, in January 1725/26, she wrote to Lady Molyneux, telling her that "it appeared that the next 6th of March he [Brydges] would be in her debt for 4 years' interest money due upon the 800 li. out of which he had paid for her two last calls upon her Affrican Stock 100 li. which taken from 160 li. the money due for 4 years' interest. The remainder will be 60 li which money he would then pay as she should order, upon the trusties signing the receipt."[38] In other words, James Brydges had helped Lady Molyneux to invest in £800 of Royal African stock and owed her £160, for four years' interest at a rate of 5 percent. But he had also paid in £100 for Lady Molyneux when the company made a call on investors, so deducting the amount for this he owed her £60, which he would pay when and to whom she desired. Brydges had his wife convey this information, leaving her to write a letter to Lady Molyneux that might have come from the pen of a broker or a bank clerk.

---

[35] As quoted in O'Day, *Cassandra Brydges*, 7.
[36] O'Day, *Cassandra Brydges*, 15.
[37] HEH, Stowe, ST 12, vol. 2 (1715–1720), 121; vol. 3 (1719–1726), 63–6, 77.
[38] As quoted in O'Day, *Cassandra Brydges*, 201.

Cassandra Willoughby Brydges's investing career began while she was single and continued during her marriage. In fact, her financial abilities may have been one of the reasons James Brydges chose her as his second wife. Cassandra is an example of a woman who used her financial knowledge not only to invest for herself but also to aid members of her natal and marital family in their investments. We will now turn to another woman who also performed the role of financial agent for the men in her family, the spinster Mary Barwell.

4.1. CASE STUDY: MARY BARWELL (1733–1825)

Mary Barwell differed from the women discussed so far in that she was a life-long spinster, not a feme covert. As a feme sole she was able to invest for herself. Nevertheless, her most impressive investments were not personal ones but those she made on behalf of male siblings. Despite being a woman, her brother Richard Barwell picked her to be his financial agent in England. While performing this office, Mary Barwell managed thousands of pounds and became embroiled in East India Company politics on her brother's behalf.

There is not much information about Mary Barwell before she became her brother's investment broker in the 1760s. She was born in 1733, the daughter of William Barwell, who had been a servant of the East India Company in India, and then a Director of the Company when he returned home to England. Mary had a number of siblings, many of them the children of her father and stepmother. In the late 1760s and early 1770s Mary Barwell was residing in London, where her friends included Margaret (Polly) Stevenson. Stevenson's mother was the landlady for an American resident in London, Benjamin Franklin. Although in her forties and still unmarried, Franklin's correspondence indicates that Barwell had attracted his interest. He mentions wanting to visit "the lovely Lady Barwell, whom he did not find at home, so there was no Struggle for and against a Kiss." Along with remarks on her person, Franklin also noted Barwell's hectic level of activity. In 1777 he inquired if Miss Barwell is "a little more at rest; or as busy as ever?"[39] She was involved in East India Company affairs and investing for her brother in these years, so Franklin may well have been alluding to these activities when he noted how busy she was. Barwell was also helpful to her friends. She offered her home to a recently widowed friend in 1778 and promised to use her connections in the East India Company to "serve" Franklin's relative Jonathan Williams Jr. in his desire to do business with the East India ships bringing tea to Boston harbor.[40]

---

[39] *The Papers of Benjamin Franklin*, vol. 17 (1770), 198–9; vol. 25 (1777), 23, 235; vol. 29 (1779), 159. <www.franklinpapers.org> (accessed Feb. 2011).

[40] *The Papers of Benjamin Franklin*, vol. 20 (1773), 230, 293; vol. 26 (1778), 361.

These examples of Mary Barwell's kindness stand in stark contrast to some of the unflattering views of her that come out in the correspondence of her family members. Barwell could rub people the wrong way and there are several indications in letters and memoirs that she was an idiosyncratic woman. Richard Barwell had to advise his sister Fanny to overlook Mary's "peculiarities" and instead rely on her advice since he thought she had good sense.[41] And there are many examples of Mary Barwell writing rather imperious, demanding, and sometimes angry letters to people, including such high profile persons as Warren Hastings, the Governor of India.[42] It was the very same imperiousness that people disliked that also allowed Mary Barwell to succeed as a female financial agent for her family.

Mary Barwell began investing in stocks for her brother Richard in 1766. Richard Barwell had served in India since 1756. He rose up through the East India Company, and eventually would be appointed to the four-man council that governed India along with Governor-General Warren Hastings. Richard Barwell would serve in India until 1780, before returning to England and becoming an MP.[43] While in India, Richard Barwell began to send letters to his sister Mary, in which he instructed her to invest money for him back home in England. He first sent her a bill for £100 and told her to apply to Anselm Beaumont for the money. Richard told Mary that Beaumont "imagines it is your own money entrusted by you to my management. You have no occasion to contradict such a supposition...but rather give him to understand you expect silence, lest it get to your father's ears he be displeased at such a disposal of your money, as you have not consulted him on the subject." Mary was about thirty-three years old at this time and as a single woman would have been capable of investing her money on her own. But Richard thought his broker would believe that Mary's father would be angry if he found out that Mary was investing as she pleased without consulting him.

Richard may have been testing Mary's investing abilities since he sent her the relatively modest sum of £100. Writing to his father around the same time Richard also asked him to invest for him. So it appears Richard was spreading his money among several family agents. Richard Barwell stated that he was worth about £12,000 at this time, so £100 was not much for him to throw his sister's way to see what she could do with it.[44] As we will see, Mary Barwell's financial acumen more than repaid Richard's bet.

---

[41] "The Letters of Mr. Richard Barwell" Pt VI, *Bengal, Past & Present*, vol. 11 (1915), 42–4.

[42] Introduction by Sydney C. Grier, *The letters of Warren Hastings to his wife* (Edinburgh: William Blackwood & Sons, 1905), 22, 224, 314.

[43] Susan Staves, "Investments, votes, and 'bribes': women as shareholders in the chartered national companies," in Hilda Smith, ed., *Women Writers in the early modern British political tradition* (Cambridge: Cambridge University Press, 1998), 273.

[44] "The Letters of Mr. Richard Barwell" Pt. II, *Bengal, Past & Present*, vol. 9 (1914), 106.

Correspondence between the siblings in 1767 reveals that Richard continued to send bills to his agent Beaumont, payable to his sister, and that he began discussing business issues with her. Mary also assisted a Captain Morris who sold goods Richard sent from India, with Mary collecting the sums due. Richard mentions paying Mary "your due's from this" and tells her that Captain Morris can be depended on to keep "the transaction a secret from our family."[45] Richard's mention of "dues" seems to indicate he paid Mary a broker or agent's fee for the financial work she was doing for him. Again though, Richard seemed to want to hide Mary's financial dealings, but whether it was to protect her reputation or his (or for some other reason), is unclear.

After a year or so of handling her brother's business affairs, it appears Mary Barwell had proven herself as his agent and was growing more confident. She asked her brother what she could do to forward his interest. He replied with no simple task. He told her to speak to Mr. Beaumont about borrowing £10,000 to invest since he had no money available in England to do so. Other letters indicate Richard Barwell was investing in East India stock with the assistance of his attorney Beaumont and his father. He wrote to Beaumont, "The disposal of my monies I leave entirely to you, but if India stock falls very low, I could wish it engaged in that stock in the names of such people as may be confided in. My father I desire to have consulted on the disposing of the votes."[46] Now Richard also began to include his sister Mary in his circle of English confidants and agents. In a letter dated 26 December 1769 he told her to speak with their father about advancing him on the Council [governing India] and he informed her that she could see copies of the business letters that were with Beaumont.[47] With these words it appears Mary's employment on her brother's behalf was no longer a secret. Now she was expected to work in concert with his male agents and kin. In a 1773 letter Richard said, "I have been pretty full on publick matters to you" and told Mary to share the letter with a Mr. Hawkesworth, a business associate.[48] Mary Barwell was now as much a business partner of her brother as Beaumont or their father.

It is not entirely clear why Richard Barwell decided to put his faith and fortune into the hands of his sister Mary. Perhaps it was because his brothers were busy making their own way in India, so Mary was the only sibling in England. He also might have found a never-married sister to have few competing ties of loyalty and so he could more easily bind her to him. But he also seemed to think Mary had ability. In a letter to their younger sister

---

[45] "The Letters of Mr. Richard Barwell" Pt. III, *Bengal, Past & Present*, vol. 9 (1914), 147, 153, 169.

[46] "The Letters of Mr. Richard Barwell" Pt. V, *Bengal, Past & Present*, vol. 10 (1915), 232–4, 250–1.

[47] "The Letters of Mr. Richard Barwell" Pt. V, *Bengal, Past & Present*, vol. 10 (1915), 254.

[48] "The Letters of Mr. Richard Barwell" Pt. VI, *Bengal, Past & Present*, vol. 11 (1915), 51.

Fanny he remarked that Mary had "great sensibility and great good sense."[49]
Richard also seems to have believed in the educability of women, or at least
women like his sister. In 1767 he wrote to her saying that he did not know why
knowledge in her sex was condemned as ridiculous, as long as it was "pursued
with prudence and used with discretion," and he wanted her to improve
herself.[50] Evidently, Richard recognized that Mary was trainable and teachable
and she did prove to be an apt pupil in finance.

Mary Barwell also took over her brother Richard's role in their wider
family's financial matters due to his absence in India. In 1773, their brother
Roger Barwell died leaving Richard as executor. Richard wrote to Mary
saying, "A full power of attorney, a probate of the will, and all the law
papers necessary to constitute you alone the manager on my behalf will be
sent to you." Richard directed Mary to collect bills of exchange and other
property from their brother's estate to pay out legacies. Richard noted that
he put "in your hands a sum exceeding £30,000, exclusive of Daniel's [their
younger brother's] fortune." He went on to say that "fortune had blessed
him with wealth even beyond my expectations" and so he reminded Mary
that, "my purse is in a great measure put into your hands and confided to
your discretion. I wish you to live as becomes my sister and you will use it
accordingly."[51] Not only was Mary her brother's deputy attorney and
executor, she was also now the manager of his estate in England. The wealth
and status he had achieved was to be shared with her. Mary Barwell's role
was similar to that of a wife or widow acting as a deputy husband for an
absent or deceased spouse. But in this case, she was the deputy partner of her
brother.

Richard Barwell also assumed (rightly or wrongly) quite a bit of knowledge
on his sister Mary's part about Indian affairs, currency, and exchange rates. In
1773 he sent her some business proposals, among them "his proposition for
reducing the rate of interest on [the East India] Company's loans from 8 to
5 per cent." He explained this proposal to her, so she could in turn explicate it
to others in England. Richard wrote, "The balance there in favor of the
Company...is not less than C.R.s [current rupees] 1,72,934. Yet in stating
this account, to render the balance as little in favor of the Company as possible,
the tribute to the King including Needjiff Cawn, is set down as an actual
disbursement from the cash . . . This is no less a sum than 26 lacs of sicca rupees
or current 3,01,6000."[52] To decipher this sentence, Mary would have needed to
have a good knowledge of accounting as well as of several foreign currencies.

[49] "The Letters of Mr. Richard Barwell" Pt VI, *Bengal, Past & Present,* vol. 11 (1915), 42–4.
[50] "The Letters of Mr. Richard Barwell" Pt. II, *Bengal, Past & Present,* vol. 9 (1914), 109.
[51] "The Letters of Mr. Richard Barwell" Pt. VI, *Bengal, Past & Present,* vol. 11 (1915), 48–50.
[52] "The Letters of Mr. Richard Barwell" Pt. VI, *Bengal, Past & Present,* vol. 11 (1915), 53.

In 1773 the Barwell family became concerned about Mary's financial management, or rather what they viewed as her mismanagement of the family inheritance. What provoked this was the bankruptcy of the merchant banker and speculator Sir George Colebrooke. Richard, however, defended and supported his sister's judgment. He wrote to Mary,

> I find my brothers extremely alarmed on the failure of Sir George, and all looking up to me to remedy the accident that may materially affect their fortunes... You may, therefore, confirm your former assurances to the family of my indemnifying any loss which may arise from your management of India stock [on] account of [the] minors or the stock placed in your hands or submitted to your management by William or James, or any of the family...

Richard did not criticize Mary's management of the family's East India stock, but he did give her fair warning of what the other siblings were thinking. He then went on to say he had confidence in her decision-making. "My brothers blame you much, remarking your zeal has gone beyond your discretion. I am so far from thinking this censure just that I confide entirely on your judgment." Richard then put the blame on whom it was squarely due, not his sister, but Colebrooke, the man to whom they had entrusted their money. It was not Mary's fault, for as Richard pointed out "With a prodigious fortune to sink to a degree of bankruptcy as Sir George has done no man could foresee." Richard noted that male financial managers were just as vulnerable as Mary. He concluded a letter full of other business he needed her to attend to, with "I apprehend very much that you have experienced many hours of uneasiness on the score of Sir George's failure, but I flatter myself that the good sense and strength of mind you possess has precluded that degree of agitation which weaker souls are affected by... "[53] Richard also wrote to his brother William, assuaging his worry and telling him he would cover any losses related to Colebrooke's failure. He did not take time in the letter to defend Mary, but he also did not undercut her, saying that he had written to her and she knew what to do.

Richard Barwell's belief in his sister Mary seems to have been correct, for under her management his estate weathered the storm of Colebrooke's financial meltdown with absorbable losses. A month later Richard responded to a letter from Mary with the words "my confidence in your good sense and discretion rendered, you perceive, the account of your management perfectly unnecessary. It however, was a satisfaction to learn from your pen the state of the large property for which I stand engaged, and it gave me pleasure to find it was so well circumstanced that I had not to replace the loss of many thousands."[54] Richard lauded Mary's management of his estate and said he trusted

---

[53] "The Letters of Mr. Richard Barwell" Pt. VI, *Bengal, Past & Present*, vol. 11 (1915), 63–5.
[54] "The Letters of Mr. Richard Barwell" Pt. VI, *Bengal, Past & Present*, vol. 11 (1915), 67.

her so much that he did not need her to give him an accounting, although he appreciated her care.

Mary Barwell, however, did not respond passively to these financial deficits, rather she took it upon herself to recover her family's lost funds. The losses of East Indian stock that the Barwells and others incurred due to the breaking of banker George Colebrooke led Mary to turn to the courts. In 1777 she filed a bill of bankruptcy against Colebrooke on her brother's behalf. Mary Barwell appeared as the lead creditor in the bankruptcy proceedings against Colebrooke. The creditors of the banker reportedly were repaid in full, although the Barwell correspondence does not verify this.[55] One hopes Mary Barwell's siblings looked more kindly on her management after she assertively protected their finances.

Despite Richard Barwell's belief in his sister's financial abilities, he was not above noting Mary's financial errors and areas in which she needed improvement. For instance, in a letter from 1774, Richard critiqued Mary's method of accounting.

> You will perceive your accounts are only deficient in mercantile method and in that clearness and perspicuity required in accounts, which for want of it must always be unintelligible excepting to the persons who are fully acquainted with the transactions on which they are founded, and a little method becomes now more necessary from the importance of the sums which fall under your management, and which will increase as opportunities of remitting my fortune to Europe may offer.[56]

Mary was evidently not employing the "mercantile method," or double entry bookkeeping, in her accounts. She was not alone in this, for many individuals of both genders did not use the debitor/creditor method, although merchants, businessmen, and keepers of estate accounts did.[57] Richard held Mary to this more "business-like" standard when he implied that her accounts would not be clear to a third party who was not familiar with the transactions enumerated. He emphasized that she needed to use more method in her accounting since the amount of capital that she was managing was growing and becoming more significant.

At the end of his letter Richard tutored Mary in accounting by rewriting the accounts she had sent him. He noted "In Mrs. Barwell's account with Richard

---

[55] London Metropolitan Archives, M/093/444–5 (1777); Dame Lucy Stuart Sutherland, *Politics and Finance in the eighteenth century* (London: Continuum, 1984), 449, n. 2. Colebrooke was a London banker and Director and Chairman of the East India Company. His extravagant speculating led to the closing of his bank in 1773 and the sale of his property. He went bankrupt in 1777. H. V. Bowen, "Sir George Colebrooke, second Baronet," *Oxford Dictionary of National Biography* <oxford.dnb.com> (accessed June 2013).

[56] "The Letters of Mr. Richard Barwell" Pt. VIII, *Bengal, Past & Present*, vol. 12 (1916), 68.

[57] See Amy M. Froide, "Learning to Invest: Women's Education in Arithmetic and Accounting in early modern England," *Early Modern Women: An Interdisciplinary Journal* 10:1 (2015): 3–26.

Barwell she debits herself for the following loans without its appearing on the face of the account from whence the money was procured." He then showed how "proper accounts could be stated thus" by crediting the balance due to him from receipts of money taken in by Mary on his behalf, as well as the balance of their brother Roger's estate transferred to his credit, and articles disbursed by Mary and thus deducted from his account. He pointed out the problem in Mary's original account: "by placing this balance to the debit of Richard Barwell and credit of Mrs. B it appears as if she had never received the money." And why "is a sum of money said to be borrowed that was never lent?" He concluded his tutorial by explaining how accounts for their brother Roger's estates should be signed by Mary as executrix by appointment of him the executor.[58] It appears that Mary was having difficulty sorting out the many persons for whom she was keeping accounts: she was managing money on her brother Richard's behalf, but now also handling accounts related to Richard's role as executor of their deceased brother, and the two accounts were to be kept distinct even though they were kept by one person, namely Mary Barwell.

Mary Barwell's accounts needed to be clear since she was thousands of miles and months away from her brother, but also because she was handling significant amounts of money for him. In a November 1771 letter to Beaumont, Richard detailed his assets in England, which now totaled a little over £50,000. The majority was comprised of money out on private loans, treasury bonds at 5 percent, Bank Consols that he had inherited from his parents, and bills of exchange. Richard left a little over half of his estate in Beaumont's hands and ordered £24,000 to "Mrs. Barwell."[59] This meant that in 1771, Mary Barwell was managing £24,000 for her brother, and this figure only grew. In a letter from November 1774, Richard stated "what monies of mine ought to come into your hands." They included the £24,000 Mary already had, as well as specie remitted, a bill of exchange, and half of the estate of their deceased brother Roger, for a total of £46,481. To this Richard added "doubtful remittances" involving sums in China and Bombay shipping, for a "Total of what will be my fortune in your hands if every remittance is made good [of] ... £52,581 17s. 5d."[60] In the mid-1770s Richard entrusted his sister with managing a portfolio of over £50,000. This was probably one of the largest portfolios in public stocks and securities managed by a woman in England at that time and was a vast difference from the £100 under her control just a decade earlier.

Mary Barwell's management of her brother Richard's financial dealings with the East India Company began to include her involvement in the politics of the Company, for the two were intertwined. In an October 1773 letter to his

[58] "The Letters of Mr. Richard Barwell" Pt. VIII, *Bengal, Past & Present,* vol. 12 (1916), 75–6.
[59] "The Letters of Mr. Richard Barwell" Pt. VIII, *Bengal, Past & Present,* vol. 12 (1916), 65.
[60] "The Letters of Mr. Richard Barwell" Pt. VIII, *Bengal, Past & Present,* vol. 12 (1916), 69.

younger brother James, Richard informed him that not only had he put Mary in charge of disbursing legacies from their deceased brother's estate, but that "I want to throw money into my sister's hands to strengthen those particular interests which must make way for our family pursuits in the East."[61] In Richard's view, the Barwell brothers, who were all in India, were to tend to the colonial side of the Indian ventures, while their sister was to manage things from the metropole.

Other historians have noted Mary Barwell's political role. Referring to Richard Barwell's appointment to the governing council of India, Sophia Weitzman stated "it is highly probable that he owed his appointment more immediately to the efforts of his sister, Miss Mary Barwell, who always remained an indefatigable worker on her brother's behalf and who, by sheer pertinacity, appears to have exerted considerable influence in official circles."[62] H. V. Bowen has also described Mary Barwell as a political agent at East India House.[63] A hint at how Mary Barwell's financial dealings and political activity reinforced and furthered each other comes in a letter Richard wrote sometime after January 1774. He references the perennial problem for East India Company servants in India, trying to remit assets from India and in Indian currency to Britain and into British currency.

> The difficulty which attends sending money to England makes me wish you would seize every opportunity of giving bills upon me for whatever amount you may be able to secure in England: it is the only safe and certain mode that occurs to me of throwing the whole of my fortune into your hands and of giving to your personal powers that additional influence proceeding from a command of money.

Here Richard equates the family money with political "influence" and urges Mary to wield it. Richard goes on to suggest to Mary:

> Now I suppose it possible by forming an acquaintance with some of the members of the Board of Admiralty to get a proffer of supplying the money required for the charge of the fleet ... and might obtain an order to the Admiral to take all or part of the money he has occasion for from me, at the fixt rates; you may be able to settle the exchange ... [and] influence the Admiralty to take your bills upon me payable in Bengal for fixt sum ...[64]

Richard then launched into the rates of exchange he would accept. He showed no compunction in asking his sister Mary to undertake the negotiation of a

---

[61] "The Letters of Mr. Richard Barwell" Pt. VI, *Bengal, Past & Present*, vol. 11 (1915), 61.

[62] Sophia Weitzman, *Warren Hastings and Philip Francis*, Historical Series, no. lvi (Manchester: Manchester University Press, 1929), 17.

[63] H. V. Bowen, *The business of empire: the East India Company and imperial Britain, 1756–1833* (Cambridge: Cambridge University Press, 2006), 105, n. 65.

[64] "The Letters of Mr. Richard Barwell" Pt. VII, *Bengal, Past & Present*, vol. 11 (1915), 298–9.

major government contract, neither doubting her ability nor the propriety of a woman negotiating with the Admiralty.

Mary Barwell might have been expected to further the financial interests of her elder brother and other siblings simply due to her membership in the family. The fact that she had remained single and had no husband or children only bound her further to her natal family. But to Richard's credit, he decided that Mary should earn her own salary for her managerial role. In 1774 Richard told Mary that "from this income [his assets in England] I appropriate the sum of £400 per annum to be received by you for your own and sole use." He gave this to her for life and if she survived him she could bequeath it. Richard ordered his executors or administrators to deliver to Mary Bank of England stock that would produce £400 a year "to be at your own and entire disposal." Before this time his attorneys had been paying her £400 per annum, but he cancelled this "as the payment of the said sum is now vested in your own hands and will from henceforth be made by yourself to yourself."[65] In other words, Mary would no longer receive an annuity from her brother's financial agents, but would now pay herself this same amount of money as a yearly salary. Whether this financial arrangement was Richard's own idea or Mary's is unclear. In any case, what Richard did was transform a dependent single sister into an independent single woman. Whether this was out of affection for Mary (which he often professed) or out of recognition for her work on his behalf, it was one more example of Mary Barwell's abilities and her brother's faith in her.

The financial and political dealings on her brother's behalf that had kept Mary Barwell busy for much of the 1770s ended when Richard Barwell retired from the India service in 1780. Richard may have even returned to England at the advice of his sister Mary who thought his "interests" would be furthered more at home than in India.[66] He returned to England as one of the wealthier nabobs of his time, with a rumored estimated worth of £400,000. Upon his return, Richard first lived "in a house belonging to an old maiden sister, Mary Barwell ... in Great Ormond Street, Bloomsbury."[67] In other words, the sister who had been his partner in business now became his household partner. But Barwell soon purchased himself a country estate at Stansted Park in West Sussex, secured himself a seat in Parliament and continued his service to the East India Company as a director. Richard Barwell also remarried and produced a large family.[68] The wealth and power Richard Barwell

---

[65] "The Letters of Mr. Richard Barwell" Pt. VIII, *Bengal, Past & Present*, vol. 12 (1916), 70.

[66] T. H. Bowyer, "Richard Barwell," *Oxford Dictionary of National Biography* <oxford.dnb.com> (accessed June 2013).

[67] *Memoirs of William Hickey*, ed. Alfred Spencer, vol. II (1775–82), 7th ed. (London: Hurst & Blacket, 1913–25), 299.

[68] Bowyer, "Richard Barwell," *DNB*; R. G. Thorne, ed., "Richard Barwell," *The House of Commons, 1790–1820*, History of Parliament Trust (Woodbridge, Suffolk: Boydell and Brewer, 1986), 149.

enjoyed certainly could be attributed to his hard work (and perhaps corruption) while in India, but Mary Barwell must also take some credit. She had managed his English capital well in his absence.

While Mary Barwell may have stopped managing her brother's money when he returned to England, she continued to invest for herself from the 1770s up until her death in the 1820s. Her income consisted of the £400 per annum from Richard and she received an annuity that she may have bought herself.[69] In 1774 Mary loaned money to a Col McLean, which she secured by insurance on his life. This was probably a smart business move since her brother mentioned McLean being late in making payments.[70] At some point Mary Barwell had enough money to invest the large sum of £10,000 in a single loan.[71] One of Mary's personal loans was to General Robert Monckton. When Monckton died intestate in 1782 Mary Barwell applied for an administration of his estate, stating herself as "creditrix by bond and judgment of the deceased."[72] Evidently, Barwell wanted to ensure she would be paid since Monckton died without a will and with heirs. A Chancery case indicates that Mary also received an annuity of £450 for three lives after signing an indenture with a Mr. Cowie. Mary Barwell continually utilized the courts to ensure she could recoup her investments.[73] She also seems to have preferred personal loans and annuities rather than investing in company stock.

Mary Barwell lived a long life, dying in 1825 when she was in her early nineties. Her will provides a final glimpse of her financial standing and her investments. It is a lengthy five-page document full of all sorts of legal intricacies, just what one might expect from her. Mary's primary bequests were to a brother and two sisters (although she had outlived many of her other siblings).[74] Most of her will was taken up with arrangements for her two great-nieces, Mary and Arabella d'Amboise, grandchildren of her brother Richard Barwell.[75] It is perhaps fitting that Mary Barwell spent so much of her will establishing and directing the financial arrangements for Richard Barwell's descendants.

---

[69] Berkshire Record Office, D/EX 345/1 (1776). In 1776 Mary Barwell, spinster, of Great Ormond Street, London is recorded as receiving an annuity from the manor of Tarring in Sussex.

[70] "The Letters of Mr. Richard Barwell" Pt. VIII, *Bengal, Past & Present*, vol. 12 (1916), 70.

[71] Keith Feiling, *Warren Hastings* (London: Macmillan & Co., 1934), 174.

[72] Andrew Cormack, "Observations on the later life of Lieutenant-General the Honorable Robert Monckton and the lives of his children," *Journal of the Society for Army Historical Research* 85 (2007), 275–85.

[73] Wyatt v. Barwell (1815), in Francis Vesey, ed., *Report of Cases argued and determined in the High Court of Chancery from the Year 1789 to 1817*, vol. 19, 2nd ed. (London, 1827), 435–40.

[74] The National Archives, PROB 11/1695/4, will of Mary Barwell, 1 Feb. 1825.

[75] Richard's daughter Louisa Barwell married Georges-Alexis d'Amboise and had at least four children, including Marie and Arabella Mathilde. "Georges-Alexis d'Amboise" Wikipedia.org (accessed March 2011).

Since no inventory of her estate is extant, it is not clear how much Mary Barwell was worth when she died at the age of 92. She mentions plate, household goods, furniture, books, china, jewels, trinkets, and a carriage. These were the trappings of a genteel lifestyle. Her address is also an indicator of her financial position. Both a fire insurance policy and her will give her address as Duchess Street in St. Mary-le-bone. This was an affluent address in the Regency period, full of mansions designed by Robert Adams. Barwell's will also includes some monetary amounts. By 1824 she was heavily invested in Neapolitan bonds—holding as much as £9,000 in this fund.[76] She stated that her executors were free "at their discretion to sell out [the bonds] and the monies arising to be put in the public stocks or funds of Great Britain or other real securities." In other words, Barwell was not strict about the stocks or securities in which her capital should be invested, but she did want her legacies to stay in the form of liquid investments that would deliver reliable dividends or interest each year. This interest was to sustain her only living brother, two sisters, and the daughters of her niece. In the end, Mary Barwell's prudent financial management and wide-ranging investment experience helped to maintain future generations of the Barwell clan.

This chapter has detailed how women, both unmarried and married, invested in stocks and securities for their families. Rather than women relying on family members to invest for them, we find instead that women served as financial agents and brokers for their kin. Single women in particular, took advantage of their feme sole legal status to invest for nephews and brothers. And widows who enjoyed the same status invested their children's portions. More surprising perhaps is that despite their coverture, married women were frequently the investing partners in a marriage, sometimes held and kept investment accounts separate from their spouses, and even invested for third parties. This investment experience meant that when a woman was older and unmarried, like Mary Barwell, she knew how to invest to maintain herself. It is to this subject that we now turn. The next chapter will examine unmarried women who invested in government securities for their retirement and old age.

---

[76] Neapolitan bonds were one the major foreign funds listed (along with sixty others) as trading on the London Exchange in the 1820s. This decade saw a boom in foreign investment options as European countries recovering from the Napoleonic wars took out loans by offering government bonds. Marc Flandreau and Juan H. Flores, "Bonds and Brands: Intermediaries and Reputation in Sovereign Debt Markets, 1820–1830." Paper delivered at Conference on Globalization and Democracy, Princeton University, Sept. 27–28, 2007. *IDEAS* <ideas.repec.org/p/cte/whrepe/wp07-12.html> (accessed Oct. 20, 2013).

5

Unmarried Women Investing
for "Retirement"

For single and widowed women in early modern England, especially those of middling and gentry status, their later years could be ones of financial uncertainty if not anxiety. They could not work and still retain their social status and yet their marital status meant they had no marital partner to aid in their financial support. The financial instruments brought about by the Financial Revolution transformed the options for these women in their "retirement" years. I use the word retirement here purposefully. Retirement is a contested notion among historians, with some arguing it is a modern concept, and others saying it only applies to those who work and have a job from which to retire. But early modern people, especially widows and spinsters, conceptualized a need for an income stream to maintain and support themselves in their later years.[1] As I will show, for middling, genteel, and elite women, stocks, securities, and state annuities became the standard for planning for these years of retirement. Public and government securities provided more timely, secure, and liquid savings compared to older forms of maintenance such as land and rents. The rate of return was not always the highest but seems to have been good enough for women to pour money into these new investment options. And as we will see, the experience of women in the early stock market shows that rate of return was only one factor in a woman's investment decisions, with security perhaps more significant.

This chapter will examine the active participation of unmarried women as government creditors and their preference for government investments to fund middle and old age. We begin by examining the numbers of female government creditors over the first half of the eighteenth century. We then focus in on the women who loaned money to one particular government fund,

---

[1] For early modern notions of retirement as well as the practice of retirement contracts for older women and widows see Susannah Ottaway, *The Decline of Life: Old Age in Eighteenth Century England* (Cambridge: Cambridge University Press, 2004); Allyson Poska, "Gender, Property, and Retirement Strategies in early modern Northwestern Spain," *Journal of Family History* 25:3 (July 2000), 313–25.

the Life Annuities of 1745. I analyze the Life Annuitants to build up a picture of the type of women who invested their capital in the government debt.

Having examined women in aggregate, the second half of the chapter presents two case studies of families of unmarried women who utilized public investments to fund their middle and old age. First we will examine the women of the Savile family—the widow Barbara Savile, her married daughter Ann Cole, and her spinster daughter Gertrude Savile. These women learned to invest on their own, held diverse portfolios, and kept detailed accounts of their investing. Gertrude Savile's stocks and securities allowed her to transition from a dependent single sister to an independent London gentlewoman. Similarly, investments in various stocks and securities formed the basis of Teresa and Patty Blount's maintenance of themselves as single gentlewomen. Patty Blount actively managed a portfolio of investments that allowed her to maintain a genteel lifestyle in eighteenth-century London. These examples illustrate the benefit unmarried gentlewomen in particular enjoyed due to the new public investment options of the Financial Revolution.

Before we turn to the numbers of women who invested in government debt for retirement, it is useful to think about why they chose this option. While it is relatively easy to find women investing in government debt, the reasons why they did so are not so readily apparent. Some clues to why women flocked to government securities are revealed in the investing saga of Agnes Herbert. Her experience illustrates that the relative certainty and reliability of public securities offered by the Financial Revolution won women over from investing in land and mortgages. Agnes Herbert was widowed in 1728. Her husband Thomas was an estate bailiff in Whittlebury, Northamptonshire. About this time Agnes began to plan for her financial future by buying a mortgage for £540 at a 5 percent rate of interest. She should have made £27 a year off of this investment. But her brother-in-law Edward's accounts for 1748 reveal that in the intervening twenty-two years she had been paid only £277 in interest while a considerable £857 (including the original loan of £540) was still due to her. This mortgage had not turned out to be a good investment opportunity. Over the next four years it seems Edward was assisting his sister-in-law in trying to get her money back, but to no avail since in 1753 Agnes was now owed over £975.[2] The fact that Agnes was turning to male relatives and acquaintances for help in recouping her investments is telling, and indicates she had no luck herself either due to her gender or her lack of financial knowledge, or both. In 1752 the mortgagee's solution to being behind on his payments to Agnes Herbert was for her to collect her money directly from his tenants (a common practice in this situation). But as she astutely put it: "and what you think is best to be done in Mr. Gardiners affair I shall be very well satisfied with and if he

---

[2] The Henry E. Huntington Library (hereafter HEH), Herbert Family Papers, HE Box 3, 103.

should comply for me to received [sic] from the tenants I fear they would take the same liberty with me as he has done [.] If it might be ordered for them to make their payments to Mr Gibbes I think it would be money well bestowed to satisfie him for his trouble but I do not know how such things should be ordered."[3] Here Agnes pointed out that if she had had no luck getting money out of Mr. Gardiner she did not think she was going to have a better chance getting it out of his tenants. And she suggested that she would rather have a Mr. Gibbes collect it than to have to do so herself. Women at this time frequently loaned money on mortgage and Herbert's predicament illustrates what could go wrong with such an investment. While mortgage lending may have appeared simple and passive on paper, not requiring much activity by the female lender, the reality of having to collect money directly from tenants was quite different.

By the following year Mr. Gibbes was collecting the money from the tenants, but he advised the Herberts that he did not think Agnes could insist on the forfeiture of the mortgage for non-payment of interest. Edward Herbert wrote to Agnes that he had let their legal advisor know about the failure of interest and that she had asked no consideration money for it and "yt was much harder upon yo for all ye time you was forc'd to break into other money wch would have produced a great deal more yn this forfeiture, besides ye continual disappointments which have grieved you greatly," and that "it is my opinion you should have half of the forfeiture especially since you have a title to the whole."[4] Herbert also added at the end of his letter that he had asked Mr. Gibbes to place her money out again at interest. He did not ask Agnes where or how she wanted her money invested. Even after admitting how badly this investment had gone for her, and that she had had to break into other funds to live on, Edward was ready to put Agnes's money into a similar loan that could (and did) result in the same problem. Three years later, in 1756, Edward had to write to Mr. Gibbes that, "My sister makes heavy complaint for want of her interest money on these new mortgages. I wish you would quicken the parties for I find their disappointing her in this manner does her great mischief & much concern."[5] It is unclear how serious this 'mischief and concern' were for Agnes, but what is certain is that she was not reaping the steady, supposedly secure interest from personal securities that she had hoped to be able to live on in her widowhood.

By 1760 it seems that Agnes Herbert was tired of having to continually dun her creditors and of not receiving any return on her loans (the whole point of an investment to be sure). A letter from her brother encouraged her to continue to invest in mortgages or to purchase land, but pointedly discouraged

[3] HEH, Herbert Family Papers, HE Box 5, Dec. 3, 1752.
[4] HEH, Herbert Family Papers, HE Box 5, Mar. 13, 1753.
[5] HEH, Herbert Family Papers, HE Box 6, April 29, 1756.

her from investing in the public funds. "I don't know in what Hands my sister can place any of the money to be paid the interest punctually; From Mr. Gardiner down to this Time, it has always been the same. And yet, a safe mortgage seems to be best, at present, unless she could lay it out in Land; The publick stocks will produce her no more than 3 per cent. If she can resolve (when she has farther consider'd) how to place it, I'll assist her all I can."[6] In Edward Herbert's cost/benefit analysis private loans earned a higher rate of interest and thus were preferable. But since Agnes Herbert could not get any of the interest, she may have preferred a surer investment with a lower rate of return.

In the 1770s Agnes Herbert finally eschewed her brother-in-law's financial advice. While he may have perceived mortgages as "safe," they had not proved to be a secure investment for Agnes Herbert. She finally "resolved," to put it in her words, to invest in a new form of property. By 1772 a man named Thomas Ward was sending her notes and paying her £540, which included dividends on investments such as East India stock. The next month he was saying if she chose it he would purchase £200 more for her in the Consols [Consolidated Annuities] issued by the government. And he was promising another £100 in interest in the next month. Compared to earlier years, Agnes Herbert's interest income was now rolling in. Once she took control of her investments and chose a different advisor than her brother-in-law, and moreover, once she decided to move her money out of private securities and land, and instead into public stocks and securities, her financial horizon improved. For Agnes Herbert at least, public stocks were much more profitable, reliable, and secure than private loans. And it was she, and not her brother, who chose and preferred to invest in public securities rather than land. What Agnes Herbert illustrates is why women chose to invest in government funds. Now we will turn to the types of government securities that interested female investors and women's relative proportion as public creditors.

One of the most popular investment choices of middle-aged and elderly unmarried women was government debt. There was a plethora of investment opportunities in the public debt beginning with the reign of William and Mary in the late seventeenth century and continuing through the eighteenth. Table 5.1. presents the proportion of women who invested in thirteen different long-term public securities offered by the British government between 1692 and 1747.

Individuals could loan money and receive a rate of interest that varied according to each government loan. Beginning in the 1700s many of the loan schemes also included a State lottery, which meant that investors would earn interest on the sums they loaned out, but were also entered into drawings

---

[6] HEH, Herbert Family Papers, HE Box 6, May 17, 1760.

for additional prizes. As we saw in chapter 2, these State lotteries were extremely popular with both men and women. Most of the government loans and lottery schemes also offered return payment in the form of an annuity. These annuities sometimes were for a term of years, but often were for the whole life of the subscriber—or even ninety-nine years.

Long-term government loans and repayment through annuities appealed to certain types of investors. Such schemes were not popular with those who wanted their capital back or a high rate of return. Nevertheless, these public funds were of particular interest to single women and widows who were looking for a steady income to see them through old age. In fact, state annuities became the most popular investment for women in the eighteenth century. As David Hancock has noted, government annuities were also popular because they were considered personal estate, and as such could be sold and bequeathed. In addition, they were free from taxation, could be purchased without fees, and could be bought in fractions. The government offered these annuities at various rates and terms from the 1690s through the eighteenth century. Interest rates varied, with the highest rates at the beginning of the eighteenth century, then dropping to a low of 3 percent in the peaceful years of the 1720s and '30s, before going up again to 4 percent when the state needed money for further military endeavors in the 1740s. The terms of the annuities also varied; sometimes they were for ninety-six to ninety-nine years, other times for lives (one, two, or three), and increasingly after the 1720s, perpetual. The government preferred perpetual annuities because they could be redeemed at any time deemed favorable for the state.[7]

Table 5.1. shows that women consistently comprised between 15 and 30 percent of investors in the government loans between 1690 and 1750, with female investors most often making up between 20 to 25 percent of overall public creditors. This illustrates that women made up a higher percentage of investors in government debt than in most public companies. What is more, for two reasons these percentages probably even underestimate female participation. One, women's money was often invested under the name of male agents and trustees, and two, historians like myself rely on samples of investors rather than complete reconstitution of long lists of public creditors for each government loan. My samples err on the side of caution, but other scholars, using different samples, have found even higher percentages of female participation in the public funds. For instance, P. G. M. Dickson found that women comprised 20.03 percent (compared to my figure of 19.05 percent) of investors in the 1707 Long Annuity and an even more significant 34.7 percent (compared

---

[7] David Hancock, "'Domestic Bubbling': 18th-Century London Merchants and Individual Investment in the Funds," *Economic History Review* 47:4 (1994), 679–702. Sidney Homer and Richard Sylla, *A History of Interest Rates*, 4th ed. (New Brunswick, NJ: Rutgers University Press, 2005), 153.

Table 5.1. Female Investors in Government Securities, 1692–1747

Type of Government Loan	Year	Interest Rate/Term	Percentage of Female Investors
Tontine Loan	1692–3	10% until 1700 then 7%/until last contributor died	19.29%
Long Annuity	1707	6.25%/ 99 years	19.05% [Dickson sample: 20.03%]
Annuity Loan	1708	6.25%/ 99 years	14.45%
5% Annuities lottery	1717	5%/ perpetual	30.16% [Dickson sample: 34.7%]
4% Annuities lottery	1719	4%/ perpetual	19.38%
14% Long Annuities	1719	14%/ 89, 96, 99 years	12% [Dickson sample: 21.3%]
3% Annuities	1726	3%/ perpetual	18.41%
Annuity	1727	3%/ perpetual	14.4%
3% Annuities	1731	3%/ perpetual	27.86%
Loan on the Land Tax	1742–3	3%/ N/A	24.9%
3% Annuities	1743	3%/ perpetual	22.27%
Life Annuities	1745	4½%/ for owner's lifetime or a nominee's	24.08%
4% Annuity	1747	4%/ for life	17.36%

Sources: Tontine Loan: The National Archives (hereafter TNA), E 401/1991–2; Long Annuity, 1707: TNA, E 401/2018 and Dickson, *Financial Revolution*, 268, Table 36; Annuity Loan, 1708: TNA, E 407/166; 5% Annuities Lottery, 1717: Bank of England Archives (hereafter BA), AC 27/330, and Dickson, *Financial Revolution*, 282, Table 38; 4% Annuities Lottery, 1719: BA, AC 27/218; 14% Annuities, 1719: TNA, E 403/1400, Dickson, *Financial Revolution*, 282, Table 38; 3% Annuities, 1726: BA, AC 27/104; Annuity, 1727: TNA, E 403/1450; 3% Annuities, 1731: BA, AC 27/131; Loan on the Land Tax, 1743: TNA, E 401/2090; 3% Annuities, 1743: BA, AC 27/143; Life Annuities, 1745: TNA, NDO/1/1; 4% Annuity, 1747: BA, AC 27/246.

to my finding of 30.16 percent) in the 5% Annuities lottery of 1717. While our findings are within a few percentage points, there is a larger discrepancy between my sample and Dickson's for the 14% Long Annuity of 1719.[8] In sum, all of my figures are conservative estimates and may actually slightly underestimate female participation in government lending.

Lists of government creditors reveal the numerically significant participation of women as public creditors. Another source that reveals the same are the wills of London's female testators during the first half of the eighteenth century.[9] A sample of fifty female testators who invested in public stocks and securities reveals that their wills most frequently mentioned the Long annuities (of the 1710s), the 3% and 4% Consolidated Annuities (of the 1750s), the Government Annuities for Lives (of the 1740s), and the 3% Annuity of 1726. Other testators were not so specific, but referred more generally to holding public, government, and parliamentary funds, or government securities.

Some of these women held both large sums of money and significant proportions of their personal estates in government funds. For instance, in her 1749 will the widow Sarah King mentioned over £3,000 that she had in the 3% Annuities payable at the Bank [of England].[10] Others held multiple government securities. Ann Astley, a single woman whose will was proved in 1757, mentioned £3,000 "which is in my name in the first subscribed Bank Annuity stock at 3 and a half per cent payable half yearly." She left half of this to her widowed sister Elizabeth Reeve as well as bequeathing to her widowed niece, Hannah Maberly, "all my title and interest in the Long Annuities" (which Astley herself had inherited from another woman).[11] Similarly, Mary Trevor, a Hanover Square spinster, stated in her will, "I am intitled for a long term of years to an annuity of £250 transferable at the Bank of England commonly called a Long Annuity..." and bequeathed the money on trust to her sisters Lucy Rice and Grace Trevor and then to her nieces.[12] In her 1766 will, Ann Ashby (a proprietor of a 1745 Life Annuity) ordered her executors to pay her four relatives legacies worth over £4,000 by "transferring to them in their respective names so much of my personal estate at the time of my death vested in any of the public funds or government securities as will be sufficient..."[13]

---

[8] This may have to do with my sample coming from the first part of the subscription book. Women usually were less numerous at the beginning, or the opening up, of a new investment opportunity and became more numerous as a subscription went on.

[9] This data is derived from a sample of fifty Prerogative Court of Canterbury wills made by women residing in London. The names of testators were chosen from *The Master Key* (L, 1742), a list of eligible London spinsters and widows that included an estimate of their estate in public stocks and securities.

[10] The National Archives (hereafter TNA), PROB 11/771, Sarah King, widow, 1749.

[11] TNA, PROB 11/833, Ann Astley, spinster, 1757.

[12] TNA, PROB 11/1063, Mary Trevor, spinster, 1780.

[13] TNA, PROB, 11/920, Ann Ashby, spinster, 1766.

As these examples show, female investors not only chose government securities for themselves, but they were the preferred choice of women making financial arrangements for their heirs or kin. When women made wills they often established financial trusts for legal minors or married female kin. They directed their trustees to "lay out or invest" the trust money in government debt. As well as putting legacies to kin into government funds, women also used this investment choice for their charitable trusts. For example, in her 1760 will Elizabeth Verney gave much of her money to her relatives, but as a gentlewoman of some wealth she also had the means and freedom to bequeath nearly £1,000 to charity in the form of government annuities. Verney left £200 in 3% Consolidated Bank Annuities to charitable uses in her family's home parish of Middle Claydon, Bucks. Her will explained that the £6 in annual interest produced by the Consols should be paid out in 20-shilling amounts to two poor families, two poor widows, and two poor maids of the parish. In all, Elizabeth Verney put £900 in government annuities, a fund that she felt confident was financially secure enough to endow these charities for perpetuity.[14]

Similarly, when the Spitalfields single woman Esther Coqueau died in 1745 she left money in government funds to establish a charity. Her charity was specifically to maintain older women in retirement. Her will stated that she devised "the sum of £2,000 in the fund of the three per cent annuities transferable at the Bank of England" to the French hospital and other charities in trust "to pay the yearly dividend to ten poor maids or widows aged upwards of 50 years and to pay each of them their respective proportions of the said dividends by equal monthly payments for and during the term of their respective natural lives." She instructed the Committee of Directors of the Hospital to appoint new women to the charity as they died off, but to keep the number at ten. And any poor widow or maid that "is of my kin she to get preference." If the government ended this particular fund or investment she ordered the directors to "lay out and invest the moneys which shall be so paid in such other Fund or Funds or Securities as they think fit."[15] Esther Coqueau was seventy-two when she died and she had never married. Presumably her investments had assisted her later years and thanks to her bequest these investments would now maintain ten more unmarried women in their old age.

It is apparent that government funds were appealing to women from the 1690s on through the first half of the eighteenth century. To get a better sense of these female public creditors let us now examine in more detail the female lenders to one government fund in particular, the Life Annuities of 1745. In 1745 the British government passed an Act to raise £2 million, out of which £500,000 was to be raised by State lottery. Each person who purchased ten £10

---

[14] TNA, PROB 11/931, Hon. Elizabeth Verney, 1767.
[15] Huguenot Library, University College London, Special Collections, H/E1/1 Extracts from Wills (1725–1842), 50.

lottery tickets would receive a 4.5 percent Exchequer Annuity for their own life or that of a nominee.[16] Four and a half percent was a decent rate of return but nothing exceptional. Out of a sample of 321 proprietors, 100 were women, or 31.15 percent.[17] This was on the higher end of female participation in public securities (see Table 5.1.). Being a proprietor meant a woman bought and owned a government annuity in her own name. Other women may have been nominees of annuities bought by males, but they are not counted here, since I am interested in women who themselves chose to invest.

All but one of this sample of 100 women were commoners, although the wealth held by them indicates many hailed from the genteel and middling classes. We can also get some sense of where these women resided since the list of proprietors included their addresses. Ninety-one separate addresses were recorded for women who purchased Life Annuities (three women purchased more than one annuity and two women had no residence listed). Twenty-five stated their residence as a parish in Westminster, ten more as elsewhere in the West End of London, twenty-three in the City of London, and seven in the county of Middlesex, or the greater London area. Fifteen lived in the nearby Home Counties (Berkshire, Hertfordshire, Kent, and Surrey), nine in English counties further afield (such as Devon, Essex, Hampshire, Suffolk, and Worcestershire), and two were women from outside England, specifically the Netherlands. In sum, 74 percent of the women who purchased government securities resided in the London area for at least some part of the year. And virtually all of the proprietors lived in England, not other parts of the British Isles.

When we look at the areas of London in which the Life Annuitants resided (see Table 5.2.), 35 percent lived in the fashionable and more expensive western suburbs of London at addresses such as Pall Mall, St James, Hanover Square, and Berkeley Square.

This is not a surprise, since such areas attracted single women and widows from the gentry, exactly the type of women with income to invest in government funds. What is more interesting is how many of the annuitants, 23 percent in all, still lived in the City—the area home to merchants, professionals, and tradesmen. While most of these women by no means came from poor families, many were probably of the middling sort. Of course, these were also the women who had firsthand or direct knowledge of stocks and securities, since their male relatives and acquaintances might well have been involved in commerce and finance. There were only three women residing in the East End, who along with the six women in the parish of St Martin in the Fields, may

---

[16] P. G. M. Dickson, *The Financial Revolution in England* (London: Macmillan, 1967), Table 25, 218–19.

[17] TNA, NDO 1/1, National Debt Office, Life Annuities, 1745. This volume lists 631 annuities. I sampled 321 of these entries, out of which 100 were women.

Table 5.2. Residences of Female Life Annuitants, 1745

RESIDENCE	WOMEN N = 91
WESTMINSTER	25
WEST END	10
CITY OF LONDON	23
GREATER LONDON SUBURBS	7
HOME COUNTIES	15
PROVINCIAL COUNTIES	9
INTERNATIONAL	2

Source: TNA, NDO 1/1, Life Annuities, 1745.

have been among the least prosperous Life Annuitants (although the mixed demographics of these areas makes this uncertain).

Only unmarried women are recorded as holding the 1745 Life Annuities in their own names, which seems to indicate that coverture prevented married women from holding a Life Annuity themselves. Wives, of course, may well have held them under trustees. Never-married women overwhelmingly dominated the female Life Annuitants, with thirty-seven spinsters and eleven widows making up a sample of forty-eight women for whom marital status was recorded. As my earlier work has shown, in the early eighteenth century adult single women outnumbered widows in the general population two to one, so this may account for some of the former's numerical dominance.[18] The proportion of widows was increasing by the mid-eighteenth century, however, and the number of adult single women declining, so there may have been other reasons that more single than widowed women chose Life Annuities.[19] It could be that spinsters were interested in a long-term investment of their capital and were comfortable tying up their funds, while widows with children may have needed more liquidity.[20]

The ages of the female Life Annuitants ranged from twenty-one-year-old Sarah Cary of Mitcham, Surrey to Susanna Robethan of St James, Westminster, who was sixty. That Cary was one of the youngest women to hold a Life Annuity seems indicative that twenty-one was the standard age of legal majority and the age required for a woman to make a contract in her own name. The average age of the female proprietors was 33.93 years, with the highest number of women in their thirties, followed by those in their twenties, forties,

---

[18] For example, in Southampton in the 1690s single women comprised 34.2 per cent of adult women as compared to widows who made up 18.5 per cent. Amy M. Froide, "Hidden Women: Rediscovering the Singlewomen of Early Modern England," *Local Population Studies* 68 (Spring 2002), 26–41.

[19] E. A. Wrigley and R. S. Schofield, *The Population History of England, 1541–1871* (Cambridge, MA: Harvard University Press, 1991), 258–9.

[20] This difference in the investing strategy of spinsters and widows also appears in private loans. See Amy M. Froide, *Never Married: Singlewomen in Early Modern England* (Oxford: Oxford University Press, 2005), 133.

and fifties. It is apparent that the Life Annuities were most appealing to unmarried women who had reached middle age and who were thinking about how to fund their "retirement" years.

The women who purchased Life Annuities in 1745 did so as an investment to benefit or maintain themselves. Almost all of the proprietors named themselves as the nominee (or beneficiary), with a mere handful of women, mostly widows, designating children or nephews as nominees. The annuities or yearly amounts the female proprietors received varied from sums as low as £5 5s. to as high as £320 (see Table 5.3.). The most common annuity amounts were £10 followed by £15. Thirty-two of the women in the sample received annuities of £25 and under. Eleven women received amounts between £25 and £50, seven received between £50 and £100, and only four received sums over £100 a year. For most women then, it seems that the Life Annuities were probably only a portion of their annual income. A woman of genteel status could not live off of £10 or £15 a year, since a few hundred pounds was the bare minimum needed to support gentility in the eighteenth century.[21]

How good an investment were the Life Annuities for the women who put their capital into them? Overall, the annuities were a good investment choice if a woman valued security over the highest possible rate of return. And this is exactly what a government fund offered a potential investor. For example, Margaret Mary Ravaud purchased the significant sum of £5,555 in lottery tickets that earned her a £250 annuity for life. The government may have been pleased to receive her £5,555 but disappointed to find they ultimately lost their actuarial bet. Ravaud, who was twenty-seven when she purchased her Life Annuity, would not die until 1800, meaning that the British Treasury had to pay her £250 annually for nearly fifty-five years. In the end Margaret Ravaud earned £13,750, almost tripling her original investment. Nevertheless, she

Table 5.3. Annuity Amounts of Female Life Annuitants, 1745

Amounts in £	Number of Women, N = 54
£0–10	1
£10–20	25
£20–30	6
£30–50	8
£50–100	7
£100–320	7

Source: TNA, NDO 1/1, Life Annuities, 1745.

[21] H. T. Dickinson, *A Companion to Eighteenth Century Britain* (2008), 151, 314. The contemporary Massie put a gentleman's income at between £200 and £2000 in 1756. Penelope Corfield, "Class by Name and Number in eighteenth-century Britain," in P. J. Corfield, ed., *Language, History and Class* (Oxford: Oxford University Press, 1991), 116.

could have made more. If she had invested her £5,555 at 3½ percent (a common interest rate in 1745) she would have earned just under £200 a year. This was less than her £250 Life Annuity from the government, but she would have retained her principal.

No matter her investment choice, Ravaud did collect much more than she had invested, and she was not alone. Out of a sample of forty-nine women who purchased Life Annuities from the British government, thirty-four, or 69.38 percent, gained on their investment. In other words, the annuities they received over time exceeded the sum they had paid in to purchase lottery tickets. Eleven women lost on their investment, and for four women it is unclear since they married and their Life Annuity was transferred into a husband's name. It took about twenty-two years for a purchaser to break even, so any woman living beyond that did well. The record holder in this sample was Mary Jane Crommelin Girandot, a spinster from East Greenwich, who lived for sixty-three years after she purchased her Life Annuity.[22]

It seems that female annuitants may have also discussed investing in government annuities amongst themselves, perhaps learning of them from other women they knew, and then investing in groups. For example, Mary Poyntz Senior, Hannah Poyntz Junior, and Mary Poyntz Junior were all single women in their mid-twenties who were related to one another. Although they lived in various locations throughout Berkshire and Kent they appeared in the Life Annuity list in a row as numbers 148, 149, and 150, respectively. Marianne Mills and Mary Chamberlen both resided in Dudbrooke, Essex and appeared one after the other as well.

I am not the first to recognize that women were prominent investors in government securities. Historian P. G. M. Dickson provided some of the initial evidence that women were prominent investors in the 1700s, but he attributed their participation in the annuities to the fact that this stock originated in the State lotteries of 1711–12 in which many small investors (e.g. women) "had a flutter."[23] With this statement, Dickson denigrated female annuitants as gamblers rather than recognizing them as rational investors. Were British women just having a "flutter"? I think not. As we have seen, women invested in government funds, whether they were related to a lottery or not. And they did so because these were safe, secure investments that could see them through their later years. These government funds were popular with female lenders from the very beginning of the Financial Revolution and remained consistently so throughout the first half of the eighteenth century. They were not gambles but rational investments. Now that we have a sense of unmarried women's interest in government funds as way to earn income in their middle

---

[22] TNA, NDO 1/1. The deaths of each Life Annuitant were recorded.
[23] Dickson, *Financial Revolution*, Table 38, 282.

and old age let us turn to some case studies of women who engaged in investing as a way to fund their later years. These studies allow us to examine the strategies and success of women who invested in stocks and securities for retirement.

5.1. CASE STUDY: BARBARA AND GERTRUDE SAVILE

The Savile women provide a particularly good example of how one cluster of unmarried women maintained themselves in their later years by investing in stocks and securities. The family included a trio of female investors: the widow Barbara Savile, and her two daughters, the wife and widow Ann Cole and the spinster Gertrude. In 1678 Barbara had married John Savile, the rector of Thornhill, Yorkshire. The couple had three children, Ann, Gertrude, and a son George. George, although the son of a clergyman, succeeded his cousin Sir John Savile as heir to the family estates and in 1704 became Sir George Savile, the 7th Baronet. His mother had been widowed a few years earlier in 1701. Although Sir George allowed his mother and never-married sister Gertrude to reside at his estate at Rufford, his rise in fortune did not generally benefit them much. In fact, much of Barbara's wealth came from estates she inherited from her maternal kin and as we will see, Gertrude's maintenance was secured not by her brother, but by a male cousin.

In the 1710s, and near fifty years of age, Barbara Savile began to invest in public stocks and securities. She continued to do so until her death in 1734.[24] Savile kept neat paper bound ledgers in which she recorded her investments from the late 1710s through to the early 1730s. She inscribed one ledger "South Sea" and labeled another bundle: "South Sea Papers and Old South Sea Papers and accompts and other Money in Funds or Bub[b]les."[25] This latter collection of various public investments also included an account book. Such a collection of investment records (or at least extant ones) is rare to find for a gentlewoman in this period.

Beginning in 1724, just four years after the South Sea Bubble, the widow Savile was buying stock in the South Sea Annuities. Like the female investors discussed above, Barbara Savile turned to annuities. The South Sea annuity stock was part of the solution to the Company's crash. They were perpetual annuities that paid a 5 percent rate of return (until 1727 when the rate

---

[24] Nottinghamshire Archives (hereafter NOA), Savile of Rufford Papers, DD/SR/219/9.
[25] NOA, Savile of Rufford Papers, DD/SR/219/9.

dropped to 4 percent) and were redeemable by the government.[26] Savile held £345 6s. 4d. worth of these annuities in 1724 and then bought another £54 13s. 8d., to bring her investment up to an even £400. The next year she bought £250 more, and by 1727 she held £1,100 in South Sea stock. With each purchase, Savile meticulously recorded the price at which she purchased the stock and from whom. She also noted that she was receiving dividends of 5 percent on her investment in the 1720s.[27] Barbara Savile showed herself to be an active and at times risk-taking investor. She made her own investments, rarely employed agents, invested money in the market on a regular basis, and increased her invested capital over time.

Periodically, Barbara Savile would tot up her investments. On June 7, 1725 she wrote:

> when I sold 300 for the Bishop I left in SS [South Sea] Stock I think–100. And at that time I had in SS Annuitys 400li. In Jul 20 1725 I bought of annuities 250li. So now in Nov 1725 I think I have in all 750. Besides dividends from the 18 of May 1724 I think for 100 for one whole year something above 6li, for 245 for half a year about 9li, and a year for 400li at 5 % 20li. Dividends in all £35.

Savile's use of the term "I think" makes her sound tentative and yet her regular purchasing and her correct math belie this. Savile also recorded how she came up with the funds to make her July 1725 purchase of South Sea annuities. She says she had £100 in her stitch purse, £40 in dividends due to her, and two bills for £100 in her possession. Altogether "I had in my house £360. I designed to buy that at 7% above the £100 17s. 10d." Savile notes that she paid 13s. 6d. in brokerage fees on the £250 in stock and that she disbursed £268 3s. 6d. in total for the stock purchase, which she says left her £91 6s. 6d. in cash. Below this Barbara Savile made a note to herself that "Tuesdays and Thursdays & Saturdays are days to buy stock and Mundays Wednesdays and Frydays are days to [she crossed out the word 'sell'] do yt other thing vizt I think receive dividends." Here we see an example of an older woman (Savile was in her late sixties or early seventies) learning how, when, and where to purchase stock, choosing her own investments, and making up her own accounts.[28]

Documentation and record keeping were important to Barbara Savile. Her 1733 will included a codicil with detailed instructions on where to find her papers and who should have access to them. She wrote, "and my will is that none of my cabinets, escrewtors [escritoire or writing desk], drawers, trunks, boxes or anything of that sort that belongs to me that has a lock on at the time of my decease shall be open'd or anything taken out of them until my two

---

[26] Ann M. Carlos and Larry Neal, "The micro-foundations of the London capital market: Bank of England shareholders during and after the South Sea Bubble, 1720–25," *Economic History Review* 59:3 (2006), 502 and n. 15.

[27] NOA, Savile of Rufford Papers, DD/SR/219/9.

[28] NOA, Savile of Rufford Papers, DD/SR/219/9.

daughters are present... and my will is that my writings and papers be perused or disposed of as my daughters think proper."[29] She entrusted these documents to her daughters because they were competent managers and account keepers in their own right.

For example, Barbara Savile's daughter Ann seems to have begun investing before her mother. In 1701, Ann Savile's father died and she, barely twenty-one, took control of her marriage portion. She placed £600 of her £2,000 dowry out at interest.[30] Ann continued to invest even more of her portion up until her 1705 marriage; putting £100 in the East India Company at 6 percent interest and £1,300 in a mortgage, and reinvesting £200 of the original £600 she had put out on mortgage in 1701. In all, she had £1,500 out at interest. Ann Savile then negotiated a marital settlement that allowed the "produce" of this £1,500 to be for her own "sole and separate use." Her husband to be, Sir Nicholas Cole, a Durham Baronet, also granted to her any interest or profits from her full £2,000 portion for her separate use.

Widowed, Lady Cole married again but this second marriage crumbled due to financial quarrels and she and her spouse separated. Once again, Lady Cole found herself a lone woman who needed to take care of herself financially. Her mother, Barbara Savile, sprang into action, helping to handle her daughter's finances, either because Ann was under coverture or because she was abroad in France (or both). Gertrude Savile's diary records her mother's trips to South Sea House as well as consultations with lawyers and their elder brother on Lady Cole's business.[31]

The Savile women were not afraid to invest money in new and perhaps risky undertakings. After all, Barbara Savile labeled her investment records as money put into "Funds and Bub[b]les." She got caught up in the early 1720s bubble mania, investing in the York Buildings Company, Welsh Copper shares, and a fishery company.[32] The York Buildings Company was originally incorporated in the 1690s to pump water from the Thames into London, but in 1719 the directors changed course and with a new infusion of capital they purchased estates forfeited by those who participated in the Jacobite rebellion of 1715. In 1720 the company tried to get into life insurance. These diversions hurt the Company's finances and they had to resort to a lottery to raise money. This is the context in which Barbara Savile invested hundreds of pounds in the company. She also sold out her shares in Welsh Copper to invest them in South Sea stock in August 1720. This was right before the South Sea Bubble burst and the worst time to invest. The £400 Savile received from selling the

---

[29] NOA, Savile of Rufford Papers, DD/SR/225/23.

[30] NOA, Savile of Rufford Papers, DD/SR/234/40.

[31] Alan Saville, ed., *Secret Comment: The Diaries of Gertrude Savile, 1721–1757*, The Thoroton Society Record Series, vol. 41 (Nottingham, 1997), 103, 109.

[32] NOA, Savile of Rufford Papers, DD/SR/219/9.

copper shares and which she invested in South Sea stock had sunk to a value of £146 13s. 3d. by late 1720. This resulted in a loss of over £250 for her. Although she was responsible for her own maintenance, Barbara Savile was obviously willing to take some risky moves in her investing.

Barbara Savile and Ann Cole did much of their investing themselves, but they also employed a female broker. In 1720, Savile, her daughter Cole, and a "Mrs. Dyett, broaker," pooled their money and bought a £500 subscription in the York Buildings Company. Neither Savile nor Cole lived full time in London, so this may be why they employed Dyett as an agent. She seems to have been a family friend or relation of the Saviles. Ann Cole named Mrs. Dyett as a broker, or buyer and seller of stocks and securities, and noted that Mrs. Dyett had bought the subscription "by the order & for the use and profit of Mrs. Dyett, Mrs. Barbara Savile & my self to wch my name is subscribed." So all three women put up the capital, Mrs. Dyett did the actual buying, and the subscription was put in the name of Ann Cole. Nevertheless, Cole recorded in a memorandum that she had put up only two fifths of the subscription money, her mother another two fifths, and Mrs. Dyett one fifth.[33] Together these three women chose their own investments, used their own money, designated one of their own gender to make the purchase, and held the subscription under a woman's name. Not one male was involved in these women's investments.

While Barbara Savile invested in some risky ventures, she also held a diverse portfolio of investments and this seems to have aided her. Her will reveals that she died in a quite prosperous state and was able to make a number of bequests to her female kin. Her testament is a matriarchal document. She wrote that since her son had an "ample" fortune of his own, and the chief part of "mine decendd to me from my mother I acquainted him with my intention of disposing of what I have mostly to my daughters and...he gave his ready consent to it." The money that Barbara Savile had inherited from her mother, transformed by her investing, now was passed on to a third generation of female kin. Savile also left lands to her sister Isabella Newton and after her sister's death to her niece (and Isabella's daughter) Elizabeth Ogle, "for her sole and separate use, with no intermeddling by her husband, her receipt during coverture as good as if she were sole," and on her death in trust to her daughter. As with her personal estate, Barbara Savile created a long matriarchal line of property inheritance. In all, Barbara Savile bequeathed real estate, South Sea Annuities, hundreds of pounds in cash, and personal estate, household goods, and plate of an unspecified value.[34]

While her mother and sister were widowed, Gertrude Savile never married. She was born in February 1696/97, sixteen years after her elder sister Ann. As a single woman, financial dependence was a concern for her. These concerns

---

[33] NOA, Savile of Rufford Papers, DD/SR/219/9.
[34] NOA, Savile of Rufford Papers, DD/SR/225/23.

began around 1721 when Gertrude was nearing her mid-twenties, an age associated with spinsterhood in the eighteenth century. As she wrote in her diary, "I begin to think I buy my meat and cloathes too dear...Chiefly the business of my dependency upon my Brother; neither father nor husband... But what must I doe, God knows, if his providence does not provide for me (which I am very unworthy of)... 'Tis far better to work honestly for my bread than thus to have every mouthful reproach me; than thus to be oblig'd to a Brother."[35] Here Gertrude pessimistically laid out the dilemma of the spinster gentlewoman—she had no financial independence without a husband or a job. As the 7th Baronet, Gertrude's brother George inherited much more wealth than did she. He did pay his younger sister an allowance (£40 for half a year when she stayed at his house), and later provided a place for her in the family's London house, but he did not hand over or let her manage her own portion. And in later life when she received an inheritance from their cousin Newton, her brother actually converted her allowance into a loan on which he charged interest. In all of these actions Sir George kept his single sister dependent on him.[36]

Gertrude Savile's financial dependency was significantly altered in her mid-thirties by news that her cousin Newton, an East India Company man, had died and left her an estate. In the short term, this news led to an improvement in Gertrude's mood in summer 1730 and to her splashing out on a fashionable new gown. The long-term impact was that Gertrude was no longer dependent on her family, with whom she often quarreled, and she would now take over and manage her own wealth. As she noted, "The most extroordinary thing relateing to myself this Year and indeed of my past Life, was the Unmerited and unexpected proof of Friendship from my poor Cosen Newton...when his Will, which he had sent to Mr. Knight two Years before, was oppen'd...to everybody's surprise, (besides a few legacys) he left me all he had." While happy for the money, Gertrude professed herself just as pleased with the thought: "I confess I take a little pride and pleasure in his distinction of me, and I own I value myself upon it." Here Gertrude notes the social, as much as monetary, value that she received from this inheritance.[37]

Gertrude Savile stopped keeping her journal, or it is not extant, for the years 1731–7. This means it is not possible to trace the beginning of her financial independence in the immediate years after receiving cousin Newton's bequest. From the few remarks she wrote later on, it seems that her cousin Dr. Ogle "offer'd, nay press'd in such a manner as coud not be refused, that he might be my Steward, and manage for me what my Cousin Newton left me; protesting he was far from being displeas'd with his Brother's kindness to me..." Despite

---

[35] *Secret Comment*, 14.
[36] *Secret Comment*, 19, 26, 236, 247. Gertrude attributed her brother's venal behavior to his expensive, seven-year long, divorce case.
[37] *Secret Comment*, 209–10, 214, 217, 219–20.

her suspicions, Gertrude says "he did after that, manage that Estate for me with great Justice, Genourosity and Friendship as long as he lived."[38]

It is too bad that Gertrude Savile's diary does not exist for these early years of financial independence, because in other years it is a useful source for revealing her knowledge and involvement in the early stock market. She began the diary in 1721, when she was in her mid-twenties, and the first non-personal news she recorded was economic. It was about the South Sea Bubble and its negative impact on people's fortunes. At Bath, Gertrude had rubbed shoulders with the son and daughter of the South Sea Director, Theodore Janssen, and even "Mr. Laws" (John Law). She admitted she "could not help liking" the latter despite the financial bubbles for which he was responsible.[39] In the 1740s she still kept abreast of financial doings, reporting a fire in 'Change Alley in March 1748 that burned over 100 houses. She wrote "'Twas said in the news pappers to be the richest spot of Ground in England if not [E]urope."[40]

Gertrude Savile's diary also shows how she frequented the places and spaces of the Financial Revolution. November 1723 is the first time she mentions going to the Bank of England and she went frequently thereafter, although sometimes she sent in her maid to receive bills for her. In 1727/28 Gertrude went to South Sea House to collect the dividend on her mother Barbara's stocks. As she aged, however, Savile seems to have employed agents to do her financial errands. In 1756 and in bad health, Gertrude noted how much she appreciated her friend Mrs. Richards; "I get her to do all my Citty business."[41]

Gertrude Savile was fortunate in both inheriting various sums from, and in being exposed to the financial accounting and investing skills of, her mother and elder sister. In the 1720s she regularly recorded in her diary that she spent time doing her accounts, whether "house recconing" with her mother, or doing her "own" accounts for one or two hours at a time.[42] Gertrude even saw accounting as a metaphor for life. In her diary, where she recorded her moods and feelings, for May 4, 1730 she described "the whole balance of account between pleasure and pain today:

Pleasure Debit		Pleasure Creddet		Balance.	
s.	d.	s.	d.	s.	d.
		5	0		
10	6	2	9½	2	8½[43]
		7	9½		

---

[38] *Secret Comment*, 229–30.   [39] *Secret Comment*, 22–3, 32–3.
[40] *Secret Comment*, 285.   [41] *Secret Comment*, 74, 100, 136, 146, 325.
[42] *Secret Comment*, 61, 69, 86.   [43] *Secret Comment*, 201.

Unfortunately, for Gertrude, this day like many others she recorded in her diary, had resulted in a pleasure deficit.

Along with her diary, Gertrude Savile also kept detailed and well-organized accounts of her wealth and investments. Her account books are extant for the years 1736–48. They begin when she was around age forty, when her mother had recently died and she had inherited a number of different properties and investments to manage. Gertrude Savile annually balanced her accounts and regularly listed her investments. As such, her accounts provide a window on an older single woman's investment portfolio in the mid-eighteenth century.

Gertrude Savile started investing in middle age and continued into her sixties. Among her accounts, Gertrude included a two-page list entitled "What I have in Stocks" for the years 1737–47.[44] This list allows us to reconstruct her trading activity and investment portfolio over this period. On April 30, 1737 Gertrude noted that she had received her half of £1,600 Old South Sea Annuity stock that had been her late sister's (Lady Cole) and that it was transferred into her name. She says that she sold £200 of the stock to pay off part of a loan from her brother, Sir George, and so £600 in this stock remained. She also had a male agent transfer to her £700 in Old South Sea Annuity stock from her mother, Barbara Savile's, estate. Gertrude noted her own financial authority in her accounts, recording "N.B. by a letter of attorney signed by [the surviving trustees of Lady Cole]...I was impowered to receive or transfer Lady Cole's [£]1,600 South Sea Annuity stock and the dividends upon it." This shows that Gertrude personally received the dividends, paid her brother his half, and transferred half of the stock to her brother and the other half into her own name. In total, Gertrude held £1,300 in South Sea Annuity stock, but she sold out £300 in May 1737 and another few pounds in 1739, to reduce her holding to an even £900.

This action illustrates how Gertrude Savile did not just inherit stocks and securities, but bought and sold them to transform her portfolio. After a four-year period during which she primarily collected dividends, in 1743 she began to make her own investment decisions. In December she bought another £100 in Old South Sea Annuities to bring her holding back up to an even £1,000. Then she began buying £100 East India bonds, one in December, one in February, and another in April 1744. She recorded the numbers for each of these bonds. She may have been speculating in East India bonds, for she sold all three out again in April and June, mere months after she bought them. In August 1744 Gertrude made another investment change. She sold out £200 of her Old South Sea Annuities for £224 and loaned the original £200 out on

44 NOA, DD/SR A4/45, Gertrude Savile Accounts, 1736–48.

bond for 5 percent interest. This was a higher rate of interest than she was receiving on the South Sea Annuities, which had been 4 percent.[45] In November she cashed out her remaining £800 in South Sea Annuities for a profitable £888 and loaned this out on mortgage, also at 5 percent. Her actions indicate that Gertrude Savile did not have a preference for public over personal securities, rather she was looking for the best rate of return. The second page of her list for 1744 reflected this change for now it was called "Money in the Stock or upon Interest." Even though Gertrude gave up on South Sea Annuities, she did not move away from public funds entirely, for she continued to hold East India bonds. And in March 1744/45 when she received £300 back from a mortgage in which she had invested, she put it into three more of these bonds. Between 1745 and 1755 Gertrude continued to buy and sell one or two East India bonds a year. The bonds started out earning between 4½ and 5 percent interest but after 1746 the interest rate fell to 3½ and then 3 percent, making them perhaps less desirable.[46]

In addition to trading in company stocks and bonds, Gertrude Savile also invested in government loans. Every year between 1745 and 1755 she purchased State lottery tickets; some were blanks, others came up £20 prizes. She usually sold them in the next year. In 1748 Savile bought ten lottery tickets for £102 5s. and sold them for £110 14s. Even with lottery tickets she was turning a profit of almost 8 percent. In the 1750s Gertrude sped up her speculation in lottery tickets. In June 1751 she bought twelve of them and in 1753 she sold twenty of them in the month of September alone, as well as another thirty-eight in October. But Savile's trading in lottery tickets died down after this. By 1757, toward the end of her book of accounts, she mentions buying, "Five State Lottery tickets which proved blanks." She also noted that she received £4 14s. 3d. for a year's interest for £300 in annuities that "I subscribed for at the same time with the lottery." It seems Gertrude Savile had now settled down to investing in government annuities tied to the State lottery—the usual investment for retired gentlewomen. But she still enjoyed a little lottery speculating. In January 1757 Gertrude bought three lottery tickets for herself, her female agent Mrs. Richards, and her maid.[47]

Like the women we have discussed so far in this chapter, Gertrude Savile turned to annuities as she aged, although in her case she established a personal annuity. In 1747 she received back the £700 she had loaned out on mortgage and sold out £400 in East India bonds. She took this £1,100 and loaned it to her nephew Sir George Savile, who in return began to pay her an annuity of

---

[45] NOA, DD/SR A4/45, Gertrude Savile Accounts, 1736–48.

[46] Pilar Nogués Marco and Camila Vam Malle, "East India Bonds, 1718–1763: Exotic Derivatives, Efficiency, and the Financial Revolution" Working Paper, 2007, http://economix.fr/pdf/workshops/2007_history_markets, Diagram 1. Accessed August 2014.

[47] NOA, DD/SR A4/46, Gertrude Savile Accounts, 1748–58.

8 percent.[48] This was three and a half percent more than she could have earned with a Life Annuity from the government, so it was a wise choice. Savile seems to have been seeking a steady, secure income in her last years, but she still was not above demanding a good rate of return, even if the annuity was from a kinsman.

Much of the wealth that Gertrude Savile inherited from kin was in the form of real estate. She usually sold this out, preferring to hold public and private securities over real property. In 1747, at the age of fifty, Gertrude sold a house she had inherited in Newcastle. Half of the proceeds went to her nephew but she also loaned him the other half in return for a 4 percent annuity. The only time Gertrude invested in real estate was to lease her own home in her old age. She did so in 1744 after her elder brother died. He was the last of her natal family and Gertrude, nearing fifty, no longer had family with whom she could reside. In the following year she acquired her house in Great Russell Street on a twenty-four year lease for £240.[49]

Gertrude Savile's accounts also provide information on both her income and expenses, thus revealing the returns a woman could earn through investing. Table 5.4. shows Savile's receipts and expenses for the years 1744–57. In only two years in this period, 1748 and 1756, did Savile spend more than she took in, and even then she had balances from previous years that covered her expenses. The amount of money Savile received each year varied widely from a high of £2,328 in 1744 to a low of £370 in 1757. The former was a bit of an

Table 5.4. Gertrude Savile's Receipts and Expenses, 1744–57

Year	Receipts	Expenses
1744	£2,328 8s. 6¼d.	£2,272 8s. 9¼d.
1745	£483 1s. 7½d.	£414 8s. 8¼d.
1746	£456 10s. 3¼d.	£456 10s. 3¼d.
1747	£1,651 11s. 11¼d.	£1,539 16s. 7d.
1748	£934 0s. 4¼d.	£936 11s. 9¼d.
1749	£597 7s. 6½ d.	£512 19s. 4¼d.
1750	£533 0s. 0d.	£511 0s. 10d.
1751	£433 9s. 8¾d.	£320 6s. 7¾d.
1752	£484 5s. 8d.	£428 18s. 3½d.
1753	£694 0s. 8d.	£661 15s. 0d.
1754	£393 3s. 4¼d.	£369 1s. 11d.
1755	£388 6s. 10¼d.	£383 7s. 8¾d.
1756	£537 8s. 2¼d.	£568 14s. 8½d.
1757	£370 2s. 11d.	£327 15s. 9¾d.

Source: NOA, DD/SR A4/45, 46, Gertrude Savile Accounts, 1736–57.

---

[48] NOA, DD/SR A4/45, Gertrude Savile Accounts, 1736–48.
[49] *Secret Comment*, 284–5, 253; NOA, DD/SR A4/45, Gertrude Savile Accounts, 1736–48.

outlier (along with 1747) because these were years that Savile received legacies from deceased kin. Nevertheless, Table 5.4. also shows that she regularly counted on an annual income of £400–500 from her investments. This puts her safely within the ranks of the gentry in mid-eighteenth-century Britain. The significant factor is that the majority, if not all, of Savile's income came from investments in public stocks and both public and personal securities. For instance, in 1744 she accounted for profits from two private loans on bond and mortgage, several East India bonds, old South Sea Annuities, old South Sea stock, a private annuity, lottery tickets, and rent on her mother's estates. The latter rents comprised only £42 out of her £2,328 income; thus land did not play a significant role in Gertrude Savile's portfolio. In the year 1748, land comprised a larger portion of Savile's income, but it was the sale of it rather than the renting of it. Out of £934 in receipts, about £300 came from land Gertrude had inherited from her mother Barbara Savile, which she sold. The remaining two thirds of her income derived from loans on bond, annuities, and lottery tickets.

In sum, the Savile women were active participants in the early stock market as a way to maintain themselves in widowhood and spinsterhood. In her middle age, the widow Barbara Savile learned how to invest and keep accounts and tried out a variety of investing options. Some of these, such as York Buildings Company and South Sea Company stock, were risky and involved losses. But overall, when she died Savile was quite prosperous. Gertrude Savile learned investing at the knee of her mother and elder sister. With the help of a kinsman's legacy she was able to set herself up as an independent single woman. Trading primarily in East India bonds and lottery tickets, she was a more timid investor than her mother, but also a prudent one. Her investments allowed her a level of independence in her old age and ensured her years of retirement were comfortable ones. It is not entirely clear whether the Savile women were exceptional or representative of unmarried female investors. We can compare them to two other single women, the sisters Martha and Teresa Blount, who also utilized investments for their retirement years.

5.2. CASE STUDY: MARTHA (PATTY) AND TERESA BLOUNT

In 1728 Gertrude Savile recorded in her diary that she had played cards at the Misses Drydens where she met "the famous Mrs. Blunts, the eldest of which was one of our party at Quadrille." Gertrude was obviously not enamored of either Martha or Teresa Blount. She noted that she lost 4s. 6d at play and that the "Mrs. Blunts, who are Papests, describ'd [the Prince] to his disadvantage—he is the better to be lik'd for being disliked by them."[50] These "famous Mrs. Blunts" as Savile referred to them, were Martha Blount (1690–1763) and her elder sister Teresa Blount (1688–1759). Although Gertrude Savile did not care for them, the sisters shared much with her for they were also never-married women who engaged in investing to maintain themselves in their later years. The Blount sisters were the daughters of Lister Blount of Mapledurham and were staunch members of the Catholic gentry. They both received educations in French convents, and Martha, or Patty, as her family and friends called her, also attended the school at Hammersmith (one of two covert nunneries in early modern England).[51] This education may have helped Patty with her future investing and accounting. Unfortunately, when their father died in 1710, the sisters were left without adequate provision. This was exacerbated when their brother Michael Blount married and asked his sisters and his mother to move out of the family home. Their friend, the poet Alexander Pope, intimated that the Blount women were financially straitened by this preemptory ousting from the family estate. It appears that their brother also did not regularly pay the allowances single sisters of the gentry customarily received from their elder brothers.[52] It became evident that the Blount sisters would have to learn how to take care of themselves.

Teresa and Patty Blount's early investing is known to us due to their close friendship and correspondence with the writer Alexander Pope. Pope was an eager, although not always successful, participant in the investment opportunities of the Financial Revolution, and he was also happy to assist his friends with their investing. Pope invested both in France and in England, starting with rents offered by the Hotel de Ville and Exchequer Bills by the English government in the 1710s, and then moving on to lottery tickets and South Sea stock.[53] In 1716 he was helping Teresa Blount invest. The timing coincides with the Blount sisters' move out of the family's Mapledurham estate earlier that year, thus their investing was directly connected to having to maintain themselves.

Teresa Blount would have been about twenty-eight when the first evidence of her investing emerges in November 1716. As a single woman, now getting past marriageable age, she may well have been thinking of her future. Pope, though helpful, also satirized Teresa when writing to her sister Patty, saying

[50] *Secret Comment*, 149.

[51] Valerie Rumbold, *Women's Place in Pope's World* (Cambridge: Cambridge University Press, 1989), 111. For the Hammersmith convent see Amy M. Froide, "The Religious Lives of Singlewomen in the Anglo-Atlantic World: Quaker Missionaries, Protestant Nuns, and Covert Catholics," in *Women, Religion and the Atlantic World, 1600–1800*, eds. Daniella Kostroun and Lisa Vollendorf (Toronto: University of Toronto Press, 2009), 60–78.

[52] Rumbold, *Women's Place in Pope's World*, 7, 60.

[53] George Sherburn, ed., *The Correspondence of Alexander Pope, vol. I, 1704–1718* (Oxford: Oxford University Press, 1956), 180, 262, 332.

"that her money like her self, shall be put out to Use to such people as will give most for it, tho' it be to whole Company." His quip both impugned Teresa Blount's virtue and confirmed that he was investing her money in some joint-stock company. He went on to say that once he was finished working on his famous poem the "Rape of the Lock," he would "consult the Elders of the City concerning her Profits in the Mammon of Iniquity and I will then write her upon that groveling subject."[54]

Pope wrote to Patty Blount again in December 1716, revealing how he was assisting both of the sisters in investing in the stock market. He told her "that I have not been unmindful of your Affairs, & that I shall omit no Occasion of doing what you order me." Pope went on to say that confidants had told him that South Sea stock would probably fall rather than rise when Parliament convened, so upon this advice he had readied £1,500 to buy. He advised, "one may certainly make advantages of money then in one's hands, which will more than answer its lying dead these two months." Pope told Patty how he planned to invest and offered to do the same for her if she gave the word:

> However I have given orders to buy 500l. for myself as soon as South Sea falls to 103: which you shall have if you have a mind to it. It will amount so to near 6 per cent: And my Broker tells me he thinks it will fall to that. But if you order me to do otherwise, with part, or all of the Sum, I have of yours, I will obey you: Hitherto I have only acted in your affair as I have done in my owne."[55]

Pope's letter is telling in many details. He shows a good knowledge of investing strategy, although he also employs a broker. He is willing to assist the Blount sisters and invest their money as he would do his own, but he also defers to Patty, saying, "if you order me to do otherwise ... I will obey you." Pope aided the Blount sisters in their investing but he did not make decisions for them.

In 1717 the Blount women were settled in London in rented lodgings in Bolton Street, Piccadilly. The street was rather new and boasted the Earl of Peterborough and other persons of quality.[56] They were independent women, one widow and her two single daughters, but Pope continued in his role as financial advisor to them. He now asked John Caryll, another member of the close-knit Catholic gentry community, and Patty Blount's godfather, if he knew of anyone who would take up to £2,000 in return for an annuity for life. Pope did not say who the annuity was for, but in a later letter from September 1717, he wrote to Teresa and Martha Blount saying "I have every where made enquiry if it be possible to get any Annuities on sound Security: It would really be an inexpressible joy to me if I could serve you..."[57] It appears that the

---

[54] Sherburn, *Correspondence of Pope*, vol. I, 375–6.

[55] Sherburn, *Correspondence of Pope*, vol. I, 379.

[56] Henry Benjamin Wheatley, *London, Past and Present: Its History, Associations, and Traditions* (London, 1891), vol. 1, 213.

[57] Sherburn, *Correspondence of Pope*, vol. I, 419, 431.

Blount sisters were not only looking to invest but also wanted a stable, secure annuity that would last into their old age; much like the women already discussed who invested in the Life Annuities.

Over the next few years, relations between Teresa Blount and Pope were volatile, and his attempts to assist her in seeking some financial security only seem to have made matters worse. Perhaps because he had not been able to find an individual who wanted to buy an annuity, he offered one to Teresa himself. Pope proposed to pay her £40 a year for six years while she remained unmarried. While scholars of Pope have wondered at this last stipulation, implying that Teresa would have resented it and that Pope may have had his own designs on Teresa, it was actually nothing extraordinary.[58] Blount was a single woman, looking for a secure and advantageous place to lodge her money. If she got married, her husband would want to make his own decisions about his wife's money, and therefore Pope may well have not wanted to be involved in a spousal matter. The stipulation may merely have been registering that fact.

For whatever reason, Teresa Blount was not happy with the annuity and Pope wrote to her exasperated. "You exprest your self desirous of increasing your present income upon Life: I proposed the only method I then could find, & you encouraged me to proceed in it—when it was done, you received it as if it were an Affront." He went on "My Friendship is too warm & sincere to be trifled with…"[59] It is easy to get distracted by the drama between Pope and Teresa Blount, but the important point here is that Teresa was thinking about how to "increase her present income upon Life" or how to improve her money so that it could maintain her in her later years.

Things seem to have settled down between the two when Pope wrote a joking letter to both sisters in September 1718. He remarked, "I heartily wish you luck in cards; not only as it is said to be a token of luck in better things, but as it doth really and effectually save money." He also wished them good husbands, and alluded to his friend John Caryll as a possibility. He then went on to give them marital advice: "These two considerations [having a country and a town house] every wise virgin should have in her head, not forgetting the third, which is—a separate allowance. O Pin-money! Dear desirable Pin-money! In thee are included all the blessings of woman!"[60] It is notable how much of Pope's thoughts and actions focus on the financial independence of the Blount sisters, whether single or married. And this only continued throughout the decades.

In 1718–19 the Blount sisters also began to invest in the State lottery and Pope assisted them in this as well. In 1718 Pope wrote to Teresa, telling her to

---

[58] Rumbold, *Women's Place in Pope's World*, 122.

[59] Sherburn, *Correspondence of Pope*, vol. I, 468, and n. 1.

[60] Sherburn, *Correspondence of Pope*, vol. I, 512.

send him her lottery order.[61] A year later Pope told Patty "I writ yesterday to Cleveland-court, to deliver you what letters came from the Lottery-office. God give you good fortune... You know I have no palate to taste it, and therefore am in no concern or haste to hear whether I gain or lose. But I won't release you from your engagement of sending me word of the tickets..."[62] By 1720 Patty Blount had transitioned from the State lottery to investing a significant sum in government loans. Pope did much of the work for her, saying "If you'll give this Bearer your Exchequer Order for 500l. I'll get them Registerd, and the Interest receivd: this being a proper time to send 'em to the Exchequer."

Most of Pope's time in 1720 was taken up with South Sea fever and he did not fail in getting the Blount sisters involved. Early in 1720 Pope was investing money with James Eckersall, a director of the Royal African Company, and discussing the need to sell lottery orders so they could purchase South Sea stock and perhaps African stock.[63] By March the Blount sisters were also now investing in the South Sea Company. Pope wrote to Teresa that he would stay in the City "till the matter of the annuities is decided; on purpose to do as you'l commission me... Your other business is at last brought about. I have borrowed mony upon ours & Mr Eckersals [lottery] Orders, and bought 500l. stock S. Sea, at 180. It is since risen to 184. I wish us all good luck in it, & am very glad to have done what you seemd so desirous of."[64] In other words, the sisters had asked him to help them obtain the coveted South Sea stock. Over the spring months, Pope was worried about when to buy and sell out to take advantage of the stock's rise. In May, he wrote their friend Caryll to say that profits had not yet appeared for him or the Blount sisters.

> The question you ask about the fair lady's gains, & my own, is not easily answered. There is no gain till the stock is sold, which neither theirs nor mine is. So that, instead of wallowing in money, we never wanted more for the uses of life, which is a pretty general case with most of the adventurers, each having put all the ready [money] they had into the stock. And our estate is an imaginary one only: one day we were worth two or three thousand, and the next not above 3 parts of the sum. For my own particular I have very little in; the ladies are much richer than I, but how rich (as you see) there's no telling by any certain rule of arithmetic.[65]

Pope linked his South Sea investments with those of the sisters, using the phrase "our estate," although he then went on to say that most of the money invested was theirs and he had "very little in." Whether this was true or not is up to debate, since some contemporaries thought Pope made huge profits

[61] Sherburn, *Correspondence of Pope*, vol. I, 468.
[62] Sherburn, *Correspondence of Pope*, vol. II, 17.
[63] Sherburn, *Correspondence of Pope*, vol. II, 30, 33.
[64] Sherburn, *Correspondence of Pope*, vol. II, 38.
[65] Sherburn, *Correspondence of Pope*, vol. II, 42.

during the South Sea craze. For instance, Robert Digby wrote two times in July 1720 to congratulate Pope and said "by this account I judge you the richest man in the South-sea, and congratulate you accordingly." Pope also confirmed to his friend Francis Atterbury that he was not one of those drowned in "the universal deluge of the S. Sea" and later said "I am sorry I was so true a Prophet in respect of the S. Sea," or at least sorry for Atterbury's losses. Pope concurred with John Caryll's "doctrine of selling out" the stock. It is likely that Pope advised this to the Blount sisters, who appear to have done all right, although it does not seem they sold out all of their stock. Pope informed Caryll, "that your relations the ladies in Bolton Street, are still gainers, even, at this low ebb; and may be pretty considerable so, if there be but any moderate rise again."[66] By December 1720 though, Pope was saying he was glad he had not made money off of others' misfortunes and was asking Caryll for money back that he had loaned him. Apparently, the South Sea Bubble had left its mark on Pope, but it is not clear from the correspondence how much it had affected the finances of the Blount sisters.[67]

Teresa and Patty Blount never married and so their investments were the most significant portion of their income as they aged. The looks and person-alities of the two seem like they would have attracted suitors. A number of portraits of the two are extant, which show that they were physically attractive. Figure 5.1. is a 1716 portrait that Pope commissioned Charles Jervas to paint of the sisters. A brown-haired Teresa perhaps upstages her blonde sister Patty, but a soft pastel of an older Patty delineates a still handsome woman.[68]

We must look elsewhere then for reasons for their singleness. The sisters' lack of dowries was certainly an impediment. And Catholics such as the Blounts had to find marriage partners within a more circumscribed circle, leading to higher rates of singleness. The Blounts' aunt, Helena Englefield, was a nun in the French convent in which the two were educated and had hoped one or both would find a similar vocation. But neither woman sought the life of a nun. Nevertheless, Teresa was open in her disdain of marriage since Pope wrote: "Some strangely wonder you're not fond to marry." So perhaps single-ness was a choice as much as a circumstance. While both sisters remained single, contemporaries insinuated that their disinterest in marriage did not extend to total celibacy.[69]

Although Patty Blount remained single, much like a widow, she eventually benefited financially from her relationship with Pope. Pope also never mar-ried and the friendship between the two deepened over the years, with acquaintances referring to them as a couple. Also significant is the fact that

[66] Sherburn, *Correspondence of Pope*, vol. II, 53–4, 57–8.
[67] Sherburn, *Correspondence of Pope*, vol. II, 60, 75, 91, 173, 241, 256.
[68] Rumbold, *Women's Place in Pope's World*, 114, 252.
[69] Rumbold, *Women's Place in Pope's World*, 59, 60, 63.

Figure 5.1. Martha and Teresa Blount (1716) by Charles Jervas.
© The Fitzwilliam Museum, Cambridge.

Pope made Patty Blount his heir. Although it is not clear if their relationship was platonic or romantic or sexual, it is apparent that the two were primary emotional partners in each other's lives. Valerie Rumbold argues that Patty Blount was neither Pope's secret wife nor his mistress, but rather his friend and the person who filled the role of his mother after her death.[70] Patty was fifty-four when Pope died in 1744, leaving a major portion of his estate to her. Pope's half-sister Magdalen Rackett resented sharing his estate with a woman who was no relation to him and who she called his mistress. Pope had helped care for his sister Rackett and her children since her widowhood in the 1720s, so he could not exactly be accused of having forgotten his duty to her. And as a single man he could bequeath his estate to whomever he wished, even a female friend like Patty Blount. Pope's sister and sons received £1,000 from him (half of which was a loan converted to a gift), while he willed Patty Blount his furniture, goods, £1,000, and the interest on the residue of his estate. In addition she received a lease on a house.[71]

---

[70] Rumbold, *Women's Place in Pope's World*, 46–7.
[71] Rumbold, *Women's Place in Pope's World*, 31, 33.

Thanks to Pope's investments and her own, Patty Blount's later years were ones of financial security. One of the executors of Pope's will, William Murray, wrote to Patty to tell her what she had inherited from Pope. "You are entitled to the interest of the residue during yr life... [which] seems principally to consist of 1000li So Sea Ann[uities] bought by your Desire, the 1000li & odd pounds in the Sun Fire Office and the money due on Ld Bathurst's bond I think 500li..." Patty Blount also received a £1,000 legacy and the lease of a house of her own, in Berkeley St., which Pope had begun to acquire before his death, perhaps in preparation for settling Patty after his demise.[72] Patty Blount was in an enviable position in her mid-fifties; she had a townhouse in a fashionable area of London, a £1,000 legacy and the interest on £2,500 invested in South Sea annuities, Sun Fire insurance stock, and private loans. As we shall see, her accounts reveal that this earned her £100–200 a year. This was just enough for a single gentlewoman to live a comfortable life in eighteenth-century London.

When Pope's other executor, George Arbuthnot, delivered his accounts to Patty Blount in 1745 they showed Pope had died with money out on four bonds totaling £3,700, as well as thirty-one shares in the Sun Fire Office purchased for £1,011, and some money in an account with the banker Mr. Drummond (a banker used by both Catholics and Jacobites). Arbuthnot informed Patty that she and the other principal heir, Pope's half-sister, would need to cover the £2,100 in legacies, wages due, and other debts. He told her, "if you and Mrs. Racket desire it all the securitys may be called in and the produce vested in such other securitys as you and Mrs. Racket shall agree on but if you are both of opinion some of them shod be continued we need only call in what is sufficient to raise the money now wanted."[73] In other words, Arbuthnot was deferring to Patty Blount, as one of the heirs, on investment decisions. She could cash out some securities to pay for legacies, and then invest in new ones, or keep the stocks and shares in which Pope had invested.

Patty Blount, like Gertrude Savile and other female heirs of stocks and securities, chose to make her own investment decisions. Instead of selling out the Sun Fire Insurance stock, as Arbuthnot had suggested, she decided to keep it. East India bonds also show up in the executor accounts, although it is unclear if Blount made this investment herself or if she inherited them. And she took some of the money Pope had had out on loan to private individuals (mostly male friends and associates), called it in, and purchased £1,000 in Old South Sea Annuity stock. This was, of course, the same stock in which the Savile women invested. As Blount and Margaret Rackett wrote to the executors in 1745: "We desire the above three bonds from Ld. Bathhurst Mr: Pannet & Mr: Allen may be call'd in & the money paid into Mr: Hoare

[72] Mapledurham Archives (hereafter MA), Bound Original letters, vol. I, William Murray to Martha Blount, July 1745.
[73] MA, Bound Original letters, vol. I, George Arbuthnot to Martha Blount, 23 July 1745.

the Bankers hands & the money apply'd [to debts and legacies] & the remainder vested in old South Sea Annuities..."[74] The interest rate Blount received due to this transfer was the same, 5 percent, so that does not explain the change. Perhaps, like other female investors, Blount preferred to invest in companies that regularly paid dividends and interest, rather than individuals who did not always disburse funds so regularly or punctually. The latter certainly proved the case with Lord Bathurst, who first did not pay the interest on the loan when it was due to Patty, and then would not pay off his bond when Blount and Racket called it in. Patty may have also wanted to end the bond with Ralph Allen, with whom she had had a falling out before Pope's death. Blount and Pope had once been houseguests of Allen when his niece informed the family that Patty was visiting Pope's rooms early in the morning. This would have been considered scandalous behavior in a single woman. Allen, who as mayor of Bath had a reputation to uphold, also balked at giving his coach to Patty so that she could go to mass, telling her to go the back way and leave the coach at a distance from the chapel.[75] Having had her virtue and her religion slandered by Allen, Patty may well have preferred not to be financially dependent on him.

Patty Blount was not merely a passive inheritor of stocks, but an active manager of her portfolio. She had no compunction about handling her inheritance as she saw fit, and she sought out relatively secure investments, such as annuities and government funds. In 1749, five years after Pope's death, she purchased an additional £411 18s. in Old South Sea Annuities. And three years later, Arbuthnot reported to Blount that "your money is now vested in East India 3 per cent Annuitys" with £830 purchased in May 1751 and another £708 the following December. He informed Patty that she would be able to receive any unpaid dividends at the South Sea House and the new dividends at India House.[76] From this it appears that Blount had sold out her South Sea Annuities and bought East India ones instead. In 1754 Blount added another two new investments to her portfolio. She acquired £250 in the 3 percent Consols, a government fund, and "annuities on Ramsgate pier."[77] The Consols became the preferred government investment for unmarried female investors when the government introduced them in the 1750s. The latter investment was explained in more detail in her account with Slingsby Bethell. In 1752 she had paid the trustees of Ramsgate harbor £500 and in return she received an

---

[74] MA, Bound Original letters, vol. I, General State of Alexander Pope's Affairs, 8 August 1745.

[75] Rumbold, *Women's Place in Pope's World*, 283.

[76] MA, Bound Original letters, vol. I, George Arbuthnot to Martha Blount, 24 June 1749 and 26 March 1752.

[77] MA, Bound Original letters, vol. I, John Blackhall to Martha Blount, 18 May 1754. In 1749 Parliament passed an act to build up Ramsgate harbor. The trustees were allowed to borrow money at 5 per cent or pay annuities of £8 10s. to raise money. Danby Pickering, *The Statutes at Large from the Magna Charta to 1761* (L, 1765), 350.

Annuity of £40 for her life. While this would have been a good investment for a younger, middle-aged woman, at age sixty-two Blount only lived another decade. This means she only received £400 of the £500 she put into the Ramsgate annuity. Blount also seems to have been trying to finally divest herself of the Sun Fire Insurance stock and trade it for government funds. Arbuthnot, still her agent, said he had "called some time agoe at the Sun fire office to know if any thing on Mr. Pope's Shares had been payed off that I might reinvest the same in Government Securitys for your benefit..."[78] Like the other women discussed in this chapter, Patty Blount saw both annuities and government funds as secure, safe investments for her later years.

Patty Blount was not, however, a passive receiver of profits from her investments. She assiduously followed the executor's handling of her investments and was not afraid to point out when she felt the men made errors. Arbuthnot had to defend some of his decisions to Blount and assure her that he did not have any of the interest or dividends owed to her in his hands. Much of the correspondence between the two was about Patty Blount's ability to collect her interest payments herself, rather than using him as a middleman. Arbuthnot assured Blount that she could have an order to receive the dividends herself, but he pointed out that she was only entitled to receive them for life; they were not inheritable. In 1762 the two also clashed over the lease of her house. Patty Blount was seventy-two at the time and it appears she was thinking and planning for her advanced old age. Arbuthnot wrote to her, saying "I find your present Lease is for thirty-one years from the 24th of June 1737 so I rec[k]on you have six years & ¼ to come." He went on to remind her that Pope had left her "the interest of his fortune for life" and after her decease it would descend to his sister, Mrs. Rackett's, sons. He said it might well make these nephews very angry if the executors renewed the lease, as Patty seems to have requested, and so she would need their agreement.[79] Arbuthnot continually had to remind Patty Blount that she was Pope's heir for life, not for perpetuity. Although she was worried she might outlive the lease, she did not.

Patty Blount's inheritance led her to begin keeping regular accounts in 1744 (or if she did keep some earlier those have not survived).[80] Blount's accounts are extant for eighteen years up until her death in 1762. At the end of the accounts, in February 1763, a new hand takes over, perhaps her niece Mary or her brother Michael (who she named as her executor). Patty Blount's accounts fill twenty-seven pages of a large ledger. She tried to keep her accounts in debtor/creditor style (balancing debits on the left with credits on the right), the merchant style of bookkeeping that the gentry slowly adapted to their personal

---

[78] MA, Bound Original letters, vol. I, George Arbuthnot to Martha Blount, 1754.
[79] MA, Bound Original letters, vol. I, George Arbuthnot to Martha Blount, 18 February 1762.
[80] MA, MS DD Blount c. 154, Martha Blount's Account Book, 1744–62.

accounts.[81] Like many of her status, Blount did not keep accounts correctly in this manner; rather she recorded items chronologically and had a tendency to list receipts and payments on both sides of the page. Blount's accounts reveal money paid to servants' wages, tradesmen's bills, and regular loans of £2 or so to her sister Teresa. By 1756 Patty began to pay Teresa's annual house rent of £15 as well as her other bills. This continued for a few years. There is no record in the accounts of Teresa ever paying these sums back, so Patty seems to have helped maintain her sister Teresa until the latter's death in 1759, when she was around seventy.

On the receipts, or creditor side, Patty Blount recorded receiving interest on the investments she both inherited from Pope and the ones she chose herself. In 1745 she noted interest payments on two loans to individuals (earning 3 and 4 percent, respectively), as well as on Old South Sea Annuities and Sun Fire Insurance shares. She collected £50, £29, £20, and £38 15s. respectively, on these four investments, for a total of £137 15s. This was a comfortable sum on which a single gentlewoman could maintain herself in old age. The money would have gone much farther if Blount had chosen to live outside of London, but thanks to Pope's assistance she had a house in London that was largely paid for through her inheritance. This removed the major expense of living in the capital. There were other expenses for a householder though, such as window and land tax (£1 7s. and £1 10s. respectively), charges for piping in New River water (12s.), and poor rates, all of which Blount recorded as paid.

Patty Blount's accounts also reveal when she began to alter the investment portfolio that Pope had bequeathed to her. Six years after his death, she invested in 3% East India Annuities in 1751 and she started to annually receive £40 from her Ramsgate annuity in 1754. Blount no longer mentioned receipts from South Sea annuities, so she may have sold out this investment to buy East India Annuities and the Ramsgate Annuity. In 1755 she was buying lottery tickets for Mary (either her servant or a kinswoman of that name). In 1757 and 1758 Patty Blount began to total up her receipts. In the first year she noted receiving £206 9s. from her investments (although she later crossed this out) and the next year recorded receiving about £181. Another undated list of Blount's investments also totals around £200 p.a. From this evidence it appears that Patty Blount had increased her investment earnings by a third from the first years after she had inherited investments from Pope. Over the thirteen years, Patty Blount had learned how to effectively manage and even improve her earnings. It is also notable that Blount preferred safe and reliable investments, such as annuities. She was earning between 3 and 4 percent on these investments. This was an average rate of return for the time, but

---

[81] For more on women and accounting see Amy M. Froide, "Learning to Invest: Women's Education in Arithmetic and Accounting in early modern England," *Early Modern Women: An Interdisciplinary Journal* 10:1 (2015), 3–26.

overall she enjoyed a higher income than when she had first inherited her investments.

Such modest profits are reflected in Patty Blount's will. She made her nephew Michael Blount her executor and left the residue of her estate to him. While the value of the residue is unclear, the named legacies she gave to Mrs. Tichborne, Matthew Swinbourne esq., Mrs. Anne Blount, and two maids, added up to £330.[82] Patty Blount's investments saw her through old age and even left her with enough to bequeath—the goal of any gentlewoman in eighteenth-century England. Such a goal was also not something we should take lightly. As we will see in the next chapter, risk was an ever present concern for female public investors, so the successful investing of women like the Saviles and the Blounts is notable. Choosing to invest in annuities, bonds, and government funds was an effective way for older and unmarried women in eighteenth-century England to avoid risk and ensure a comfortable retirement.

---

[82] Robert Carruthers, *The life of Alexander Pope: Including extracts from his correspondence*, 2nd ed. (London: Henry G. Bohn, 1857), 464–5.

6

Gender and Risk in the Early Stock Market

Investing in England's early stock market was, of course, inherently risky. And like men, women investors sometimes lost their money. The best-known case of financial risk and loss in this era was the South Sea Bubble of 1720, but there were many other bubbles, no less devastating to individual investors, even if less scarring to the nation. In modern-day investing parlance women are considered more risk averse than men.[1] Whether this is truly the case and whether we should apply this assumption to the past is still up for debate. For instance, Ann Laurence's work on the Hastings sisters reveals that these eighteenth-century gentlewomen exhibited varied "investment strategies" and had differing financial "outcomes." She posits that a woman's gender did not determine her attitude to risk, rather each individual investor's comfort with risk varied. Ann Carlos and Larry Neal's article with Karen Maguire on women speculators in the Royal African Company during the South Sea Bubble found that in the aggregate women who traded shares "at worst broke even on their activities or had positive speculative gains" compared to men who lost overall.[2] Thus research so far reveals that at least some female public investors were not risk averse but were speculators and active traders in stocks.

This chapter will take a different approach to the question of gender and risk. It will investigate how women were involved in and responded to incidents of financial fraud and speculation between 1690 and 1750. First we

[1] Some examples include, Tahira Hira and Cäzilia Loibl, "Gender Differences in Investment Behavior" (Aug. 31, 2006) www.finrafoundation.org (accessed June 2015), Catha Mullen, "Real Data Suggest Gender Biases in Investing" (Feb. 5, 2014), and Suba Iyer, "Overcoming Gender Irrationality for Better Investing" (March 5, 2014) <blog.personalcapital.com> (accessed June 2015).
[2] Ann Laurence, "Women Investors, 'That Nasty South Sea Affair' and the Rage to Speculate in Early Eighteenth-Century England," *Accounting, Business & Financial History* 16:2 (July 2006): 245–64; Ann M. Carlos, Karen Maguire, and Larry Neal, "Financial Acumen, Women Speculators, and the Royal African Company during the South Sea Bubble," *Accounting, Business & Financial History* 16:2 (July 2006): 219–43.

will examine one of the biggest risks women could face, that of fraudulent financial brokers. Then we move on to some of the financial scandals of the era and how they impacted women. While female investors were definitely hurt by the most famous crash of the era, the South Sea Bubble, there were other lesser known bubbles that proved risky as well, such as the London Orphans Fund, the Mine Adventurers Company, and the Charitable Corporation. Lastly, this chapter will explore women's role in creating risk rather than merely being victims of it. The Financial Revolution provided illicit opportunities for women to make money by defrauding others. As we will see, it was not only men who benefited from financial fraud.

One of the first ways women encountered risk when investing in public stocks and securities was through the financial agents and brokers they entrusted with their capital. If these brokers were incompetent or criminal, women stood to suffer the consequences. Concerns about women being swindled or defrauded by brokers were part of the critique of stockbrokers, or jobbers, from the early years of the Financial Revolution. Sometime around 1720, the female poet Anne Finch, Lady Winchelsea, satirized women's resort to brokers in her poem "Ombre and Bassett laid aside." Commenting on women switching from gambling to investing, she says:

> Ombre and Basset laid aside
> New Games employ the Fair,
> And Brokers all those hours divide
> Which Lovers used to Share...
>
> With Jews and Gentiles undismay'd,
> Young tender Virgins mix,
> Of Whiskers nor of Beards affraid,
> Nor all their Cousening tricks.
>
> Bright Jewels polished once to deck
> The fair ones rising Breast
> Or sparkle round her Ivory Neck
> Lie pawn'd in Iron Chest.[3]

In her poem, Finch comments on ladies turning from their card tables and games to "gambling" in stocks and shares. She says these women forgo trysts with their lovers to meet instead with their stockbrokers. Typical of the anti-Semitism one finds in the literature on stockbrokers from the time, Finch represents brokers as venal and foreign Jews. She also alludes to these foreign men spending time alone with young and tender virgins. Such brokers evidently imperiled both a woman's chastity and her purse. According to Finch's

---

[3] Scholars attribute this unsigned manuscript poem to Anne Finch. "Anne Finch's unpublished poetry taken from manuscripts and rare books" <www.jimandellen.org/finch/finchtexts. html> (accessed September 2013).

poem, the way that women got the money to play the market was to pawn their jewels, which ended up in the broker or lender's iron chest, while the female investor presumably lost all.

In his mid-eighteenth-century guide to investing, *Every Man his own Broker*, Thomas Mortimer also critiqued brokers and presented a solution for the female investor. Mortimer posited that one of the reasons brokers had emerged in the first place was to assist women in need of investment advice. "The original design of employing brokers must certainly have been for the convenience of the ladies, for whose service these gentlemen are always ready..."[4] The author's assumption (shared by others) was that women would need assistance and a male mentor if they were to invest in the market. This created a problem since naïve or ignorant women would supposedly be easy targets: "for really many an innocent young lady, who has but just heard of 'Change Alley', may reasonably imagine these are the identical Bulls and Bears she has been told of." Mortimer's solution was not to suggest that women should learn how to do their own investing but rather that they should rely on a male relative or friend for assistance rather than a professional male broker.

> As I cannot imagine any lady so destitute of relations and friends, as not to be able to find one gentleman, who would be so obliging as to transact her business for her in the funds, especially when it shall appear, that it is the most simple and easy affair in the whole circle of business... And why should not every gentleman, in the same manner, assist his sister, his cousin, or any other female relation, or friend, when she wants to lay out a sum of money in the funds, or to sell a sum out of them?[5]

Mortimer goes on to say that "I am certain, that when I have fully demonstrated not only the practicability, but likewise the facility, of rendering this service to the ladies, no gentleman will refuse to devote half an hour occasionally, to the agreeable employment of delivering the fair sex from all connections with this medley [of tradesmen] whom the mammon of unrighteousness has transformed into Stock-Brokers."[6] Mortimer assumed that a man known to a woman would not swindle her and he presented men investing for their female kin as an act of charity.

Mortimer's faith that male kin would be wise and honest investors is somewhat ironic when read alongside examples of real women who employed male relatives as financial agents to the detriment of their material condition. For example, Agnes Herbert (who we met in chapter 5) saw barely a penny

---

[4] Philanthropos [Thomas Mortimer], *Every Man his own Broker: Or, a Guide to Exchange Alley* (L, 1761), preface, xi–xii. Philanthropos appeared as the author on the first edition, but by the third edition Mortimer appeared as the author.

[5] *Every Man His Own Broker*, preface, xi–xii.

[6] *Every Man His Own Broker*, preface, xii.

from her investments while she let her brother-in-law invest her capital in mortgages. It was only when she took control of her investments herself and put them into East India Company stock and government Consols that she began to receive any profits. If Herbert lost out due to her brother-in-law's financial assistance, Elizabeth Freke (discussed in chapter 3) found herself in an even worse financial position due to her male cousin.

In her widowhood, Elizabeth Freke had trouble extracting profits from her deceased husband's Irish lands (all of which he had purchased with money lent by her father or with capital his wife had "improved" by her own investing). Elizabeth blamed much of her difficulty on her cousin John Freke, who served as co-executor with her of her husband's estate. Although the ideal was that kin would work to help ensure the financial security of a widow, in this case Elizabeth Freke's trust in her cousin proved risky. Elizabeth had given her power of attorney to cousin John Freke when he went to Ireland to prove her husband's will there. Taking advantage of his legal authority, John Freke, "my pretended truste" as she called him, "gave away from me to my son my deer husbands estate in Ireland hee gave me of 750 pounds a year." She asked rhetorically whether this was "kind or faire" for cousin Freke, her trustee, to give away her Irish estate to her son who had £800 a year settled on him already.[7] Elizabeth found herself legally vulnerable, with her male cousin taking advantage of his position and rewarding her son over her.[8]

The Irish estates that Elizabeth Freke's husband settled on her for life never provided as much income as she was promised. This was not only because cousin John Freke had leased them to her son for a much lower rent than they were worth—£350 in yearly rent instead of the £800 a year at which her late husband had valued them. Much more problematic was that despite the sweet deal he received, her son Ralph was constantly in arrears on his payments to her and when he finally would pay her it was only part of what he owed. Even cousin John Freke was embarrassed by this, writing to Elizabeth "I should nott have bin soe long silent had nott your sons conduct made me ashamed."[9] Elizabeth Freke wrote back to cousin John. She could not help herself from reminding him that he was the one who stuck her with this "very foolish lease" and that he had promised "to be my paymaster your selfe of my rentt and of my sons good usage and gratitude to me."[10]

Elizabeth Freke came to rue allowing her cousin John Freke to act as her financial agent. Three years into her widowhood and fed up with both her son and cousin, she moved to take financial matters back into her own hands. In May 1710 she wrote to John Freke:

---

[7] Raymond Anselment, ed., *The Remembrances of Elizabeth Freke, 1671–1714*, Camden Fifth Series vol. 18 (Cambridge University Press/Royal Historical Society, 2001), 106, 257.

[8] *Remembrances*, 21–2, 24, 28.

[9] *Remembrances*, 130–1.   [10] *Remembrances*, 132–3.

"I doe think itt butt prudent in me that all my small abbillityes now loose should be more properly and sattissfacttorily now settled by you in my owne name and to my own disposall—as well whatt is in your hands as my years funds with this returne of my sons...Nott being att all sattisfyed (finding your partiallitye soe great against me)..."[11]

Freke effectively fired her cousin John Freke as her financial and legal agent. She asked for her money to be put in her own name and at her own disposal. And she said she was not at all "satisfied" with how John had run her affairs. She did not trust her cousin since she felt he had acted against her own financial interests in the past and she feared he might do so again. Such candor by a woman against a male financial agent, and one who was a relative, was rare and quite damning. Freke's example illustrates that relying on male kin as financial agents was by no means risk free.

The example of Elizabeth Freke should give pause to Thomas Mortimer's advice that male kin were the best financial agents for their female family members. On further reading, it becomes a little clearer that Mortimer recommended the use of male kin as agents not to help women investors but to assist men. "If, in consequence of a compliance with my plan, these gentlemen should lose the fair sex, their greatest support falls to the ground, since one of their principal emoluments arises from the management of the fortunes of women."[12] Here Mortimer lets the cat out of the bag. Men materially benefited from managing the fortunes of their female kin and losing access to that money would be detrimental for these men. Thus investing for female kin was not so much an act of charity but a prudent act of self-preservation on the part of men. The female investor was left between a rock and a hard place: did she entrust her capital to an unknown stockbroker or to a venal male kinsman? Or, did she read *Every Man his own Broker*, and learn to handle her own finances as many of the women discussed in this book so far did?

Brokers were but one risk that women investors faced. The companies in which they lodged their capital were another. The next section of this chapter will explore the risks that female investors faced in the uncertain and new world created by Britain's Financial Revolution. First we will examine the best-known example of financial risk, the South Sea Bubble, and its particular impact on women. The South Sea Company was originally founded in 1711 to trade in the South Atlantic and Pacific oceans, and more particularly to provide slaves to the Spanish empire. Finding their trade confounded by England's wars with Spain, in 1719 the company became involved in finance, offering to take over part of the government debt. They did so by converting the debt into company shares and opening it up to buyers through various stock subscriptions. South Sea stock rose from the low £100s at the beginning

---

[11] *Remembrances*, 132–3.   [12] *Every Man his own Broker*, preface, xii–xiii.

of 1720 to a height of £1,050 in June, after which it began to fall, before crashing in September. Insider trading, bribes to politicians and peers, and purchases of stock based on loans and partial payments all contributed to the collapse.[13]

Commentators took to prose, poetry, fiction, and non-fiction to discuss the negative repercussions felt by unlucky investors caught up in the South Sea Bubble. While much of this literature was satirical in nature, and must be taken with a grain of salt, the detail that is supposed to lend a realistic air to these pamphlets is what interests me here. For instance, this commentary continually emphasized that the Bubble's victims included both men and women. So far there has been no specific research done on how the South Sea Bubble affected women, but contemporary evidence reveals female victims just as readily as male ones. For example, the title of one satirical piece was: *Observations on the Spleen and Vapours: Containing Cases of Persons of both Sexes, and all Ranks, from the aspiring Director to the humble Bubbler, who have been miserably afflicted with those melancholy Disorders since the Fall of South-Sea.*[14] This pamphlet was presented in the form of a doctor's case notes on patients who had all been misadventurers in the Bubble. While Midriff was most likely a pseudonym, the writer had some medical knowledge and was perhaps one of the first in history to connect financial crisis to mental illness.[15] Defrauded women investors figure prominently in the doctor's case notes. For example, his second case is that of Lady Arabella Blackham, who "had never been well since the Fall of the Stocks, having put all Miss's [her daughter's] Fortune into the South-Sea, with an Intent to marry her to Sir John Frisk's eldest Son." Not only had this Lady lost the money that was to be her daughter's portion, but she had borrowed the money to invest on the security of her jewels and silver plate, and her own suitor had recently broken off a prospective match with her due to her losses. The theme of women risking (and losing all) for the sake of a good marriage was echoed by another patient, a "middle ag'd Widow Lady, who was miserably in the Vapours, for she had sold the Life-Rent of her Jointure" for what she thought would be a better maintenance in South Sea stock and the chance to marry a young attorney

---

[13] For recent accounts of the South Sea Bubble see John Carswell, *The South Sea Bubble* (Stroud: Alan Sutton, 1993) and Helen Paul, *The South Sea Bubble: An Economic History of its Origins and Consequences* (Abingdon: Routledge, 2010).

[14] Sir John Midriff, *Observations on the Spleen and Vapours: Containing Cases of Persons of both Sexes, and all Ranks, from the aspiring Director to the humble Bubbler, who have been miserably afflicted with those melancholy Disorders since the Fall of South-Sea, and other Public Stocks* (L, 1721). Eighteenth Century Collections Online (hereafter ECCO) <www.galegroup.com> (accessed October 2013). Vapours were symptoms associated with nervous disorders or hysteria in the early eighteenth century. The spleen was believed to be the seat of melancholy or morose thoughts. Oxford English Dictionary <www.oed.com> (accessed September 2015).

[15] David Walker, Anita O'Connell, and Michelle Faubert, *Depression & Melancholy, 1660–1800*, vol. 2: *Medical Writings* (London: Pickering & Chatto, 2012), 35–6.

who handled her business. Not only did this widow end up without a husband, she also lost her jointure, which was what she had to maintain her if she remained unmarried. According to this pamphlet, the South Sea Bubble ruined both women's marriage prospects as well as their long-term financial security.

Observations on the Spleen and Vapours also highlighted how the bubble affected women in the City. The fictional example for this group of women was Mary Duroy, the wife of Thomas Duroy, a mercer residing in the Strand. Duroy was "very much in the Vapours" because of her husband "who kept all Affairs to himself, and never would acquaint her with any Thing he did, but went on his own Way to ruin himself and his whole Family." Mr. Duroy had gone off stock jobbing each day, spending the family's money, while Mrs. Duroy "like a good Wife, kept in the Shop all the while." The mercer's wife said she was angry at not being consulted on family business matters and at having to work all day while her husband went off and gambled the family's money. The doctor, however, attributed her distress to not having received a coveted gold watch out of her husband's investment profits. While this woman may have attributed her family's distress to the South Sea Company's actions, the author blamed her for her own venality.

The pamphlet's satirical case notes continued with a bevy of female patients from the urban trades and crafts occupations. One, the wife of a salesman, was the opposite of Mrs. Duroy, for she was the one who goaded her husband into investing since other men "were getting Estates in the South-Sea, and setting up in Coaches." Other couples imperiled their relationships and families with the acrimony that ensued due to bad investments in the South Sea Company. The "wife of John Tape, Haberdasher of Small-Wares" also pushed her husband to invest and "from the Time they Sunk, he never ceas'd upbraiding her . . . until he made the Woman not only miscarry, but in that Weakness almost distracted." Mary Firkin, the wife of Jonathan Firkin, cheesemonger, and Mary Pickle, the wife of James Pickle, salter, did not drive their husbands to invest because of their greed; instead "both these good women had persuaded their Husbands very earnestly not to meddle with the Stocks." But these men prevailed by promising their wives the household goods of their dreams: silver spoons, teapots, new carpets, and easy chairs. In this case it was male investment that had familial repercussions and was the "Cause of their Wives Disorders." These examples illustrate how the South Sea fraud disrupted family and marital relationships as well as upending livelihoods.

According to *Observations on the Spleen and Vapours*, women who lost it all in the Bubble (either independently or through the actions of their husbands and fathers) were likely to fall victim to illness, alcoholism, and despair. The author noted that there were a "number" of other women affected by the South Sea Bubble, but he did not include their names, since they had succumbed to alcohol abuse, which was "not altogether becoming their Sex." He explained that women were more prone to melancholy, for men were kept busy turning to other businesses to try to recover some of their losses "while Wives and Daughters had Time to think, and had therefore laid those Things more to Heart." Some women took events so hard that they even took their own lives.

This was not mere fiction, for the press regularly reported cases of male, and to a lesser extent female, suicide due to the fallout from the South Sea Bubble. Historian Julian Hoppit doubts the Bubble affected the general economy much, but he does acknowledge that "it is certainly notable that numbers of suicides in London were 40 per cent above trend levels in 1721."[16] Some of the men involved directly in the South Sea Company could not bear the public censure and took their own lives. We know from real accounts in the press that Eustace Bludgell plunged "overboard into the Thames from a rented boat his pockets weighted with stones." Charles Blunt slit his own throat with a razor. And James Craggs the Elder supposedly overdosed on poison or opium. Sadly, Craggs's death doubly affected his three daughters to whom he had left his estate, since the government went after it.[17] Although a fictional pamphlet, *Observations on the Spleen and Vapours* mirrored fact.

Sometimes even murder was a consequence of the South Sea Bubble if we are to believe an account from the *London Journal*. The paper reported that a seventy-year-old wife of a mechanic living near St James's who had persuaded her husband to subscribe for a South Sea Annuity, "has led so miserable a Life by the Old Man on that Account that a few Days ago she put an end to it (by hanging her self)."[18] Both fictional pamphlets and news accounts noted that the South Sea Bubble affected men and women as well as whole families. Although caused by men, the effects of the stock's collapse were gender-blind since so many women were investors. Three years after the Bubble women still comprised 20.9 percent of the holders of South Sea stock.[19] At a minimum then, one fifth of those affected by the Bubble were women.

Another source for exploring the repercussions of the failure of the South Sea Company is the popular series of South Sea Bubble playing cards. The

---

[16] Julian Hoppit, "The Myths of the South Sea Bubble," *Transactions of the Royal Historical Society* 12 (2002): 158. He cites Michael McDonald and Terrence Murphy, *Sleepless Souls: Suicide in Early Modern England* (Oxford: Oxford University Press, 1990), 276–8. Hoppit also argues that we need to take the satires on the South Sea scheme with a grain of salt.

[17] Barbara Gates, *Victorian Suicide: Mad Crimes and Sad Histories* (Princeton: Princeton University Press, 2014), 82. Edward Pearce, *The Great Man: Sir Robert Walpole: Scoundrel, Genius and Britain's First Prime Minister* (New York: Random House, 2013), 119. Malcolm Balen, *The Secret History of the South Sea Bubble* (London: Fourth Estate, 2002), 212, 220. "Craggs, James (1657–1721)," *Dictionary of National Biography* (London: Smith, Elder & Co., 1885–1900) <en.wikisource.org> (accessed July 2015).

[18] *London Journal*, issue 97, 1720. *17th and 18th Century Burney Collection Newspapers* <gdc.gale.com> (accessed October 2007).

[19] P. G. M. Dickson, *The Financial Revolution in England: A Study in the Development of Public Credit, 1688–1756* (London: MacMillan, 1967), 282, Table 38.

illustrations on the cards feature a striking gender parity in the effects of the Bubble (see Figure 6.1.). Issued in 1721, the year after the collapse, eighteen out of the fifty-two-card suite (or 35 percent of the cards) featured women. The cards chronicled women who had risked their money in South Sea stock as well as those who had lost it. For instance, the Six of Diamonds features two women and the motto:

> A certain Lady when the Stocks run high,
> Put on Rich Robes, to Charm Her Lover's Eye,
> But South Sea falling, Pawn'd her fine Brocades,
> And now appears like other homely Jades.[20]

While this elite woman suffered a decline in her standard of living due to stock losses, others are puffed up by pride when they make profits. For instance, The Ten of Hearts card displays:

> A Lady, who when Bubbles and South Sea were high,
> Pamper'd by Pride sets up for Quality;
> No less than Peers, must be allow'd to Woo her,
> And with disdain, Discards her Pristine Lover.[21]

Pride, of course, goes before a fall. The next card in the suite, the Jack of Hearts explains the woman's rise and fall:

> A South Sea Lady having much improv'd,
> Her Fortune proudly Slighted him she Lov'd,
> But South Sea falling, sunk her Fortune low,
> She would have had him then, but he cry'd no.[22]

Other women who profited off of South Sea stock saw their marriage prospects improve. The Jack of Clubs illustrates a tea table of never-married women who had done well enough in South Sea stock that they now had fortunes to attract husbands:

> Here Ancient Maids, that ne'er Defil'd the Smock,
> Boast of their Great Success in South Sea Stock;
> Says one, when Poor, tho' Young, no Man would Sue me,
> But now I'm rich, Six Irish Captains Woo me.[23]

These cards present investments in South Sea stock as integral to women's marital prospects, both causing a loss or an improvement in marital prospects depending on the woman's luck.

---

[20] Harvard University, Baker Library, Harvard Business School (hereafter HBS), 8874_006. Women investors in the South Sea Company also feature on the following cards: the Two and Jack of Diamonds, Four, Ten, King, and Ace of Hearts, Seven and Queen of Clubs, and Five, Eight, and King of Spades.
[21] HBS, 8875_010.   [22] HBS, 8875_011.   [23] HBS, 8876_011.

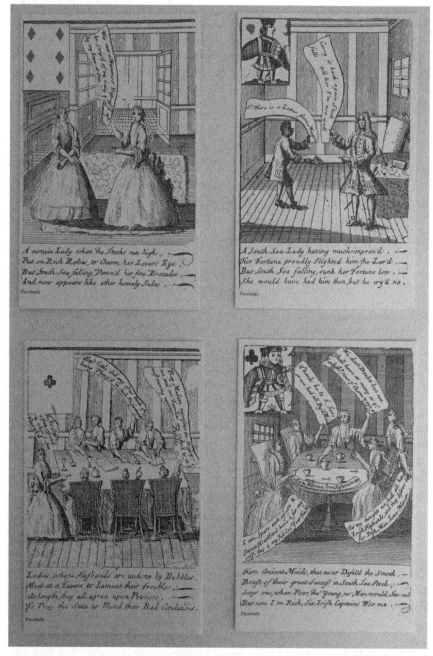

Figure 6.1. South Sea Bubble Cards: Six of Diamonds, Jack of Hearts, Jack of Clubs, Ace of Clubs.

From Collection of the Author. (Facsimile of South Sea Bubble Playing Cards, first published 1720, repub. by Harry Margery, 1972.)

Other Bubble cards show the risk inherent to investing. The Eight of Clubs shows a woman investor tricked by her agent. A stockjobber buys shares for his female neighbor but charges her twice the price for them, and she in turn determines to roast him.[24] The Nine of Hearts illustrates a merchant "bilk'd by Stock like Thousands in the Nation," who goes to prison for debt, leaving behind a weeping wife as well as children who try to console their mother.[25] These cards feature the familial repercussions of the Bubble and the more serious financial distress of the middling sort.

While fiction most often represented women as victims of the South Sea Bubble, some women who lost their money fought back against the Company and expected the government to address their concerns. The Ace of Clubs card features:

> Ladies, whose Husbands are undone by Bubbles,
> Meet at a Tavern to Lament their Troubles;
> At length, they all agree upon Petitions,
> To Pray the State to Mend their Bad Conditions.[26]

Again fiction and reality blurred, for just as the lady petitioners on the Bubble card stand up to the South Sea Company, so too did the real female investor Eleanor Curzon. As we will see in chapter 7, Curzon took advantage of a legal technicality (the clerk's mistaken transcription of her name as "Edward Curzon" in the company's books) to get back the money she had subscribed to the South Sea Company. While the company's stock had fallen to dismal lows and most subscribers had to make do with the government's partial bail out offer of between one third and one half of the value of the money they had invested (and that in stock and not cash), Curzon received her £1,000 back in full.[27] The South Sea Company fought Curzon's case hard, most likely because the precedent could have been financially disastrous for them. They transferred the case from the equity to the plea side of the Court of Exchequer and ultimately appealed to the House of Lords, but at every stage Eleanor Curzon triumphed.[28] Although she had risked her money she also was willing to fight to recover it.

Women who had done business with, or who were related to the infamous Directors of, the South Sea Company, also found themselves victims. A number fought back, however, refusing to give up their assets when the government confiscated the estates of their husbands and fathers. One such woman was Susannah Blunt, the wife of John Blunt, the Director who is

[24] HBS, 8876_008.   [25] HBS, 8875_009.   [26] HBS, 8876_001.
[27] Richard Dale, *The First Crash: Lessons from the South Sea Bubble* (Princeton: Princeton University Press, 2014), 146–8; Dickson, *Financial Revolution*, 181–7. And see the act "to Restore the Publick Credit," 7 Geo. I, stat. 2.
[28] The British Library, 19h2, Appeals to the House of Lords, no. 27, The South Sea Company v. Eleanor Curzon.

credited with conceiving the South Sea scheme and who was at the center of its downfall. The *Tatler* reported that Sir John Blunt's wife and three daughters came to the door of the House of Commons where they delivered the petition "The Case of Sir John Blunt, as it relates to his Lady."[29] Susannah Blunt was the daughter and widow of men successfully involved in the investment opportunities of the Financial Revolution. Her father, Richard Cradock Sr., was a Director of the Hudson's Bay, Royal African, and East India companies, as well as the Bank of England. Susannah's second marriage had been to Benjamin Tudman, a goldsmith who was also a South Sea Company director. Twice widowed and with a sizable estate, in 1713 she married John Blunt, her second spouse to be associated with the South Sea Company.[30]

In her petition to Parliament, Susannah Blunt appealed to the MPs to leave her separate estate untouched when they seized her husband's assets. Blunt declared she was as much a loser in the South Sea as any investor. Her case explained that before their marriage Sir John had promised:

> he would make a considerable Addition to her Fortune, and publickly declared it; and therefore did put several Sums into South Sea Stock and Subscriptions for her Use and Benefit, which he hath brought with the Gain thereof, into the Inventory of his Estate. So that she has no manner of Profit or Advantage from the Rise of the Stock; and that she hath, by a former Husband, Eleven Children and Grand children; and her Children's Fortunes being in the Redeemable Annuities, subscribed into the South-Sea Company, the greatest part thereof is sunk and lost thereby.[31]

Her argument here was three-fold: her South Sea assets were held as separate estate from her husband and as such should not be counted as his assets (which were liable to seizure); secondly, she had many dependents, both children and grandchildren from her past marriages, and needed her own estate to care for them; and thirdly, she was a victim of the South Sea Company's losses as much as the next person, since she had put her children's inheritance in government annuities which had then been converted into South Sea stock. Despite her and Sir John's efforts, the Blunts incurred considerable losses. Sir John Blunt's estate was valued at £183,000 but he was only allowed to keep £1,000 (which was later raised to £5,000).[32] When John Blunt died in Jan. 1732/33 he bequeathed £13,000 to his family, so evidently he had somewhat recovered financially. His widow Susannah Blunt died a decade later, in 1743. She made bequests to

---

[29] The *Tatler,* issue 101, Jan. 7, 1721.

[30] Susannah (Cradock Banner) Blunt (1668–1743) in David Man, "The Families and Descendants of Susannah & Sarah Cradock," 108, 208 <www.manfamily.org/bibliography> (accessed November 2013).

[31] The *Tatler* issue 101, Jan. 7, 1721.

[32] The Henry H. Huntington Library (hereafter HEH), "Inventory of Sir John Blunt," in *The Particulars and Inventories of the Estates of the late South Sea Company Directors* (L, 1721), 234.

her family of £2,000 in South Sea Annuities along with a few thousand more pounds.[33] Lady Blunt seems to have survived, although not entirely thrived from, the South Sea Bubble.

While many women lost money in the South Sea Bubble, some of them did so because they had asked the Directors of the Company to invest for them. When Parliament later examined the Directors and inventoried their estates for seizure, the numbers of women caught up in the losses came to light. For example, John Blunt's estate inventory revealed that not only had he invested money for his wife and daughters, he had done so for numbers of women, ranging from ladies down to those of the middling sort. For instance, he owed Mrs. Rebecca and Frances Town £900 (which they had paid in money to him and he had put in South Sea stock, and now held in trust for them). He also owed Mrs. Day of Bristol money on dividend, £100 to Lady Catherine Jones, and another £300 that he subscribed in his and another man's name for Lady Pearshall. In addition, Blunt had £500 of Elizabeth Wilcox's money and the same amount paid into the fourth subscription for Mary Braithwaite. And he had loaned money to a number of women, perhaps to buy South Sea stock.[34] Likewise, another South Sea Director, Robert Chester, owed various debts to women. Chester had invested for a number of female kin. He owed £525 to his cousin Mary Chester, although he had paid her an interest payment plus £509 in July 1720, which appears to have been South Sea profits before the bubble burst. He owed another £274 to his cousin Ann Chevall and a more considerable £1,140 to his sister Jane Chester. The latter included £1,200 in South Sea stock in his own name, but held in trust for Jane. The Director also held £800 in stock in trust for his sister Elizabeth and at least £500 each for his sisters May and Theodosia Chester. In all, his accounts mention sums invested in South Sea stock for ten women, totaling over £25,000.[35]

Women who had clamored for the supposed "sure bet" South Sea stock often faced the sobering reality that they had risked all and lost. It is not clear that either gender did better or worse in the aftermath of the South Sea Bubble, but there are examples of both genders engaging in risky and speculative behaviors, and both genders paying the price. The South Sea crisis was so widespread it affected almost all ranks and both genders, albeit in different ways. Some of the worst off would have been women who invested all their capital and for whom there were fewer economic options than their fellow male losers.

Although the South Sea Bubble is the best-known and remembered financial crash of England's early stock market, we have neglected to examine the many

[33] "The Families and Descendants of Susannah & Sarah Cradock," 235, 239, 241.

[34] "Inventory of Sir John Blunt," *The Particulars and Inventories of the Estates of the late South Sea Company Directors.*

[35] "Inventory of Robert Chester," *The Particulars and Inventories of the Estates of the late South Sea Company Directors.*

other corporations that went belly-up or engaged in financial fraud in the early years of the Financial Revolution. Women's finances took a toll as much as men's. A full thirty years before the South Sea Bubble, trouble was already brewing in what was a particularly risky era in early English finance. In the 1690s hundreds if not thousands of women found themselves the victims of the financial mismanagement of London's Court of Orphans. London's Corporation had been raiding the orphan's money (similar to raids on modern-day pension funds) to make loans and pay expenses. The result was that by the late 1680s there was no money left to pay even interest to the orphans whose inheritance money was lodged there. The London Court of Orphans had been established in the thirteenth century as a safe and secure place to lodge the inheritances of London freemen. The court was responsible for drawing up an inventory of the deceased freeman's estate, determining the amount due to his orphan, and deciding where the inheritance would be held until the orphan's majority. The executor (often the freeman's widow) could hold the inheritance, or the money could be paid into the city's Chamber and held there. In the sixteenth century the Chamber loaned out orphans' inheritances on recognizance to private individuals. Charles Carlton estimates that between the 1560s and the 1680s the Chamber loaned millions of pounds of orphan's money to private creditors. These were popular loans because the sums could usually be held for a long period of time, the maturity dates were known well in advance (when the orphan turned twenty-one or married), and the interest rates were low. The "recognitors" had to pay "finding money," or interest, to the orphan. The Corporation set the rates and revised them periodically. By 1659, 5 percent was the rate on all loans up to £1,500. These interest rates were low compared to the market rate of the time, which was between 10 and 12 percent.[36]

By the seventeenth century it became more common for families to make orphans' inheritances available as a form of public rather than private credit. The money the Chamber of London owed to the freemen's orphans grew from £182,795 in 1585 to a high of £558,920 in 1681. Between the years 1628 and 1682 executors had loaned London's Chamber almost £1.5 million. They did so because ironically they thought it was the safest place to lodge the orphans' money. Carlton says that it is not true that the Corporation forced executors to lodge orphans' money in the Chamber, rather they chose to do so. Unfortunately, this led to the orphans' money being "entangled with the city's worsening financial crisis."[37] Before the seventeenth century London had not borrowed much at all from this fund, but by the 1600s the city was in need of funds and the Corporation used the orphan's money to pay its bills.

---

[36] *The Manuscripts of the House of Lords, 1678[–1693]*, H. M. Stationery Office, 1892, 172–9. Charles Carlton, *The Court of Orphans* (Leicester: Leicester University Press, 1974), 13, chapter 3, esp. 43, 50–1, and 83–5.

[37] Carlton, *Court of Orphans*, 90.

Disastrously, by 1682 the Corporation was not able to even repay interest on the principal of the orphan's money. Scholars have blamed the Corporation's default on the 1672 Stop of the Exchequer, but Carlton says this also is fallacious. In fact, in 1672 "the Crown owed London a mere £1,240, all of which was repaid within four years." Rather, Carlton says London's financial collapse was due to the expenses of the Civil Wars and the financial losses of the Great Fire, as well as the failure of the city to keep up with its growth and to modernize its revenues. It turns out the city had been dipping into the Orphan's Fund to cover its losses for decades. False accounting allowed this to go undetected.[38]

It took over a decade for the orphans to begin to wrestle their inheritances out of London's Chamber. In the meantime, the city made partial interest payments of 2.23 percent instead of the 4.6 percent the orphans had previously received. Carlton figures that in 1688 the chamber owed £508,355 to 617 families of orphans and using a factor of 3.77 children per family he surmises that the London Chamber's financial crisis affected 2,326 orphans. This is almost 1,000 more people than the 1,400 "distressed orphans" mentioned in a petition to the House of Lords. Either way, thousands of young men and women whose money had been loaned to the Corporation were affected. The orphans tried to recover their money by first going to the courts, then appealing to the monarchs, namely Charles II and James II, and finally trying to sway public opinion through a number of pamphlets.[39]

One such pamphlet, *A Dialogue between Francisco and Aurelia, two unfortunate Orphans of the City of London* (1690), reveals the difficulties faced by both male and female orphans.[40] It begins with a young man named Francisco asking a young woman named Aurelia what she is doing at London's Guildhall. She responds, "Sir, think you that Young Women have no Business in Guildhall?" Francisco remarks that due to her mentioning her hatred of the City's alderman he thinks she must be "one of the orphans of the City of London." Aurelia concedes this is true and finds he is also "one of the same unhappy Number" and that they are both at the Guildhall to pursue their business before the court, although so far to no avail. They both say their fortunes are in a "desperate" condition and that they live on hope only. And then the couple's dialogue turns to narrating the facts of their predicament. Aurelia says,

> But 'pray', Sir, give me leave to enquire of you the Reasons, or Occasions, of the Practice of putting the Orphan's Money into the Chamber of London; by what Authority demanded, and whether our Deceased Parents were not influenced by Custom, and had a wrong Notion of the Matter; for could they have foreseen

---

[38] Carlton, *Court of Orphans*, 51, 82, 90–3, 96.   [39] Carlton, *Court of Orphans*, 97–101.
[40] *A Dialogue between Francisco and Aurelia, two unfortunate Orphans of the City of London, Guildhall, November 3, 1690* (L, 1690). Early English Books Online (hereafter EEBO) <eebo.chadywyck.com> (accessed December 2013).

what has since happened, they would as soon have ordered their Executors to
have laid out their Money in Ruffs and Farthingal[e]s, as to have put it into the
bottomless Pit, the Chamber.

Francisco admits that the practice was at first intentionally "Good and Pious."
The Lord Mayor and Court of Alderman became the trustees of the widows and
orphans. And he concedes that for "several scores of years" the Orphan's Fund
worked. But first the costly Civil Wars of the 1640s made calls on the "sums in
the Chamber." The money was not paid back so that new orphans' money was
used to pay the old. And then the "Stop of the Exchequer" when the government
repudiated its loans during Charles II's reign, also hurt the Orphan's Fund.

Aurelia mentions more problematic reasons for the loss of the orphan's
money, including rumors that city buildings and guildhall dinners were paid
for out of the Orphan's Fund. She also deplores that a young man, born and
educated to be a gentleman, but whose money lay in the Chamber, might have
to take "some mean Office to keep from starving" or even become a highway-
man to make his fortune. Francisco commiserates with her that it is a pity that a
Young Gentlewoman whose money "lay sleeping" in the Chamber might have
to engage in "some mean Employ" or work for some ungrateful and unworthy
Lady, or marry some "inferior Fellow," or worst of all, expose her virtue, due to
her poverty. Aurelia sighs and asks if there is any hope of recovering their
fortunes. Francisco responds, as "Much such Hopes as a Dying Patient has,
when he sees his Physician shake his Head." Aurelia hopefully says she has
heard the City might sell some land to pay these debts, but Francisco is dubious,
so she says they must pray that Parliament will do something. Francisco echoes
these thoughts and with their hopes set on Parliament the two depart home.
According to this pamphlet the prospects for the defrauded orphans depended
on their gender: men who lost their inheritance would have to turn to jobs that
were beneath them or a life of crime, while women's options also included
menial work, as well as a bad marriage or a life of prostitution.

Unfortunately for this fictional pair and the real creditors they represented,
the real Parliament stalled, introducing so called Orphans' bills throughout the
1690s to no avail. Women and their families petitioned Parliament for relief.
For example, in 1693 Ann Wright's petition stated that eleven years earlier, in
1682, she had loaned the Chamber £600 at 5 percent and for security she
received two bonds in return. But she had only received one half year's interest
at 1 percent in all that time. Wright should have earned £330 on her invested
portion but instead had only received a mere £3—less than 1 percent of what
she was owed. She told the MPs that "being fatherless and motherless, [she
was] reduced to great Streights" and asked for her money back.[41] In the same

---

[41] *Journal of the House of Commons: volume 10: 1688–1693* (1802), 838–9. British History
Online <www.british-history.ac.uk> (accessed August 22, 2014).

year, three women presented a petition to the House of Commons. Frances Bradbury, Ellen Pank, and Grace Bell said their father Thomas Bradbury had put £250 in the Chamber of London "at small interest," evidently because he thought "it the securest Place; and which he intended as a Provision for the Petitioners, who are in mean Condition."[42] They also asked Parliament to relieve them. Likewise, in February 1694 Elisha Patching and Patience Dod petitioned Parliament explaining that in June 1688 their aunt, Ursula Drake, had loaned £600 to the Chamber of London. "The credit [of the Chamber] failing, the said Ursula laid it so much to Heart the 600l. being all her Dependence, that she shortly after died..." As her administrators, her niece and nephew continued to pursue their aunt's inheritance while blaming London's Corporation for their aunt's death.[43]

Despite these petitions, it took twelve years and six attempts at a bill before the London orphans finally achieved redress. The 1694 "Act for the relief of orphans and creditors of the City of London" combined the city's debts into an Orphan's Fund on which the Corporation paid 4 percent interest. The fund traded openly as stock and the city paid the interest through raising various rates and taxes. Although this solution started out shakily, by the eighteenth century the fund had grown substantially. The Corporation eventually paid off all of the debt in 1832 and ended the Orphan's Fund. The use of the Chamber to lodge orphans' portions had long since ended, declining precipitously after 1694. Carlton notes that the advent of new financial options, such as the Bank of England, meant that families had other options for lodging inheritances, at better rates of interest, and with better security.[44]

The Orphan's Fund was not an isolated case of financial fraud and risk in the 1690s. Also in this decade there was much speculation involving lead mines throughout the British Isles. When Sir Carberry Price discovered mines in Wales, he created a company and divided the mine into shares. Great profits were predicted but instead the company went into debt. In 1698 Sir Humphrey Mackworth stepped in and bought the enterprise, reorganizing it into the Mine Adventurers Company. And thus began one of the more speculative and fraudulent ventures of the early years of the Financial Revolution. Koji Yamamoto goes so far as to call it "probably the most sensational financial scandal before the South Sea bubble." He also notes that the fraudster Mackworth was quite hypocritical, presenting himself as a pious and charitable public servant. A Tory gentleman and founder of the Society for the Promotion of Christian Knowledge, Mackworth argued that the company's mines would bring wealth to Britain and help employ the poor. He also proposed to

[42] *Journal of the House of Commons: volume 11: 1693–1697* (1803), 35. British History Online (accessed August 22, 2014).

[43] *Journal of the House of Commons: volume 11: 1693–1697* (1803), 108–9.

[44] Carlton, *Court of Orphans*, 97–101.

donate money to the poor from the mines' future profits (shades of the socially-conscious businesses of today). And such a charitable focus persuaded some, especially women, to invest.[45] For instance, among the names of investors in 1700 was Mary Astell, the High Church Tory author and charity school founder.[46] Mackworth's political and philanthropic credentials fit closely with hers. Unfortunately, however, Mackworth bilked a lot more people than he helped.

Realizing the venture he had bought was in debt for some £15,000, Mackworth proposed a lottery to recapitalize the company.[47] The "unwary shareholders" of the Mine Adventurers Company agreed to the lottery scheme and Mackworth adeptly created demand by advertising the lottery widely in a number of pamphlets and newspapers. When the subscription books opened on September 1, 1698 they were quickly filled with £26,490 of investment capital. The lottery drawing was set for March 1698/99. As W. R. Scott understatedly put it: "Unfortunately it turned out subsequently that there was an element of dishonesty in the promotion of the company."[48] First, there was out and out embezzlement. Evidently, Mackworth and the manager William Waller had diverted £2,000 in cash, £20,345 in stock, and 624 shares from the company to themselves.[49] Second, the investment opportunities and lottery chances were not as good as advertised. There were concerns about the "fairness of the drawing with allegations that Mackworth and his friends obtained a disproportionate number of prizes."[50] After the lottery there were now 700 proprietors of shares in the Mine Adventurers Company. Despite continued debts the share price for Mine Adventurers stock was steady and its public image was one of success until 1707. "Underneath the whole enterprize was honeycombed with fraud," however, and word leaked out when the managers started quarreling between themselves.[51] Parliament looked into the company's affairs and found that Mackworth was withholding news about mine failures and propping up share prices so that he and others

---

[45] Koji Yamamoto, "Piety, Profit and Public Service in the Financial Revolution," *English Historical Review*, vol CXXVI, 521 (Aug. 2011), 811, 818, 823.

[46] *A List of All the Adventurers in the Mine-Adventure. May the 1st, 1700.* (L, 1700). ECCO (accessed October 2013).

[47] My discussion of the Mine Adventurers Company is largely based on W. R. Scott, *The Constitution and Finance of English, Scottish, and Irish Joint Stock companies*, vol. II (Cambridge: Cambridge University Press, 1912), 443–56.

[48] Scott, *The Constitution and Finance of English, Scottish, and Irish Joint Stock companies*, vol. II, 446.

[49] Folger Shakespeare Library, 169–927q, William Waller, *The Mine-Adventure Laid Open; Being an Answer to a Late Pamphlet, Intitled, A Familiar Discourse, &c. published by William Shiers* (L, 1710).

[50] Scott, *The Constitution and Finance of English, Scottish, and Irish Joint Stock companies*, vol. II, 447.

[51] Scott, *The Constitution and Finance of English, Scottish, and Irish Joint Stock companies*, vol. II, 450.

could sell their shares at a profit. Investors began to suffer. Dividends were deferred and the company's bank suspended payments on its notes, although certain "favoured depositors" were paid.

It was at this time that the creditors of the bank began to demand their money and the shareholders in the company began to ask questions. Mackworth managed to assuage them and blame Waller for the company's monetary losses. The two attacked each other in print. But the creditors were not happy with the proposal that their bonds should be converted to "blanks" that could earn 6 percent interest but would not share in any future profits of the company. In 1710 the creditors of the Mine Adventurers Company lost confidence in the managers and convened in coffee houses to hold separate meetings. They decided to petition Parliament. When the House of Commons began to investigate the company they found major mismanagement: decisions were made and business conducted without the Directors being present, the company books had been altered, and when they opened the company chest they found no money inside. Mackworth and Waller turned on each other, but the House of Commons held Mackworth, along with company secretary William Shiers, and treasurer Thomas Dykes, guilty of fraud; they also forbade the men to leave the country or sell off their assets.[52]

The company's creditors and shareholders joined in petitioning Parliament for some sort of financial settlement. What they got was most likely a disappointment. The 1711 Mine Adventurer's Act valued the company's shares at £20, which would be written down by one third (meaning the value would be reduced by this much) and credited to shareholders. Bond-holders had the value of their blanks written down by a little less, or one fifth. Legal cases brought by the company's investors and creditors continued for the next seven years when in 1718 Mackworth amazingly reappeared and once again took over the company. He was successful in the short term but evidently his fraudulent ways had not changed much. The shareholders once again deserted him and turned to Parliament for redress. But the company survived into the later eighteenth century with women continually comprising significant numbers of shareholders.

The financial shenanigans of the Mine Adventurers Company were a serious risk to female investors. This was because the company garnered one of the highest levels of female investment in any public security outside of government funds. A list of the adventurers drawn up in May of 1700 included the names of 211 women.[53] These women made up 28.8 percent of the total

---

[52] *The History and Proceedings of the House of Commons: volume 4: 1706–1713* (1742), 135–68 <www.british-history.ac.uk> (accessed January 10, 2014).

[53] *A List of All the Adventurers in the Mine-Adventure. May the 1st, 1700.* Yamamoto says there were "no less than 150 female investors" but the number was actually significantly higher—211. Yamamoto, "Piety, Profit and Public Service in the Financial Revolution," 813.

731 investors. The list of those eligible to vote in company affairs only included the person's name, so it does not provide a lot of detail on the women investors. Twenty-nine of the 211 women (or 13.7 percent of women investors) held titles such as Lady, Dame, Honorable, Countess, or Marchioness. This was a relatively high number of elite female subscribers for a company of the time. Nevertheless, the other 86 percent of female investors were non-elites who might not be able to weather financial losses so easily. Four years later, in another list of the members of the Mine Adventurers Company the total number of adventurers had dropped some to 676, but the percentage of women shareholders had actually gone up to 29.58 percent.[54]

Almost forty years later, gender was still a salient characteristic for shareholders of mining companies managed by the Mackworths. An issue of the *London Daily Post* from September 1739 ran an announcement addressed "To the Ladies of the Hon. City of London." These City women were informed that at a recent meeting of the General Court for the Society for the Mineral and Battery-Works, the Governor gave 500 shares of the corporation to several gentlemen in order to carry out a proposal presented by Sir Thomas Mackworth for manufacturing copper and brass.

> And whereas the Ladies of this City have formerly contributed generously to some Proposals of his [Mackworth's] for the Public Utility, he entertaining a grateful Sense thereof, doth freely give among such of them as shall be dispos'd to enter into this Undertaking, the remaining 500 shares, not exceeding ten Shares to any one, provided that by the 10th of October next they accept the same, and pay at the appointed Time the Calls for the more vigorous carrying on the said Works ... to the amount of 18,000 l. as the Value thereof appear'd to indifferent Appraisers.

Three calls (options to buy a specified amount of stock at a specified price) would be issued in the upcoming season, with each call being 30s. a share. Because "the Addresses of many Ladies not being at present known to the Governor, he humbly begs Pardon for taking this Method of giving the Notice hereof." The newspaper advertisement informed any interested female investors, that he, the Treasurer and the Accountant of the company would be available from 9 in the morning till 3 in the Afternoon, at Mr. Donnolly's Office up Stairs on the Royal-Exchange. He added that he hoped to get permission from the Court to extend the time to buy "as the Ladies may find this Notice too short." The announcement was signed: "I am, with the greatest Respect, Ladies, Your most devoted Servant, DAVID AVERY."[55] This

[54] *A List of the Names of the Governour and Company of the Mine Adventurers of England. November the Twenty third, 1704.* (L, 1704). ECCO (accessed October 2013).
[55] *London Daily Post and General Advertiser*, issue 1532, Sept. 22, 1739. 17th and 18th Century Burney Collection Newspapers <gdc.gale.com> (accessed October 2008).

advertisement was significant since it was rare for women to be so directly and publicly sought out as investors.

The company's announcement was noteworthy in a number of other ways. First, women were addressed directly as investors without any reference to husbands or other male kin being involved. They were told when and where they could buy shares in the company and that they could meet directly with the officers. And second, women had already invested in some of Thomas Mackworth's other business ventures, so he was targeting them once again. Thomas Mackworth was Sir Humphrey's cousin, and had been involved in the Mine Adventurers Company from the beginning, although he and Sir Humphrey were several times at odds over the latter's financial mismanagement. Sir Thomas Mackworth was not without taint himself, however, since he was also involved in the management of another fraudulent company in the 1730s—the Charitable Corporation.[56]

Women then were significant holders of risky and speculative ventures such as the Mine Adventurers Company, and may have held well over a third of the stock precisely because mining ventures sought out female investors in particular. Whether men like the Mackworths targeted women because they thought they were easy marks is unclear. But we can say that some women may have been persuaded into this risky investment due to the machinations of these men.

While the frauds outlined so far predated the South Sea Bubble, the crisis of 1720 did not end corporate cases of financial mismanagement and outright fraud in England. There were also a surprising number of financial scandals and Parliamentary investigations in the early years of the 1730s, a mere decade after the South Sea Bubble. Two of the biggest involved the York Buildings Company and the Charitable Corporation. In fact, the two companies shared many of the same managers and directors. The financial troubles of the York Buildings Company are worthy of more research. And it is apparent that women were involved.[57]

Less well-known than its sister scandal, the South Sea Bubble, the meltdown of the Charitable Corporation also scarred investors, a large proportion of whom were female. The Charitable Corporation was established in 1707 to provide emergency loans to the working poor who gave property on pledge as security. The loans were funded by establishing a corporation and offering

---

[56] "Sir Thomas Mackworth," History of Parliament Online. <www.historyofparliamentonline. org> (accessed June 2014). Thomas Mackworth was on the Committee of Accounts for the Charitable Corporation in 1726. Thomas Hansard, *Cobbett's Parliamentary History of England*, (1811), 47–8.

[57] David Murray, *The York Buildings Company: A Chapter in Scotch History* (1883). The Internet Archive <www.archive.org> (accessed December 2013). A. J. C. Cummings, *The York Buildings Company: A Case Study in Eighteenth-Century Corporation Mismanagement* (University of Strathclyde dissertation, 1980).

shares to public investors. The corporation was deemed charitable because it offered low interest loans (10 percent) in contrast to the exorbitant rates charged by individual pawnbrokers (up to 30 percent). Some investors were drawn to investing in the Charitable Corporation as an early modern version of ethical or socially-conscious investing (wherein individuals put their capital into companies that further social or ethical causes). This may have been why many women invested in the Charitable Corporation. At the same time an investor could think of themselves as "doing good," they could also turn a nice profit by investing in the Charitable Corporation. The company boasted 10 percent dividends between 1725 and 1730, dropping to a more modest but still substantial 6 percent the year after.[58]

A list of shareholders in the Charitable Corporation from 1731 includes the names of 333 investors. Of these, 97 were female, which indicates that 29 percent of investors in the corporation were women when the company was on the verge of financial collapse. As we have seen, this was on the high side of female proprietorship for a public stock. A list from three years later, in 1734, shows there were even more women holding Charitable Corporation shares. Out of 352 proprietors, 116 were female which meant 33 percent of shareholders were now female.[59] This was the highest level of female investment in any public security other than the government debt.

By 1731 accounts of mismanagement, fraud, and embezzlement of Charitable Corporation funds had become public. Perhaps because the country had gone through this a decade before, the creditors mobilized and petitioned the government relatively quickly. *The Present State of the Unhappy Sufferers of the Charitable Corporation Consider'd* (1732) publicly presented the case of the swindled investors. The proprietors of the Charitable Corporation appealed to Parliament to assist them. In response to those who protested this could not be "stiled a public calamity" the publication protested that:

> *Persons of all Degrees, Sexes, and Ages* have had their Fortunes swallowed up by the late fraudulent Management, *many of them such as were willing to secure the regular Interest of what they had saved thro' the Course of an industrious Life, that it might afford them a comfortable Support in their Declining Years... Orphans and Widows*, the most helpless and distressed Characters in ordinary Life, have, from These Frauds, had their Misfortunes doubled, and their Small Pittances of Support utterly dissipated... [60]

[58] *A Short History of the Charitable Corporation* (L, 1732). ECCO (accessed June 2012).

[59] "A List of the Proprietors of the Charitable Corporation...1 October 1731," in D. Mowbray, *The Report of the Gentlemen Appointed by the General Court of the Charitable Corporation* (L, 1732) ECCO (accessed June 2012); "A List of the Sufferers by the Charitable Corporation, Entitled to Relief from the Lottery granted for that purpose," *Gentlemen's Magazine* v. 4 (May 1734), 235–7.

[60] Italics my own. HEH, 280426, *The Present State of the Unhappy Sufferers of the Charitable Corporation Consider'd. With Reasons humbly offer'd for their Relief* (L, 1733), 18, 24.

Some commentators thought that never-married women in particular should be excused for having ventured their money in Bubbles and that they were particularly deserving of help.

> Single Women and others uncapable of Trade, or the Management of great Estates, whose Substance is in Money, and Income but small, have the most plausible Excuse for venturing into these Projects. But let these consider whether a secure Interest, tho' small, is not better than to run the Risque of losing their All in Hopes of a greater, and whereby they are often left without Means of repairing a broken Fortune.[61]

These contemporary commentators recognized that women, especially widowed and single ones, were putting their money at "risque" in ventures such as the Charitable Corporation, but that these women ran this hazard because they had few other options to maintain themselves. For them, the repercussions could be disastrous since they might lose "their all." And lest we think this was just a ploy to engender sympathy for investors by dwelling on the consequences for widows and orphans, we should remember that the subscriber lists verify the considerable number of women who had invested in the Charitable Corporation.

The Charitable Corporation's creditors now waited for Parliament to make up their losses, which were not only financial. The authors warned "several struck with the vast and unexpected shock of their whole fortune being destroyed, have added the loss of life to the miseries induced by the late wicked management" while there remains some hundred of distressed families who have no other support for their hopes "but that confidence they place in the equity and tenderness of the British Legislature towards British Subjects."[62] Just like during the South Sea Bubble the talk was of suicide and families ruined by corporate greed.

In 1733 the proprietors of the Charitable Corporation stock began a suit in the Court of Chancery. Included among the 212 named defendants were fifty-two women. This means that 25 percent of the defendants were female, which although high, was actually 8 percent less than the overall percentage of female proprietors. Among the defendants were women such as Harriott Pitt, possibly the mother of the future Prime Minister, Pitt the Elder.[63]

Another source documenting the Charitable Corporation's defrauding of women investors appeared in a 1734 issue of the *Gentleman's Magazine*. It was a "List of the Sufferers by the Charitable Corporation entitled to Relief from a

---

[61] *Gentleman's Magazine* v. 2 (March 1732), 649.

[62] *The Present State of the Unhappy Sufferers of the Charitable Corporation Consider'd*, 18, 24.

[63] *The Present State of the Unhappy Sufferers of the Charitable Corporation*. Prime Minister William Pitt the Elder's mother was Harriet Villiers Pitt, who died Oct. 21, 1736.

Lottery granted for that purpose."[64] This list includes 304 names, 116 of which belong to women. This reveals that 38.16 percent of the people swindled by the directors of the Charitable Corporation were women. This was the highest percentage of female participation in any public security I have found for the period up to 1750. Such numbers suggest that women were disproportionately disadvantaged by this particular financial scandal. The list included the amount each "sufferer" had lost and the amount each received out of the proceeds from the lottery. Every person received back approximately 48 percent of what they had invested. Women and men got back the same percentage of their investments. So for instance Sarah Lane who had lost £50 in the company was "allowed" £24 7s. 6d. of her investment back. Similarly, but on the higher end of the scale, Constance Craig who had invested £2,752 16s. 1d. received £1,341 12s. Rather than making a profit, the women who bought shares in the Charitable Corporation suffered the loss of half of their investment.[65]

Even worse was the method Parliament settled on to pay back the "sufferers" in the Charitable Corporation: a lottery. This lottery issued 125,000 tickets at £4 each for a fund of £500,000. But only £79,120 of this fund was allotted to pay the subscribers who had suffered at the hands of the Charitable Corporation, while £400,000 was reserved for lottery benefit tickets or prizes. If the prizes had been 20 percent lower the Corporation's shareholders could have been paid back in full. As Table 6.1. illustrates, over half (or 68 out of 116) of the female investors in the Charitable Corporation had invested less than £200 in the company. Perhaps they had not put all of their capital in this one investment. On the other hand, almost 20 percent of women had invested more than £500. And a few women had invested thousands of pounds. This may well have been their entire nest egg. All of them got back less than half of what they had invested, a risky venture indeed.

The types of women who invested in the Charitable Corporation varied. They included the daughters of Francis Asty: the spinster Elizabeth Asty who died in 1736 and had a memorial put up to her in Bath Abbey and her sister Henrietta who married Christopher Wyvill in 1738 and died four years later; Mary Tothaker, also a spinster, resident in St Andrew Holborn when she died much later, in 1767; and Rebecca Torriano, the widow of a merchant and mother of eleven when she invested in the Charitable Corporation. Also included among the investors were the memorably named Clementina and Martha

---

[64] "A List of the Sufferers by the Charitable Corporation, Entitled to Relief from the Lottery granted for that purpose," *Gentlemen's Magazine* v. 4 (May 1734), 235–7.

[65] Beverly Lemire says "of those owed money, over 55 per cent of the women were owed under £200 while 72 per cent of the men were owed under £500." Beverly Lemire, *The Business of Everyday Life: Gender, Politics, and Social Practice in England 1600–1900* (Manchester: Manchester University Press, 2005), note 57; *The Report of the Commissioners appointed to examine, state, and report, who of the Sufferers in the Charitable Corporation are Objects of Compassion* (L, 1733), appendices A–F. ECCO (accessed July 2010).

Table 6.1. Female "Sufferers" in the Charitable Corporation

Monetary Amount Lost in the Charitable Corporation	Number of Female Investors N = 116
£0–49	20
£50–99	21
£100–199	27
£200–299	14
£300–399	3
£400–499	9
£500–599	7
£600–699	3
£700–799	2
£800–899	2
£900–999	0
£1,000–1499	1
£1,500–1,999	1
£2,000–2,499	3
£2,500–2,999	3

Source: "A List of the Sufferers by the Charitable Corporation, Entitled to Relief from the Lottery granted for that purpose" *Gentlemen's Magazine* 4 (May 1734), 235–7.

Swordfeger, the daughters of Simon Swordfeger, who was secretary to Charles Boyle, Earl of Orrery. The family was Catholic and Jacobite; and perhaps it added insult to injury that some suspected the Charitable Corporation's managers had embezzled its assets to aid the Pretender. It seems the Charitable Corporation's collapse, happening a mere decade after the South Sea Bubble, was just as severe for the hundreds of women who lost half or more of their money to this later fraud.

So far this chapter has explored some of the risks incurred by women investors in public stocks and securities during the 1690s–1730s. While women were indeed victims of financial risk, we should recognize that they could also be agents of financial fraud. The Financial Revolution provided new opportunities for women to bilk unsuspecting would-be investors. The last section of this chapter will examine some examples of such women. For example, London's Old Bailey criminal court saw an increase in cases of theft and forgery of new financial instruments from the 1690s onward. In 1690 Mary Young and her husband stood charged of passing forged bills of exchange. While Robert Young was the forger, it was his wife Mary who passed the forged bills and received money in exchange; £9 on one occasion, and a significant £200 on another.[66] Other women forged bonds or notes for money due them. One of the more audacious, although perhaps ill-advised,

---

[66] *Old Bailey Proceedings Online* (hereafter *OBP*), t16900115-25, case of Mary Young, 15 January 1690. <www.oldbaileyonline.org> (accessed July 2010).

attempts was by Mary Butler, alias Strickland, in 1699. She was indicted for forging a bond in the name of Sir Robert Clayton for £40,000 "with a Condition to pay 1200l. a Year, with interest, and after the decease of the said Sir Robert, there should be 20,000l. paid her within six Months." Butler made multiple mistakes in this criminal endeavor, which tipped off several people. First, the financial amount of the bond was incredibly large, and second, she alleged the involvement of Clayton, the most famous banker in the City.[67] She still was fortunate though, since soon after forgery was changed from a misdemeanor to a felony punishable by death.[68]

Women also were implicated in the forging of stocks and shares. In September 1755 the widow Mary Skelton and Susannah Knight appeared at the Old Bailey for "forging and publishing a promissory note dated May 10, 1755 for the payment of £20 under the hand of John Waters, first clerk of the Million Bank, with the intent to defraud Thomas Wheat." In this case, the court found both women to be innocent.[69] Theft of bank notes, stocks, and shares could also be accomplished by forging other paper. The *Universal Museum* reported that in late 1762 a broker named Mr. Rice had absconded to the continent. His wife did not get away but was taken at an inn "by one of the clerks belonging to the South-Sea house. There were found in her custody bank-notes to the amount of near five thousand pounds." It appears that Mr. and Mrs. Rice had defrauded another woman, a Mrs. Pearce from Yorkshire, of several thousand pounds "by means of a forged letter of attorney."[70] Mr. Rice was caught and brought back to London where he confessed to forgeries involving the South Sea Company and the Bank of England to the much larger amount of £50,000. Nevertheless, he insisted he was the only one involved, perhaps trying to save his wife. The courts thought otherwise.

Other women focused their fraud on the lottery. For example, in 1715 Jane Mower faced the accusation of having stolen twenty-eight lottery tickets.[71] For Mower, lottery tickets represented a form of wealth and future security. The court proceedings reveal that Jane Mower was a housekeeper for Thomas Smith and took advantage of her employer being away to steal "a great quantity of plate, household and wearing linen, and apparel, to a very great value; and 28 Lottery

---

[67] *OBP*, t16991011-19, case of Mary Butler, alias Strickland, 11 Oct. 1699. Butler was lucky enough to be convicted of merely a misdemeanor, but she was fined the large sum of £500.

[68] Forgery became a felony first for paper financial instruments issued by the government (State lottery tickets, Exchequer bills) and the Bank of England. By 1725 forgery of East India and South Sea Company stocks and bonds was also punishable by death. And in 1729 forgery of all private paper instruments (bonds, bills, promissory notes, wills, even receipts) became a felony punishable by death without benefit of clergy. Randall McGowen, "Making the 'Bloody Code'? Forgery legislation in eighteenth-century England," in Norma Landau, ed., *Law, Crime and English Society, 1660–1830* (Cambridge: Cambridge University Press, 2002), 121–30.

[69] *OBP*, t17550910-43, case of Mary Skelton & Susannah Knight, 10 Sept. 1755.

[70] *Universal Museum*, vol. 2 (Jan. 1763). ECCO (accessed October 2007).

[71] *OBP*, t17151207-40, case of Jane Mower, 7 Dec. 1715.

tickets, for the Year 1710, value 224 l., some rings, 2 silver watch[es], and 71 guineas." Mower's employer, Thomas Smith, became suspicious when she did not follow him to his family's country home. Returning to London he found his goods missing, and going first to "Exchange Alley, and puts up his lottery tickets; by which means he discover'd" who had sold them. It was John Kelley, a soldier who was "keeping company" with Jane Mower. In her defense Mower said, "That Mr. Smith had made a Bargain with her in his Wife's Lifetime, to come and live with him, if his Wife should die, and be his Bedfellow: That after his Wife was dead, he claim'd her Promise, and She went to live with him, and he put her into Possession of all he had: That she was with Child by him; upon which he order'd her to take a Room on t'other side the Water, and gave the Lottery Tickets for her Security." It appears this was a case of a woman seduced and now pregnant with a bastard child claiming that her lover had given her the lottery tickets for her financial security. The story got even more complicated, but for all parties concerned, the lottery tickets, valued by the court at around £224, were a central part, while the other stolen goods in question dropped out of their separate narratives. The court found Jane Mower and John Kelley guilty of grand larceny and receiving, respectively. Kelley was branded for his lesser charge, and Mower had her death sentence respited thanks to her pregnancy. It is not clear if her financial fraud doomed her in the end or not.

By engaging in forgery and theft, of financial instruments or otherwise, women took a risk. These female criminals had something in common with female investors. They both were striving to improve their economic condition. Crime, of course, was illicit and punishable, while investing was licit and at first sight unpunishable. But women were punished for risky investments; they lost their money. Much of the time, women were not necessarily seeking out risk, but exposure to the new investment options of the Financial Revolution left them open to it. Bad management and outright fraud on the part of brokers and company directors led to many women losing a portion of their capital rather than increasing it. But there is no evidence that this experience led women to invest less. I have not found one example of a woman who said she would avoid investing in public stocks and securities, even after the South Sea Bubble. Evidently, these women had faith that the new market in stocks and securities would reward them with profits more than it would punish them with losses. Risk then was something female investors in public funds had to learn to meet and manage. The financial agency of such investors is what we will turn to in the next and last chapter.

7

The Financial and Political Agency
of Female Investors

The Quaker gentlewoman Mariabella Eliot turned twenty-one in the year 1757. Upon her entry into adulthood she also came into her inheritance, one that was predominantly made up of public stocks and securities. Eliot was the fourth generation to have the intriguing first name of Mariabella. The tradition had begun with her great-grandmother Mariabella (Bleake) Farmborough, born in 1627, continued with her grandmother Mariabella (Farmborough) Briggins, born 1665, descended to her mother Mariabella (Farmborough Briggins) Eliot, born 1708, and then to herself. Four generations of Mariabellas shared a name, but they also shared something else: they were all investors in public stocks and securities. Such a generational chain of female investors was rare, although as we have seen it was common for mothers and daughters, sisters and brothers, and aunts and nephews to pass on investing knowledge and advice.

At the same time she came into her inheritance, Eliot began keeping a well-organized book of accounts (although a male scribe did the actual accounting). She was fortunate enough to inherit a significant amount of wealth from her mother and father as well as from her grandmother, grandfather, two aunts, an uncle, and a cousin.[1] These legacies came in the form of a range of the investments made available by England's Financial Revolution. Eliot's ledger indicated that she inherited ten different public stocks and securities, in addition to cash and real property. It was a considerable fortune worth about £6,721. She received £4,000 in "Orphan stock" (the London Court of Orphan's Fund) from her grandmother Mariabella Briggins. She also inherited £790 stock in 3½% Bank annuities from her mother Mariabella Farmborough Eliot, while her father John Eliot left her £2,425 worth of stock in the 3% Consols. In 1758 her cousin Tibey bequeathed her £1,225 in Consolidated Bank Annuities and £200 in Reduced Bank Annuities. A year later she received

---

[1] London Metropolitan Archives (hereafter LMA), ACC 1017/925, Ledger of investments, Mariabella Eliot.

bequests from her Uncle Philip's estate, which included £1,500 of Reduced Bank Annuities, a considerable amount in East India bonds, and 3½% Bank Annuities worth some £1,687. Eliot also received shares in the London Assurance Company worth £162, £550 in Bank of England stock, £125 East India stock, and three Lead Mines shares worth £15.[2]

Mariabella Eliot did not just passively hold onto the stocks and securities that she inherited from her family and content herself with collecting dividends. Instead, within a year or two of her inheritance she began to alter and actively manage her stock portfolio. Eliot also put investments she had inherited into her own name, and in doing so, transformed her inheritance into her own stock portfolio. For instance, she sold out her London Assurance and Lead Mines shares for just a bit more than they were worth when she inherited them, but she also chose to hold onto her Orphan stock. She earned £160 in annual interest on the Orphan stock at the rate of 4 percent. Since this was a relatively high interest rate for the time this may explain why she kept it. Eliot also kept her East India Company stock (through at least the 1750s), but she transferred this holding into her own name. This shows that she viewed it as her own wealth and perhaps intended to keep it for some time. Eliot also kept the Bank of England stock she had inherited, but she chose to increase her holding by investing even more of her capital in the Bank. After inheriting £550 in Bank stock in 1757, three years later she bought £450 more to make an even stock holding of £1,000. Eliot also took her cash inheritance and invested it in stocks and securities. For instance, in 1759 she used £300 bequeathed her from her uncle toward a purchase of £600 in East India Company bonds.[3] Although a young single woman, Mariabella Eliot was not a passive holder of stocks she had inherited, rather she was a confident trader and investor.

Mariabella Eliot's assured behavior can also be glimpsed in her positive attitude toward investing in government funds. In 1759, her uncle Eliot left her £1,500 in Reduced Bank Annuities. Eliot chose to purchase more and by 1762 her holdings had increased to £3,600 stock in Reduced Bank Annuities. This fund was Eliot's second largest investment; although she inherited one third of her investment, she purchased two-thirds of it herself.[4] Similarly, Eliot inherited a modest £105 in Consolidated Bank Annuities from her father's estate in 1757. She chose to purchase first another £700 and in the following year another £200 to make up a total of £1,000 stock in Consolidated Bank Annuities which she held until at least the mid-1760s.[5] In addition to these two government funds, Mariabella Eliot also held thousands of pounds in 3½% Reduced Bank Annuities and 3% Bank Annuity Consols. While she usually

---

[2] LMA, ACC 1017/925, Ledger of investments, Mariabella Eliot.
[3] LMA, ACC 1017/925, Ledger of investments, Mariabella Eliot.
[4] LMA, ACC 1017/925, Ledger of investments, Mariabella Eliot.
[5] LMA, ACC 1017/925, Ledger of investments, Mariabella Eliot.

purchased and held on to stock rather than selling it, her holdings in the latter fund show her engaging in some profit-taking. In 1757 Eliot inherited £2,525 in 3% Bank Annuity Consols from her father. Three years later, she followed the dictum "buy low," and purchased an additional £575 in stock. She did so again in 1762, buying £3,000 more. In that year Eliot now owned £6,200 of Bank Annuity Consols (which were worth £5,422). In 1763 as the price of the Consols rose to the highest they had been while she had held them, Eliot sold off £200 at a modest profit. She still held £6,000 in the Consols, which made them her largest investment, and more than half (or £3,500) was stock she had purchased herself.[6]

In January 1769 Mariabella Eliot died at the young age of thirty-three. She had never married and at her decease she was a wealthy woman, worth tens of thousands of pounds, all of it neatly accounted for in the rows and columns of her ledger of investments. She had not let her investments sit, rather she had actively managed her stock portfolio, adding new investments, topping up old ones, and slowly amassing a genteel fortune. Eliot illustrates how a woman who inherited stocks and securities could exercise financial agency by transforming such wealth into a stock portfolio reflecting her own personal choices and investment strategies. In Mariabella Eliot's case, she preferred to hold a mixture of government funds and company stocks, in rounded amounts between two and six thousand pounds each, and to hold onto these investments for years at a time.

Women who inherited investments in the public funds can sometimes appear to be passive investors. One might think women only held stocks because they inherited them in the form of marriage portions and jointures. Or trustees held the money and women received the dividends or profits only. While it is true that some women relied on investment income and did not actively trade in stocks and shares, this stereotype does not apply to all women. Mariabella Eliot is a prime example of how women who came into public investments via inheritance could buy, sell, and refashion their portfolios according to personal investing preferences, strategies, and risk tolerance.

*   *   *

Mariabella Eliot was a woman who exercised financial agency. In her case, Eliot's agency resulted in an extensive stock portfolio that made her a wealthy young woman. But female public investors also exercised other types of financial agency. This chapter will examine how women's capital could translate into moments or opportunities for female agency and authority during the first half century of the Financial Revolution. The types of financial agency explored here include how women actively managed and transformed portfolios of investments, how women functioned as financial agents or brokers, and how women exercised political and public power through their

---

[6] LMA, ACC 1017/925, Ledger of investments, Mariabella Eliot.

investments. A case study of the lace trader turned public investor Hester Pinney will provide an example of the varied types of financial agency a female investor could exercise. Pinney is an example of a woman who began her adult life as a shopkeeper on the Royal Exchange. She took the profits from her trade and began to invest in government loans and company stocks. She did so well that she amassed a personal fortune in the tens of thousands of pounds. Her friends and family recognized her financial acumen and asked her to serve as a financial agent and invest for them. Pinney was so successful as a businesswoman that she not only served as a financial agent to her kin, like other women we have seen, but also to a man to whom she was not related, which was rare for an early modern woman.

7.1. CASE STUDY: HESTER PINNEY (1658–1740)

Bristol University holds an item in its Special Collections evocatively titled "Hester's Red Box." Within it is a treasure trove of financial papers and accounts belonging to the lace trader and businesswoman Hester Pinney. Pamela Sharpe has introduced us to Pinney's mercantile activities, but Pinney's financial accounts have never been analyzed or discussed in any detail. This is significant, since the papers provide a substantial chronicle of a woman's investments in public stocks and securities over a fifty-year period. This is also an unusual find for a woman born into the merchant class, who never married and thus had no children to preserve her papers. Hester Pinney's accounts and correspondence reveal that she started out investing modestly, taking advice from her brother Nathaniel, and showing herself cautious about risk-taking. Over time, Pinney emerged as an active and independent trader who was not afraid to speculate in the market and who became the key financial agent in her extended family and beyond.

Hester Pinney was born in 1658 in Broadwindsor, Dorset, the daughter of the clergyman John Pinney and his wife Jane. Her father was a Presbyterian minister who was ejected from his living due to his dissent from the Church of England. He then turned to lace trading which became a family business for the Pinneys. Hester's older sisters Sarah and Rachel Pinney went to London where they sold lace, linens, and bows out of a stall at the Royal Exchange. Hester followed her sisters in 1682, working with them at the Exchange and making house calls to customers' residences around London. When Sarah, the eldest sister, married in the mid-1680s Hester and Rachel continued to work and lodge together in London. Rachel then married and Hester's father and her brother Nathaniel thought the unmarried Hester should shut up shop and come home. Showing the first signs of what would become her trademark independence, Hester did not stop trading. Her father was not happy about

Hester's proclivity for independent living, particularly objecting to her lodging and doing business in taverns. But the Pinney men did acknowledge that Hester worked hard. Showing her financial skills, Hester brought the sisters' lace trade back after her sister Sarah's mistakes. Her brother Nathaniel noted that Hester worked early and late and did menial work—living by her needle and speciality laundering.[7]

Hester Pinney is notable for taking the profits she made from a relatively humble trade and investing them in Britain's emerging stock market. While she perhaps was not entirely unusual, the documentation of her life and investing is more so. Pinney's transition from lace trader to financial investor and broker was by no means inevitable. First of all, she was not particularly well-educated. This is not surprising since she was a younger daughter in the large family of a dissenting minister. She had been bred to trade, serving only an informal apprenticeship with the women in her family. Though Pinney could read and write, Sharpe points out that it often took her up to three attempts before she could produce a good letter. And although Pinney could keep accounts, her brother complained about their presentation. Sharpe suggests she was more verbally articulate, persuasive, and certainly had a practical knack for profit-making. Hester Pinney's access to and familiarity with the geographical spaces of the Financial Revolution no doubt also helped educate her in investing. As we saw in the introduction to this book, in addition to working in the Royal Exchange, Hester frequented coffee houses, the East India House, private banking houses, the Bank of England, and the Exchequer while going about her brother's business and then her own investing. Pinney provides a telling example of how a lack of a formal education was not a barrier to women's entry into finance.

Hester Pinney's first forays into investing began in the late 1680s, when she was in her thirties. In this decade there were not yet many public investment options, so investing primarily meant putting money into personal loans and mortgages. In February 1687 her brother Nathaniel wrote from Bristol to Hester who was in London. He asked if he could "draw on her money" for about £300. Even though Nathaniel did not currently know of a place to put her money out at interest, he affirmed he would "turn it to your advantage, besides supposing you know not well where to lodge it safe during your being in the country."[8] Nathaniel's letter reveals a number of points: first, he was establishing himself as more "in the know" about financial investing than his (slightly older) sister, second, he assumed Hester needed a safe place to lodge her money while she traveled, in essence a banker, and third, he assumed she would want some profit or "advantage" from lodging her money. Nathaniel

---

[7] Pamela Sharpe, "Dealing with Love: The Ambiguous Independence of the Single Woman in Early Modern England," *Gender & History* 11:2 (July 1999), 209–32.

[8] University of Bristol Special Collections (hereafter UB), DM 58, Pinney Papers, Box 3, folder II.

noted, somewhat patronizingly, that he was glad she had saved up so much of her earnings. So it appears that we can date the starting point of when Hester began to take her earnings from trade and use them as investment capital to the 1680s.

In the early 1690s both Hester and Nathaniel were loaning out their capital on private bonds and mortgages. In 1693 the siblings had to sue to get their money back from one bond and by the mid-1690s they had hundreds of pounds invested in mortgages. A 1696 letter from Nathaniel to Hester alludes to her capital. He said, "You are now mistress of a very good estate, such a one I am sure as you never thought of securing together in all your life." Hester's total wealth at this time is unknown, but in 1696/7 she had £5,000 invested in a mortgage; a "good estate" indeed. Rather than put her at ease, her brother thought her wealth had instead led to some anxiety. Nathaniel went on: "and I think really you are now more uneasy under it than when you was not worth a groat and cannot be content though it be far greater in proportion to your sex than any of your relations."[9] He said she was always complaining of their father's unkindness and how she had had so little "out of the family." Nathaniel's point about Hester having more money in proportion to her sex stands out. He may have thought women, especially single ones, did not have as much need for wealth as did married men like himself.

It was in the mid-1690s that Hester and Nathaniel Pinney began to transfer their capital from private investments into public investments in companies and the government. A note from 1694 indicates that they had money in the Exchequer at 6 percent. In 1695 Nathaniel mentions other investments, saying that they had lost money in Briscoe's [land] bank due to its failure and that he had lent their money to the King on the land tax.[10] The Pinneys stuck with the latter investment in 1696, putting more money on the land tax loan, which Nathaniel noted paid 8 percent interest.[11] The Pinney siblings were looking for a good rate of return and new places to invest money. Hester seems to have worried more than her brother did about losing on their investments. And since they had made out badly in their investment in Briscoe's land bank she was not entirely without reason.

A March 1696/97 letter from Nathaniel highlights Hester Pinney's concern about investment losses and refers to Hester asking for more security on their loans. Nathaniel took Hester's concerns personally and his correspondence from the 1690s reveals the tensions elicited by the siblings' investments. In December 1696 these strains hit a high note when Nathaniel retorted that if

---

[9] UB, DM 58, Pinney Papers, Box 3, folder II.

[10] Various land bank schemes were floated in the 1690s, including John Briscoe's, but none of these banks (which issued notes secured with land instead of money) were successful. See W. R. Scott, *The Constitution and Finance of English, Scottish, and Irish Joint Stock Companies to 1720* (Cambridge: Cambridge University Press, 1911), vol. 3, 246–52.

[11] UB, DM 58, Pinney Papers, Box 3, folder II.

Hester had trusted him with the "disposal of her money" he would have put it in Sir Jo's [Sir Jon Thomas's] hands on land security but she was "uneasy" about this. He then shockingly says he wished her "in the grave" and that he could not "tell what your apprehension of me" is but he did not deserve the imputation. Despite his anger, he closed with advice to Hester that if she put out her money in London "take great care you are not cheated" because tradesmen's bonds were dangerous.[12] This letter reveals a host of conflicts between the siblings when it came to money and investing. It appears Hester was questioning the investment choices her brother was making for the two of them, that perhaps Hester was more risk averse or at least more cautious than her brother, and that Nathaniel preferred "land security" while Hester may have been pushing to invest in stocks and securities. Nathaniel's last words imply Hester was entertaining investment options in London separate from his capital and his management. This letter marks the beginning of Hester's financial independence. The student was about to become the master when it came to investing in the options made available by the Financial Revolution. It is probably not a coincidence that Hester Pinney was now in her late thirties. She, like many women who never married, was transitioning into a more independent phase of life, one that I have characterized elsewhere as a phase redolent of "autonomy, activity, and authority."[13]

Despite their "financial birth pangs" the Pinney siblings continued to have a close relationship for another quarter of a century. Moreover, after Nathaniel's death Hester would continue to manage the financial affairs of his widow and minor son. A change occurred however in the late 1690s; their roles reversed and Hester began to serve as a London financial agent for her brother rather than he managing her affairs. For instance, in 1707 Nathaniel and his wife sent their "hearty thanks for receiving our money at the Exchequer and India house and [for paying Nathaniel's bills and] . . . for the care you take of our child [Jack] at school."[14]

Breaking away from her brother, Hester rather than Nathaniel was the Pinney who pursued investments in government securities. Their differing views on investment can be seen in Nathaniel's 1705 statement: "I can't think what greater advantage there can be in lending the Government money . . . I don't think it prudence in [illegible] to be more concerned in public funds than we are upon already." His primary qualm seems to have been that the government would only pay 5 percent interest or less. Interestingly, when he wanted Hester to loan him money a few years later he offered her 5 percent.

---

[12] UB, DM 58, Pinney Papers, Box 3, folder II.

[13] For the independence of middle-aged single women see Amy Froide, "Old Maids: the lifecycle of single women in early modern England," in Lynn Botelho and Pat Thane, eds., *Women and Ageing in British Society Since 1500* (Aldershot: Ashgate, 2001), 89–110.

[14] UB, DM 58, Pinney Papers, Box 3, folder II.

In 1710 Nathaniel was still pessimistic about investing in the government, although Hester was not. He warned his sister: "I suppose the present prospect of the times will discourage you from trusting more of your substance with the government. If I had never so much money I assure you I would venture no farther and can't forbear advising you to the same, and could even wish you had not concerned yourself in the lottery though what your advantage has been on drawing I never yet heard." Despite his chidings and misgivings about government investing, Nathaniel could not keep himself from wondering if Hester had won a prize in the State lottery. Nathaniel Pinney's dislike of government securities emerged again in late 1713 on news that the Pretender might invade which would produce "tumults and wars...and all public payments must during those commotions be stopped...what will become our Exchequer securities is high time to consider." He thought he in particular would be in a difficult situation since he relied on the government payments to pay certain "encumbrances," but he also warned Hester not to put any more money in this fund.[15]

In these years Hester Pinney invested for and provided financial advice to a number of family members. In 1705 the Pinney family invested together in the Exchequer annuities. Nathaniel bought an annuity of £50 per annum, Hester purchased two of £40 each, and her sister Rachel Scrimshire bought one that paid her £15 p.a.[16] In 1714 Pinney also assisted her sister Scrimshire in investing in Bank of England stock. Hester sent her sister a bill for £100 and wrote in her accounts, "then at the Bank bought a £100 21s. 5d. being a £100 stock with her money in my own name." It was Hester that went to the Bank, purchased the stock, and held it in her own name for her sister. Rachel Scrimshire was a widow, so she could have done this business herself, but she may not have been in London or may not have felt comfortable doing so. In 1731 Hester also paid for £300 of Bank stock that was transferred to her sister Mary Pinney. And Hester continued to do financial business for her brother. In the 1710s and the first half of the 1720s Hester collected dividends at East India House and the Exchequer for Nathaniel and made payments for him as well. Periodically the two siblings examined accounts together and signed off that they were balanced. Hester also held many of Nathaniel's financial papers and written proof of his investments, including three exchequer orders for £42, £80, and £50 respectively, and in 1702 a mortgage, which he said he was glad was "safe in her hands."[17]

By the second decade of the 1700s, Hester Pinney's position as financial advisor and agent for her family was firmly in place. Her role is particularly visible during the rise and fall of South Sea stock in 1719 and 1720. Nathaniel

---

[15] UB, DM 58, Pinney Papers, Box 3, folder II.
[16] UB, DM 58, Pinney Papers, Box 2, folder XII.
[17] UB, DM 58, Pinney Papers, Box 2, folders III and XII.

wrote to Hester in 1719 asking her for information about their government [Exchequer] annuities and the impact of the company's taking over the government's debt. He told Hester: "I should be glad to hear from you about South Sea company and should with you be sorry should our 99 year annuities be put in there." In a letter dated 1 July 1720, the month before the South Sea Bubble burst, Nathaniel wrote to Hester saying each week's newspapers acquainted him with the thousands of pounds Hester had added to her fortune. He "rejoices" for her but grieves because as her money increased "mine might have done so too..." Nathaniel had avoided subscribing his annuities into South Sea Company stock, but since stockholders (like Hester) were making amazing profits, he now wanted in.[18] In August 1720 Hester was in London, serving as Nathaniel's agent. She was trying to sell his annuities. He told her "I must leave it to you to do the best you can for me." His plan was to have Hester sell his annuity to either the banker George Colebrooke or to the Million Bank and then for her to use the £588 to buy South Sea bonds. Nathaniel obviously wished to be in London himself: "I find it a sad thing to be so far removed from the scene of action." He also asked Hester to send her further opinion and advice as well as letting him know what others were inclined to do in the market.[19] Nathaniel was a mere bystander, but Hester Pinney was right in the midst of the hurly burly of the South Sea Bubble.

Nathaniel continued to pester Hester for help in investing in South Sea stock. At an unspecified date in 1720 (sometime in the Fall based on the stock price) Nathaniel asked Hester "if you will be so kind to me now as to buy for me which may be done by a broker two stocks capital in the South Sea company which I am informed by those who read the news are fallen to 300li." He goes on to say the company made him pay £800 for the same amount of stock before the bubble burst, "which shows my loss... to be near 20,000 pounds, a loss sufficient not only to give and aggravate the gravel [kidney stones]" but to kill a man. He also told Hester that his orders were not subscribed with those of her own and sister Scrimshere (for whom Hester was acting as an agent). And he says his "ruin" is that the same was not done for him as was for her and his sister. It is not clear who he is blaming—the company? A broker? Hester? In any case, he "begs" her to buy the shares for him. It seems Hester did so because in August 1721 she collected dividends for both herself and Nathaniel.[20]

We can assess Hester Pinney's performance as a broker by the Pinneys' fortunes in South Sea stock. While Nathaniel missed out on any major profits in South Sea stock, he also avoided major losses. It is not clear how Hester Pinney fared, but she certainly was not ruined. She did mention a small

---

[18] UB, DM 58, Pinney Papers, Box 3, folder II.
[19] UB, DM 58, Pinney Papers, Box 3, folder II.
[20] UB, DM 58, Pinney Papers, Box 3, folder II.

"injury" or loss having to do with the lottery, but Nathaniel dismissed this as nothing compared to his "great losses" and said he was glad that her fortune continued to increase. So it seems Hester was savvy enough to avoid being one of the major losers in the Bubble.

One way Hester Pinney may have protected herself was by diversifying her holdings. She put her capital into a number of different investments, including government loans, company shares, and lottery annuities. Her papers provide a sense of her portfolio. As already stated, around the turn of the eighteenth century she invested in Briscoe's land bank and an Exchequer annuity.[21] In the first decade of the 1700s Hester held stock in the East India Company and she began to put capital into the Bank of England, buying £200 of stock.[22] (See Figure 7.1.) Hester continued investing in Bank of England stock, purchasing a total of £300 in shares at three separate times between June 1714 and November 1715. In 1718 she started to invest in government debt by putting money in the 5% government annuities. She subscribed a total of £50 15s. in the "lottery Annuities" in her own name. This same year she also invested the larger sum of £294 15s. for a £300 share in the 4% Annuities. Hester's lottery tickets came up blanks, but she recorded the numbers and the £8 8s. annuity she would receive on each of these two tickets.[23] In April 1719 it was this annuity that was transferred into the capital stock of the South Sea Company in that company's takeover of the national debt.

We can analyze Hester Pinney's stock portfolio and how it evolved, because she kept accounts of her investments over a fifty-year period. In the 1690s Hester invested her money in private loans to individuals. She made loans to at least nine different men and women and advanced an overall sum of £2,063 1s. 6d.[24] By the first decade of the 1700s Hester's money was now lodged in public investments. In addition to the 1704 annuity, she was receiving quarterly payments from the Exchequer and the East India Company. By 1719 Hester was receiving higher quarterly payments from the East India Company, meaning she had invested more money at some point.[25] And by the later 1710s Hester had begun investing in another public company, the South Sea Company. Over the years Pinney moved her capital from private to public securities and increased her investing in both range of options and amount of capital invested.

In the 1720s Hester Pinney focused much of her investing in South Sea stock. As early as 1715 she had paid some £243 8s. 9d. for £250 of South Sea stock, when it was still trading below par. A year later, she bought another £200.

---

[21] UB, DM 58, Pinney Papers, Box 2, folder III.
[22] UB, DM 58, Pinney Papers, Box 2, folder IV.
[23] UB, DM 58, Pinney Papers, Box 2, folder IV.
[24] UB, DM 58, Pinney Papers, Box 2, folder III.
[25] UB, DM 58, Pinney Papers, Box 2, folder III.

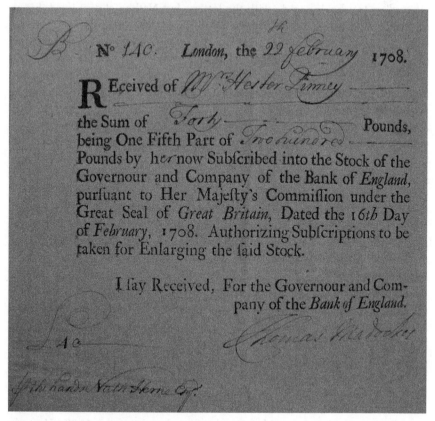

Figure 7.1. Bank Stock certificate (1708).

With the permission of the Pinney Archive, held in the University of Bristol Library Special Collections. DM58/Folder IV/Miscellaneous receipts to Hester Pinney.

As stated above, it is not exactly clear what happened to Hester's investment in the Bubble year of 1720, but a few years later, Hester was back to buying South Sea stock for herself and as a financial agent for George Booth. Between 1723 and 1726 she bought shares in the South Sea Company at seven separate times, usually in £500 or £1,000 share increments. By July 1726 she held £7,170 worth of stock in the company (including £3,000 which she may have inherited from Booth). These stock investments were a huge jump from the modest amounts of £200 and £300 she had invested in the 1710s. And we know this was Hester's own stock, since she carefully recorded whether she was buying stock for herself or for others.[26]

---

[26] UB, DM 58, Pinney Papers, Box 2, folder IV. George Booth made his will in 1717 and named Hester Pinney as his sole executrix. Booth added a codicil March 31, 1726 and Pinney proved his will in July 1726, so he died sometime in spring of that year.

In the 1720s and 1730s Pinney was also investing her capital in South Sea Annuities and in Bank of England stock. Between 1728 and 1738 Hester usually purchased modest amounts (£33, £100, or £150 at a time) of South Sea Annuities. In March 1731, however, she did buy a sizable £1,000 share and in 1737 made another major purchase of £722 19s. 7d. In 1738 Nathaniel records buying a bit more "for sister" to "make up her sum of £7,050 in the New Annuities."[27] Hester Pinney was also regularly investing in the Bank of England. Between 1720 and 1733 she bought shares at seven separate times. In 1720 she purchased £150 stock, five years later she bought another £800, and after another lapse of six years she purchased another £400 in 1731. The following year Hester made her largest purchases of Bank stock; £700 and £500, respectively. In 1733 she bought another £500 in stock, making her total investment in Bank of England shares an impressive £3,350.[28]

As Table 7.1. shows, Hester Pinney invested her money in a variety of public investments, at least nine in all. Research by Carlos, Fletcher, and Neal has shown that women (and men) usually only invested in one or two stocks. They found that in the 1690s, 87.4 percent of men and 97.5 percent of women owned only one stock. Out of a sample of 708 female shareholders in the Bank of England, the East India, Royal African, Hudson's Bay, South Sea companies, and the Million Bank, 691 held one stock, sixteen held two, and only one person held three. The percentage of women who held more than one stock did increase over time. By the years 1719–23 out of a sample of 6,394 female shareholders, 5,663 held one stock. This was a drop from 97.5 percent in the 1690s to 88.57 percent three decades later. And more women held multiple investments, with 601 owning two stocks, 120 holding three, and ten holding four.[29]

Table 7.1. Investment Portfolio of Hester Pinney, 1701–38

Type of Investment	Year Investment made or recorded	Total Amount Invested
Briscoe Land Bank	1701	Half of £100
Exchequer Annuity	1705	£80 annuity
5% Government Annuities	1718	£50 15s. annuity
4% Government Annuity	1718	£300
East India Company Stock	1709–20s	£1,800–6,400 *
South Sea Company Stock	1719–38	£7,170
South Sea Company Annuities	1728–38	£7,050
Bank of England	1710–33	£3,350

Source: University of Bristol, DM 58, Pinney Papers. *These total holdings are extrapolated from quarterly dividends of £18–64.

[27] UB, DM 58, Pinney Papers, Box 2, folder IV.
[28] UB, DM 58, Pinney Papers, Box 2, folder IV.
[29] Ann Carlos, Erin Fletcher, and Larry Neal, "Share Portfolios in the early years of financial capitalism: London, 1690–1730," *Economic History Review* 68:2 (2015), 588, Tables 3 and 4, 590, Tables 6 and 7.

Pinney's stock portfolio, however, was much more diversified than Carlos et al.'s sample of women from either the 1690s or the 1720s. And she was not alone in holding multiple stocks. As we saw earlier in this chapter, Mariabella Eliot held ten different public stocks and securities. Most of the individual women discussed in this book put their capital into at least two or three different public investments, and it was common for them to hold as many as four or five public stocks and securities. It seems that examining different types of sources, in particular women's account books and financial papers rather than shareholder lists, better brings to light women's ownership of multiple stocks. Female public investors were much more diversified than we have thought up to now.

While diversification may have been one sign of Hester Pinney's financial acumen another was that she was also a financial agent for others. As we have seen, most of the men and women for whom she invested were related to her. But Hester Pinney also served as the secretary and financial agent for the Honorable George Booth, a man to whom she was not kin.

Hester Pinney was not the only woman to serve as a financial agent for a male to whom she was not related. As we saw in chapter 4 Mary Wortley Montagu invested in South Sea stock for a male friend. Ann Carlos and Larry Neal have also uncovered the widow Johanna Cock's financial brokering in the 1720s. After inheriting shares from her husband, Cock became an active broker and dealer in Bank of England stock during the South Sea Bubble years. In 1720, for instance, Johanna Cock was the thirteenth largest purchaser and the twenty-first largest seller of Bank shares out of more than 2,000 traders. She traded not only on her own account but for "a large number of other individuals," all of whom were men.[30]

Another woman who served as a financial agent for a man was Mrs. Sarah Beake of London whose name appeared in Benjamin Poole's accounts in March 1711. He recorded, "this day Mrs. Beake delivered my 6 annuity warrants to Mr. Windham at Mr. Dives office at ye Exchequer & I am to call for them in 3 weeks hence." Poole continued to employ Beake on his exchequer business for the next three years. He also recorded that she was with him when he left a copy of his will at his cousin Mary Lowther's house.[31] When Benjamin Poole died in 1714 his daughter Margaret took over the account books that recorded the family's public investments. Margaret Poole carefully recorded the profits from money invested in Exchequer bills, Bank of

[30] Ann Carlos and Larry Neal, "Women Investors in early capital markets, 1720–1725," *Financial History Review* 11:2 (2004): 198, 205–8.

[31] Henry E. Huntington Library (hereafter HEH), STBF, BOX 14 St vol. 445, no pagination. This volume is cataloged as Margaret Poole's Cash Book, 1708–1714. It was actually kept by her father Benjamin Poole until his death in January 1714.

England shares, and East India and South Sea Company stock. Although Margaret, an adult single woman, handled some of her own financial affairs, she continued to employ Sarah Beake on financial business. In January 1714 she paid Beake for "our expenses." In October 1715 Poole "cleared" accounts with Mrs. Beake and paid her a "commission" of £3 for her services (which included disposing of some plate worth £36). In 1714–15 Margaret Poole had Sarah Beake collect her dividends on East India and South Sea stock. She wrote to Mr. John Grigsby to pay her half year's dividend of £59 11s. on c. £1,300 in South Sea Stock to Mrs. Beake. She also wrote to Mr. Charles DuBois at East India House asking him to pay her dividend to Sarah Beake "whose receipt would be a sufficient discharge." Sarah Beake continued to serve as a financial agent for the Pooles into 1717 at least.[32]

Women such as Johanna Cock and Sarah Beake worked as financial agents for men, but Hester Pinney's position differed somewhat in that she also had a close personal (and it seems romantic) relationship with George Booth, the man for whom she did financial business. Hester Pinney's involvement with George Booth began in the late 1680s when she was employed on her brother Nathaniel's business and in contact with Nathaniel's attorneys, one of whom was Booth. In a letter from December 1690, Nathaniel asked Hester to use her "interest with Mr. Booth" in their financial affairs. What Nathaniel meant by "interest" is ambiguous.[33] He could be referring to the fact that Hester was in London and could meet with Booth, or perhaps Booth's affection for Hester was already apparent. At some point in the 1690s Hester went from dealing with Booth on her brother's business to becoming Booth's financial agent. In 1697 she even recorded loaning £100 to Mr. Booth...[34] In 1717 Booth appointed Hester Pinney his paid secretary—an uncommon position for a woman. Hester became his agent in many financial dealings.

Hester Pinney was not only Booth's financial partner, she was his life partner as well. Hester was the only one of her sisters not to marry. Although she remained single, she had a forty-year relationship with Booth. Pinney enjoyed the legal and financial freedoms of a feme sole, while also cohabitating with Booth after his wife's decease. And when Booth himself died he made Hester his executrix and primary heir. Hester Pinney experienced the financial security of a widow even though she had never married. For instance, a little before his death in 1726 Booth wrote out a warrant that allowed Hester to collect the dividends on £3,000 of his South Sea stock. Hester had just this amount of stock transferred into her name after Booth's death, so this seems to have been part of her inheritance. Booth also transferred real estate to Hester, including the manors of Monken Hadley and West Ham as well as some

---

[32] HEH, ST 445, Margaret Poole Cash book, 1714–1719, no pagination.

[33] UB, DM 58, Pinney Papers, Box 3, folder II.

[34] UB, DM 58, Pinney Papers, transcriptions of letters, Box 2, folder III.

houses in London.[35] Pinney spent a large amount of time in litigation over securing her titles to these properties. Her desire to establish her claim to the property may explain why she was eventually buried in the chancel of St Mary's church at the manor of Monken Hadley.[36]

The other male in Hester's life, her brother Nathaniel Pinney, died in 1724. After his decease Hester continued as the financial advisor to his widow, Naomi, and his son Azariah Pinney II. In March 1725 Naomi wrote to Hester thanking her for receiving £53 at East India House and the Exchequer, and asking her to keep it in her hands after deducting £10 for mourning for herself. Naomi Pinney wrote that she hoped "they made no scruple in paying it...but Mr. Edward wrote me sometime since he could not receive any more from South Sea until he had a new power of attorney from the Executors or Administrators...a precaution he says they are obliged to use to prevent fraud." Naomi notes that there is "a pretty deale of money in his hands which he received before the Christmas dividends became due...so there seems to be a necessity for me to Administer."[37] Naomi's lack of legal knowledge is striking for the wife of a prominent merchant. It appears she did not know that companies required up to date powers of attorney for agents to collect dividends and she was dragging her feet on administering her deceased husband's estate. (Surprisingly, Nathaniel Pinney, an established London merchant and investor for over forty years, had died without a will, hence the need to administer the estate.[38])

Six months later, Nathaniel's widow Naomi Pinney was getting her financial house in order, thanks to Hester Pinney who offered her advice and assistance from London. In October 1725 Naomi sent Hester the warrants to collect dividends from East India House and wrote "when you have the leisure and ability I hope you will go abroad and receive this as you have also that at the Exchequer." Naomi was contemplating buying leasehold land for her son Azariah but feared the price was too high and turned to her sister-in-law for guidance on where to invest. "I am in great perplexity about it and once more desire your advice" she says.[39] Naomi noted that with the next Christmas dividends she would have £500 in all and would have to borrow the rest to make up £1,000 (the sum she presumably wanted to invest in land). Naomi also admitted that she had not yet administered her husband's estate: "I have delayed it as long as I could, being unwilling to bear the trouble and expense of

[35] UB, DM 58, Pinney Papers, Box 2, folder XII.
[36] Sharpe, "Dealing with love," 224. It is surprising, but the Pinney family correspondence provides no inkling that Hester's affair hurt her reputation among kin or associates. Her sister Rachel engaged in an even more improper affair with the husband of her deceased sister (a relationship within prohibited degrees), so perhaps Hester's behavior was less of a concern.
[37] UB, DM 58, Pinney Papers, Box 2, folder XI; Box 3, folder II.
[38] UB, DM 58, Pinney Papers, Box 3, folder II.
[39] UB, DM 58, Pinney Papers, Box 2, folder XI.

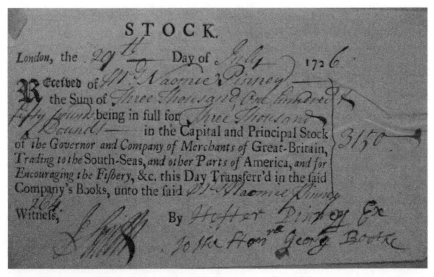

Figure 7.2. South Sea Stock certificate (1726).

With the permission of the Pinney Archive, held in the University of Bristol Library Special Collections. DM58/Folder IV/Miscellaneous receipts to Hester Pinney.

a London journey." She may have been hinting that she wanted Hester to take on the administration. Naomi acknowledged that it had to be done soon, since without a correct power of attorney she had not received any monies from the South Sea Company for the last three years. By 1726, Naomi was thanking Hester for helping her and her son with the land purchase and enclosing orders to receive monies at both India House, and now finally, South Sea House. (See Figure 7.2.) She added: "I hope you will soon receive at both places." Thanks to Hester's assistance, the onerous financial work of the widowed Naomi was accomplished. She had finally administered her husband's estate, purchased land for her son, and started to put her investments in her own name.[40]

In 1727 Hester Pinney began to financially advise the next generation of Pinneys. Her nephew Azariah, who was about nineteen and engaged in his studies, began to write to his Aunt Hester about financial issues. He thanked her for continuing to receive their money at South Sea and India House and was "sorry you should run any hazard in keeping it by you, but hope now stocks are lower, you may have an opportunity of lodging it safer."[41] The Pinneys did not need to live off of the money generated by their stocks, instead they sought to reinvest it. Hester was performing the role of banker and financial manager for them, looking for places to advantageously put out their money. Between 1725 and 1732 Hester continued to receive Naomi

---

[40] UB, DM 58, Pinney Papers, Box 2, folder XI.
[41] UB, DM 58, Pinney Papers, Box 2, folder XI.

and Azariah's money in East India stock, South Sea annuities, and Exchequer annuities. They also drew money on Hester, using her as their banker.

In 1731 Azariah sent Hester their account, signed by his mother and asked her to sign, witness, and return it to him. Although now twenty-three, Azariah was not entirely confident in his accounting or his financial knowledge and he continually deferred to his aunt. He wrote that he hoped the account was right and "if you find any error please to return the papers and I will draw new ones." Azariah also mentioned a sum of £592 that his mother received quarterly, but the odd number "made the interest difficult to reckon... [so] I have put the full of interest of 600li for two years... but if you do not approve this method please to let me know..." And lastly, Azariah asked Hester a question about whether South Sea annuities could be renewed. In this exchange Azariah showed an inability to compute interest on an unrounded sum and a lack of knowledge about financial instruments.

In 1732 Azariah was again confused over the machinations of the South Sea Company and wrote to Aunt Hester for advice on what stock being "sunk" meant. He added, "I beg you will inform me of this matter in your next."[42] Five years later, in 1737, Azariah admitted he did not know the new interest rate on South Sea Annuities and asked Hester to inform him. Another letter explained his lack of knowledge and reliance on his Aunt: "because I do not take in the London papers so knew nothing of it till your last letter."[43] It was lucky for Azariah that he had an older, female relative who was experienced and competent in financial investments, for as the man of his family, Azariah Pinney was not. The correspondence between Hester Pinney and her nephew Azariah reveals a woman knowledgeable about investing in stocks and securities and a younger man looking to her for tutelage in financial matters.

Hester Pinney lived into her eighties. When she died in 1740 she left significant bequests to a number of kin, including three living siblings, a niece and a nephew, and various "cousins." Her largest legacies went to her sister and nephew in the forms of public stocks. Pinney left half of her stock in the Bank of England to her sister Rachel Scrimshire and all of her South Sea stock to her nephew Azariah Pinney. In total, Hester bequeathed over £11,100.[44] Pinney's economic life was an active one. She started as a lace trader on the Royal Exchange but became over time a major investor in public securities, a financial secretary, a broker for her relatives, and a financial advisor

---

[42] UB, DM 58, Pinney Papers, Box 2, folder XI.

[43] UB, DM 58, Pinney Papers, Box 2, folder XII.

[44] Hester Pinney's will, PCC 3 Mar 1739/40, as transcribed in *Notes and Queries for Somerset and Devon*, vols. 7–8 (1901), 345. She bequeathed over £1,100 in legacies plus her Bank stock and South Sea stock, which I estimate at over £12,000.

for her nephew. She managed over £11,000 of her own wealth and bequeathed it to the next generation of her family. Such financial agency is notable for a poorly-educated, single woman from a trading family in Dorset.

*   *   *

While Pinney exercised many types of financial agency she does not seem to have exercised another significant type of agency: the political influence female public investors earned via their capital. The remainder of this chapter will examine the political power of women investors in public funds. A number of women parlayed their capital into political power on an individual level. In chapter 4 we saw how Mary Barwell, who served as her brother's financial agent, was able to wield considerable control in East India Company politics. In her case, her power came not through her own capital but through her management of her brother's vast fortune. Another example of a woman who used her wealth and investments to gain a political voice was Eleanor Curzon. Eleanor Curzon was a formidable woman and investor who defies easy characterization. Investing thousands of pounds in various stocks and securities she twice put herself forward as a public and prominent litigant against fraudulent stock companies.

Eleanor Curzon was born in 1691, in the initial decade of the Financial Revolution. She was the daughter of Sir Nathaniel Curzon, Baronet, and his wife Sarah (née Penn). Like many of her siblings, Eleanor never married, so as a feme sole she was able to control her own finances. Several of her unmarried siblings predeceased her—her sisters Elizabeth and Sarah died in 1705 and 1718/19, and her brother Sir John Curzon in 1725—which led to Eleanor holding much of the family wealth. Her father also died in 1718/19 and left her an inheritance. Curzon set up an independent household in London, residing at the fashionable address of George St., Hanover Square. A picture of the young adult Eleanor hangs in the family estate at Kedleston Hall, Derbyshire (see Figure 7.3.). She is dressed in a sumptuous blue fabric and seated at a desk with a small book in her hand. She appears plain and tall and stares directly at the viewer, a slight smile playing on her lips.[45] Perhaps Curzon is enjoying a small chuckle, foreshadowing the havoc she will cause for one of the biggest companies of Britain's Financial Revolution.

In her adulthood, Eleanor Curzon's family reckoned she was an effective financial agent. Many of them named her to execute their estates. For instance, Eleanor was the executrix of her mother's will in 1727/28 and the administrator of her brother William Curzon's estate in 1749. Her friend and fellow investor, Lady Anna Elianora Shirley, also made "Mrs. Elinor Curzon" her

---

[45] National Trust Collections <www.nationaltrustcollections.org.uk/object/108772> (accessed Jan. 30, 2014). The possible date given for the portrait is 1703. This is unlikely since Eleanor would have been twelve years old and the portrait is clearly of an adult woman. More likely would be 1713 when Eleanor would have been twenty-one or twenty-two and of marriageable age.

Figure 7.3. Eleanor Curzon by Michael Dahl (reputed 1703).
CMS_108772(2) Collections–Public © National Trust / Andrew Patterson.

executrix, leaving her a diamond ring in thanks. But since Curzon and Shirley died within six months of each other, it is not clear if Curzon lived to fulfill the office. As well as being close friends, Curzon and Shirley also were involved in investing together. Shirley was a major investor like Curzon; she made gains of up to £7,000 on Royal African stock alone in 1720. And in the 1730s she had holdings in the York Buildings Company along with Curzon.[46]

Eleanor Curzon was a prominent investor in a number of public stocks and securities. A check of the subscriber lists from various public investments reveals that she held £3,500 stock in the Million Bank in 1732, £2,000 East India stock in 1747, and £2,000 Bank of England stock in the 1740s. And from other records we know she held stock in the South Sea and the York Buildings companies. *A Master-Key to the Rich Ladies Treasury*, a catalogue of London's rich single and widowed women published in 1742, estimated Eleanor Curzon's

---

[46] She was the daughter of Robert Shirley 1st Earl Ferrars and died May 1754. Ann M. Carlos, Karen Maguire, and Larry Neal, "Financial Acumen, Women Speculators, and the Royal African Company during the South Sea Bubble," *Accounting, Business, & Financial History* 16:2 (July 2006), 220, 237, 239; *A Report from the Committee to whom the petition of [the creditors and subscribers of] York Buildings . . . was referred* (L, 1735), 13. *Eighteenth Century Collections Online* (hereafter ECCO) <www.galegroup.com> (accessed May 2013).

worth at £20,000.[47] This estimate seems about right, since Curzon bequeathed over £15,000 when she died twelve years later.

Eleanor Curzon's involvement in the politics of joint-stock investment began in 1720, when she was about thirty. She, like so many others, had invested in South Sea stock in the frenzied months before the Bubble. But unlike most, her investment became the basis for a series of court cases. In the midst of South Sea excitement, Curzon bought £1,000 of stock in the third subscription. She paid down £100 for her subscription but the clerk at South Sea House noted her name incorrectly. One can see how such a mistake might have been possible in the bustle of South Sea mania in late spring 1720. It seems Eleanor Curzon's name appeared on a subscriber list in June 1720, but in the ledger of over 100,000 proprietors her name "was transcribed by mistake as Edward Curzon." This small mistake of gender and name would allow Curzon to exploit a legal loophole and manage what no other South Sea investor was able to do: regain her original money.

After the Bubble burst the South Sea Company did not have enough money to pay back investors. Instead they offered £100 of stock in the company for every £400 each investor had paid in. Not only did the burned shareholders receive only one fourth of what they had invested, but they received it in a form that was no longer a desirable investment. Eleanor Curzon "coming amongst other proprietors of the said subscription to claim her stock, for the £1,000 by her paid in" found only Edward Curzon listed and "imagining that the original lists of subscribers were either destroyed or not to be found" and that it would be difficult to prove her a subscriber, "she refused to accept such stock."[48] Instead, she brought an action against the South Sea Company on the plea side of the Court of Exchequer to recover her original £1,000 investment. Against considerable odds she won and "obtained judgment for recovering the sum together with costs of suit." The South Sea Company counter-sued Curzon, saying she should have to abide by the Act to restore public credit like everyone else, but in 1722 the company lost again. They appealed the decision once more, but the Company's appeal was dismissed. Eleanor Curzon had taken on the South Sea Company and won, through a legal technicality for sure, but her dogged pursuit of her case stands at odds with the many men and women who fatalistically accepted their losses.

It is perhaps not a surprise then, that in the 1730s we see Eleanor Curzon once again embroiled in company politics. Curzon, now in her forties, got involved in the shareholder elections of the York Buildings Company. A report detailing the holders of York Buildings stock as of January 18, 1733–4 revealed that the Governor of the Company, Solomon Ashley, held

---

[47] *A Master-key to the Rich Ladies Treasury, or the Widower and Batchelor Directory* ... by a younger brother (L, 1742), 19. ECCO (accessed May 2013).

[48] "The South-Sea Company—Appellants vs. Eleanor Curzon Respondent 11 Mar 1722" in *The English Reports: House of Lords (1677–1865)*, vol. 4, 1092–4. Google books (accessed October 2013).

over £44,000 in stock. This stock was not held in his own name but under the names of three men and one woman, Eleanor Curzon. She held over one fourth of Ashley's stock, or £11,175 3s.[49] Other women also held various amounts of stock in trust or had stock transferred over to them, so that as "friends and supporters of the Direction" they could cast votes in the General Court meetings and help control elections.

Curzon was not alone in exercising the right to vote in company elections. Proof of women's voting rights comes from various sorts of corporation documents. Lists of subscribers or shareholders in company stock regularly designated which individuals were eligible to vote or to serve as officers in a corporation. These qualifications were designated in the lists by a notation next to a subscriber's name, usually a star or an asterisk. The number of asterisks next to a shareholder's name indicated their eligibility to either vote in company elections or serve as a company Director. Voting qualifications were based on how much stock a person held. Commonly, £500 entitled an investor to vote for the Directors of the Company at annual General Court meetings. What is significant is that designations of voting rights and office holding were made without reference to gender. For instance, *A List of all the Adventurers in the Mine-Adventure* (1700) noted at the outset that "Those marked *** are qualified by their Shares to be Elected of the Select Committee, And those marked ** are qualified to Vote in a Grand Committee; and those marked * are qualified to Vote in a General Meeting: And no Person has more then [sic] one Vote."[50] Both men and women adventurers appeared in the list with no asterisk next to their name or one asterisk; while forty-three out of 731 total adventurers had two asterisks next to their name. These included six women: four women with the title Mrs. and two ladies. Another four women had three asterisks next to their names: Mrs. Elizabeth Childers, Mrs. Dorothy James, the Honourable Philippa Mohun, and Mrs. Mary White. These women were not only eligible to vote but also to be elected to the Select Committee. While these numbers are small, they indicate that women were not excluded by their gender from voting in company elections or holding company offices.

The Mine Adventurers Company was not unique in including female shareholders among those eligible to vote. The Bank of England, East India Company, and South Sea Company all did the same. In June 1712 the latter corporation published a list of the names of those "Who are qualified to Vote at the ensuing Election for Governor, Sub-Governor, and Deputy-Governor" and Directors. Shareholders had between one and four votes depending upon how much stock they held.[51] Those with one asterisk next to their name had

---

[49] *A Report from the Committee to whom the petition of [the creditors and subscribers of] York Buildings...*

[50] *A List of all the Adventurers in the Mine-Adventure. May the 1st, 1700* (L, 1700). ECCO (accessed October 2013).

[51] *A List of the Names of the Corporation of the Governor and Company of Merchants of Great Britain Trading to the South Seas...* (L, 1712). ECCO (accessed October 2013).

one vote, those with two asterisks had two votes and were eligible to serve as Directors, those with three asterisks had three votes and were eligible to serve as Governors, as were those with four asterisks who also had four votes. A total of eighty-eight women appeared as shareholders. Most of them (seventy-three) had one asterisk next to their name, which allowed them to vote. Three women had four asterisks, five women had three asterisks, and seven women had two asterisks next to their names. These women were eligible to hold offices in the South Sea Company. The list also included an excerpt from the company by-laws concerning elections. The by-laws used gender inclusive language, referring to shareholders, voters, and even prospective Directors as "persons." The by-laws also mentioned votes that "he, she, or they" might be entitled to cast.[52] The South Sea Company was the most explicit of all the corporations that women's capital equaled a political voice.

While women investors were eligible to vote in company elections, what women investors did in practice is more difficult to discern. Susan Staves has also noted that women could theoretically attend and vote in General Court meetings of various corporations, but was not able to find much evidence of women doing so.[53] Huw Bowen's work on the General Court meetings of the East India Company shows that the Court met only for the mandated minimum of five times a year, and excited little interest before 1760 (when the company's politics became more turbulent). And for the two decades after this stockholder attendance was still generally low. Between 1766 and 1773 "the available evidence points to an average attendance of... about eight to ten per cent of those entitled to attend," meaning that most shareholders did not attend, no matter what their gender. But a contemporary noted the diversity of General Court attendees, including "old women of both sexes."[54] Such a quote simultaneously tells us that women did attend General Court, or shareholder, meetings at the same time it shows a pejorative attitude toward some of the male voters. These old women of the male sex may have been derided for being overly cautious or concerned when voting in company matters.

More direct proof of women voting in shareholder elections comes from the Minutes of the East India Company before 1750. In March 1677, the General Court minutes of the East India Company noted that questions had arisen regarding the procedure for electing the Governor and officers of the company. "The Counsel opine that the elections must be made by adventurers who are present and not by votes sent in, that widows interested in the joint stock

---

[52] *A List of the Names of the Corporation of the Governor and Company of Merchants of Great Britain Trading to the South Seas...* (L, 1712). ECCO (accessed October 2013).

[53] Susan Staves, "Investments, votes, and 'bribes': women as shareholders in the chartered national companies," in Hilda Smith, ed., *Women Writers and the early modern British Political Tradition* (Cambridge: Cambridge University Press, 1998), 259–78.

[54] Huw V. Bowen, "The 'Little Parliament': The General Court of the East India Company, 1750–1784," *The Historical Journal* 34:4 (Dec. 1991), 859–60, 863. Patrick Tuck, ed., *The East India Company, 1784–1834*, vol. 6 (New York: Routledge, 1998), 2.

may be allowed to bring in their votes, but not minors."[55] This seems to indicate that widows who inherited stock had a vote but could also vote by proxy without being present. The Minutes of a meeting in 1702 record "That in all elections of managers and in all future elections no vote of any person shall be received until he or she shall have taken the following oath, vizt. I. A.B. doe swear that I have five hundred pounds in the capital fund of the new united stock in my own name and right."[56] The minutes explicitly mention men and women voting. A half century later, a 1749 newspaper advertisement addressed itself "To the Proprietors of East-India Stock." It read "Gentlemen and Ladies, Tomorrow is appointed for taking your Approbation, by Way of Ballot, to a Scheme proposed to you by your Directors for discharging of your Bond Debt" in the form of lowering the rate of interest on shares.[57] This announcement specifically included female proprietors amongst those who would be voting. It also shows that the Court of Directors was wooing women's votes.

It was this same voting function that Eleanor Curzon performed in the York Buildings Company elections. Her financial agency and active involvement in the companies in which she invested ensured a level of wealth throughout her later years. Curzon died in 1754 when she was in her mid-sixties and was buried near her parents at Kedleston. In her will, she left over £15,480 to relatives including her sister, her nephew, his children, and several cousins. She also named a number of female and male friends to whom she bequeathed £100 legacies. She left money to the poor in all three parishes to which she had some attachment, although the sums were modest, £20 or £30 each. And she bequeathed the residue of her estate to her brother Sir Nathaniel Curzon and his son Assheton Curzon, and made them her joint executors. Nathaniel got another present in that she set aside £1,000 to augment the land of the family estate at Kedleston. This single woman's judicious investing in stocks aided her family's landed patrimony.[58]

Her nephew Assheton Curzon remembered Eleanor at her mother's family seat at Penn church in Buckinghamshire. He put up a memorial featuring her profile in relief, a white marble urn, and the following words:

This Monument was placed here An. Dom. 1765, to the Memory of Mrs. Elenor Curzon, by her dutiful and affectionate Nephew Assheton Curzon. She was Daughter of Sr Nathaniel Curzon, Bart. of Kedleston, and Sarah his Wife, who

[55] Ethel Bruce Sainsbury, *A Calendar of the Court Minutes of the East India Company 1677–79* (Oxford: Clarendon Press, 1938), 25.

[56] The British Library, India Office Records, B/255 General Court Minutes 1702–1734, 9.

[57] *Whitehall Evening Post or London Intelligencer*, issue 607, December 30, 1749. *17th and 18th Century Burney Collection Newspapers* <www.galegroup.com> (accessed October 2007).

[58] The National Archives, PROB 11/812/248, will of Elenor Curzon, spinster, St. George, Hanover Square, 10 Dec. 1754.

was a Penn, born the 25th of Oct 1691; and buryed in Kedleston Church, near her Parents, the 15th of Dec. 1754.

This Lady was a great example of Piety, had a constant attention to the Poor; steady in Friendship to those with whom she was most nearly connected; and of an affable behavior to all her acquaintance. These, and many other virtues of which she was possessed, must make all who cast their eye on this stone reflect upon her memory with reverence and regard.[59]

It is notable that her nephew and heir made no mention of Eleanor Curzon's formidable legal, financial, or political skills, nor to the great wealth she possessed in financial investments. Although her investing set Assheton up in life, he preferred to note his aunt's piety, charity, and virtue. These were, of course, much more ideal feminine qualities in the eighteenth century. Curzon's epitaph, however, elided some important parts of her character. Not every woman would have been comfortable suing the South Sea Company and taking the case as far as the House of Lords. Perhaps her nephew did hint at this aspect of her character, for Eleanor Curzon's epitaph does not contain the word "modest."

Eleanor Curzon's story is somewhat remarkable, but the political agency she exercised due to her financial investments was not. In some ways Curzon's actions are analogous to what Margaret Hunt has uncovered for women who held and traded in another type of financial instrument: the pay tickets that the British navy and East India Company issued to seamen.[60] Hunt has found that it was common for sailors to give their wives (or sometimes mothers and sisters) power of attorney, allowing these women to exercise an unprecedented level of legal authority under coverture. One of the "powers" these women obtained was the ability to collect their husband's pay from the ship owner or Navy. A sailor's pay was made through a "pay ticket"—a sort of promissory note that guaranteed payment at a future date. Women with power of attorney and in possession of a pay ticket could collect their sailor husband's pay. These pay tickets began to circulate themselves as a form of currency and Hunt has found that some women became brokers and traders of these pay tickets. For instance, in the 1700s Margaret Stewart was known as "a Solicitrix for Seamen in helping them to sell their Tickets" and to receive their pay. Stewart was well known at the Navy Office where she "had good interest" or connections. Hunt notes that although "we are accustomed to thinking of the job of solicitor as a male monopoly" there is no sense from the records that it was odd for a woman to work as a financial agent for seamen and their families.[61]

[59] George Lipscomb, *The history and antiquities of the county of Buckingham* (1847), vol. 3, 289.
[60] Margaret Hunt, "Women and the fiscal-imperial state in the late seventeenth and early eighteenth centuries," in Kathleen Wilson, ed., *A new imperial history: culture, identity, and modernity in Britain and the Empire, 1660–1840* (Cambridge: Cambridge University Press, 2004), 29–47.
[61] Hunt, "Women and the fiscal-imperial state," 36–7.

In addition to these brokers, navy wives and widows exercised financial agency from the 1690s on by directly lobbying Parliament for their husbands' pay. These women forged a direct relationship with the fiscal-military state through their control over and trade of pay tickets. Their management of these financial instruments directly led to their claim of a political voice, whether in petitioning the Navy board or lobbying Parliament. As with Eleanor Curzon, the financial activities of women were one avenue to political agency.

7.2. FINANCIAL PATRIOTISM

So far we have been looking at individual female investors and how their capital allowed them to exercise a level of public and political power. Female creditors also exercised agency as a group or in the aggregate. One of the primary ways they did so was to the benefit of the fiscal-military state. Women who invested their capital in joint-stock companies, the Bank of England, and the government directly influenced the economic, political, and military success of these British institutions. As we have seen, women made up between 15 and 30 percent, and averaged a quarter, of investors in government funds.[62] If they had chosen not to lend their capital to fund the national debt the government would have had significantly less money with which to wage war, establish colonies, and engage in global trade. Whether intentional or not, female investors were functionally "financial patriots." Some women, such as Eleanor Curzon, Mary Barwell, and of course, Sarah, Duchess of Marlborough, were cognizant of the political power they wielded due to their capital. Others, like Hester Pinney, were perhaps not. But this does not mean that we should ignore the functional "financial patriotism" of female public investors during the Financial Revolution.

My evocation of "financial patriotism" to describe the actions of female public investors depends on Linda Colley's assertion that "an active commitment to nation was often intimately bound up with an element of self-interest."[63] By investing in their country and its commercial ventures, women not only aided their own finances, they also contributed to the commercial and financial success of the nation. The Financial Revolution allowed women a means to participate in and literally support the British state, as well as its foreign wars, colonial endeavors, and imperial pretensions. The adaptability, innovation, and risk bearing inherent in Englishwomen's adoption of new forms of property benefited both them and the nation.

---

[62] See Table 5.1. in chapter 5.

[63] Linda Colley, *Britons: Forging the Nation 1707–1837* (New Haven, CT: Yale University Press, 1992), 55.

Some women who loaned money to the government were aware of and proud of their patriotic role in doing so. Sarah Churchill, for example, was able to translate her management of the Marlborough family trust into political influence. The Duchess of Marlborough, who was the single largest creditor to the British state in the 1730s, complained that her care for her country went unappreciated. The Duchess claimed, "I lent such sums to the government as reduced the interest from six per cent to four per cent; thinking it would have had a good effect for the security of the nation; and at that time he [Sir Robert Walpole, her political nemesis] could not have compassed such sums without me." She complained that instead of showing any appreciation for her loan, Walpole had recently informed her "that he will take no more of the [Marlborough] trust-money," in other words he did not want her money even if the government was seeking out funds.[64] Walpole's refusal can be read as a tacit admission of the clout the Duchess gained via her funding of the national debt. Sarah Churchill, however, painted herself in a positive light by equating her loans to the government with patriotism. In 1737 she also noted her interest in serving her country, saying "and I should be as willing to give my vote for anything that concerned the good of the nation as any man living." Even though Churchill did not have a literal vote, perhaps she viewed her capital as a vote of another sort.

Contemporaries sometimes recognized and lauded the patriotic contribution of those who loaned their capital to the nation in its time of need. Anne Murphy says that, "some contemporary commentators argued that investment in the public funds was a patriotic duty." For instance, the periodical the *Athenian Mercury* told its readership that the Million Adventure of 1694 was "necessary for the defence of the nation." When Samuel Jeake bought his tickets in the Million Adventure he too noted it was "to support the government in the War against France."[65] Moreover, such patriotism was not limited to men. For example, in 1702 when he took Ann Crisp's loan of £100 to the Exchequer, Peter Pell noted the money would be used "towards carrying on a vigorous war against France."[66] This was not a sum given to the nation for some vague purpose, but for national defense. And although a woman, Ann Crisp could wage war against the national enemy if not in person then through her financial contribution.

Similar attention to women who loaned money to the nation can be found in the 1720 pamphlet entitled *The Case of the Annuitants Stated And Compar'd with other Creditors of the Government.* Its author sympathized with

[64] *Private Correspondence of Sarah, Duchess of Marlborough [with sketches and observations of her]* 2d ed., 2 vols. (London, 1838; reprint New York: Kraus, 1972), vol. II, 179.

[65] As quoted in Anne L. Murphy, "Dealing with Uncertainty: Managing Personal Investment in the Early English National Debt," *History* 91:302 (2006), 208–9.

[66] HEH, Herbert Papers, Box 2, Folder HE 29.

those who had lost their money in the South Sea Bubble and noted especially those public creditors who had been cajoled into exchanging their government annuities into South Sea stock and annuities whose value crashed in the Bubble. These so-called Annuitants for ninety-nine years—20 percent of whom were women—had loaned their money to the government during the wartime years of 1705–7. As this author pointed out, these creditors deserved bailing out because they had "advanced their money to the Government" directly to aid in fighting its enemies. Moreover, these public investors could have loaned their money to the Bank of England or to the East India Company at the favorable rate of 8 percent interest. But instead they chose to aid the nation and got "little more than 6 per cent per Ann[um]" in return for their money. The author argued that these public creditors deserved continued payment "for the Service they did, in lending their money in its greatest Exigencies, upon easier terms than had been obtained from any others."[67] In other words, the annuitants (many of whom were widows, single women, and orphans) had foregone profit in service to the nation.

Contemporaries also recognized the financial patriotism of investing in domestic rather than foreign stocks. John Law's Mississippi scheme, set up to aid the French government's debt, drew many investors across the channel.[68] But when England formed the South Sea Company it was seen as a domestic rival to Law's company. Appeals were made to investors to stop their support of the age-old enemy France and instead invest in British stocks. For example, Francis Tolson's "A Poem on his Majesty's Passing the South-Sea Bill" evoked this sense of financial patriotism.[69] Tolson lauded the South Sea Company that would "revive BRITANNIA's Fame, And His [King George] who all her Wealth restores..." Tolson reminded British readers that when they invested in the Mississippi scheme they helped France and hurt Britain. "If FRANCE is still in Pomp array'd, And shall we poorly give her Aid... To mount her Sickly Glories higher, 'Till we consume our selves in the exotick Fire?" He then exhorted his readers: "For Shame ye BRITONS Home return!" Tolson told his readers to return their money from France. "No more let Mississippi be, the darling Idol of Mankind: BRITAIN can now boast her SOUTH-SEA, As nobly form'd, as well design'd." Tolson's poem ended with the lines: "Nobly resolve, and boldly dare, /Be PATRIOTS all, and all Unite!" Significantly, Tolson explicitly associated investment in the domestic South Sea Company with patriotism.

[67] HEH, Rare Book 57014, Anonymous, *The Case of the Annuitants Stated, And Compar'd with other Creditors of the Government* (L, 1720).

[68] For a recent examination of John Law and the Mississippi Bubble, see Larry Neal, *I am not Master of Events: The Speculations of John Law and Lord Londonderry in the Mississippi and South Sea Bubbles* (New Haven, CT: Yale University Press, 2012).

[69] Francis Tolson, "A Poem on his Majesty's Passing the South-Sea Bill" (L, 1720). ECCO (accessed October 2013).

Whether intentional or functional, recognized by contemporaries or forgotten, female public investors performed an important role. Through their investing they helped not only themselves but also the British nation that was dependent on the money of private citizens, both male and female, for funds. As one contemporary noted, investors in government annuities helped accomplish "the greatest events in the glory, welfare, and preservation of these realms."[70] The financial contributions of female public investors enabled Britain's rise to global dominance in the eighteenth century. Of course, the flip side of this is that women investors were directly implicated in colonial power, imperial wars, and the transatlantic slave trade. Did women who invested their money in South Sea Annuities or Royal African Company stock stop and think about the slave trade that their funds facilitated? I have not been able to find any examples of female shareholders expressing any qualms over their investments. But from our perspective this does not excuse these women of course. If we are to recognize women as financial capitalists then we must recognize their financial agency in both its positive and negative forms. During the Financial Revolution British women adapted to, benefited from, and encouraged capitalism. As such we need to restore these women to their integral agency in the narrative of British financial capitalism.

---

[70] Thomas Mortimer, *Every Man his own Broker*, 7th ed. (London, 1769), 155–6. As quoted in Hancock, "Domestic Bubbling: 18th-Century London Merchants and Individual Investment in the Funds," *Economic History Review* 47:4 (1994), 679–702.

8

Conclusion

Examining female public investors during the Financial Revolution reveals that women were much more involved in the world of early finance than we have realized. Literate and urban women, women of the middling sort, and gentlewomen were comfortable with simple arithmetic, keeping accounts, and calculating rates of interest. They not only kept accounts for themselves, but they did so for others. The skill set that we have long known early modern women possessed so that they could help out in the family trade, run the household, or in the case of genteel and elite women, help manage the estate, positioned them to take part in the changing financial world of the late seventeenth and early eighteenth centuries.

Women who were in need of an income stream, whether due to singleness, widowhood, or as we have seen in the cases of Elizabeth Freke and Martha Hutchins, a bankrupt or ne'er-do-well spouse, could now turn to the market in stocks and securities for a steady rate of return. Private moneylending had long been an option for femes soles with capital on hand who either were not able to engage in trade or felt it would lower their status to do so. Extending credit also was something women could do well into their old age, as opposed to more physical labor. The Financial Revolution increased the opportunities for lending and increased the demand for the capital of private individuals. Women as much as, or maybe even more than, men, were eager to invest in public companies and government funds.

This book has brought to light some of the reasons women were attracted to these new financial opportunities. Women preferred these new credit opportunities for their decent rates of interest, their relative security, their reliability of payment, and for their easy liquidity. Collecting quarterly dividends or interest payments from a corporation or the Exchequer turned out to be much more regularized and reliable than trying to get rents, interest payments, or annuities out of relatives and private individuals. As we saw in the case of Agnes Herbert, female lenders found that private individuals had a tendency to put off their creditors, impose on their good will, make excuses, or at the very least pay late. Companies, however, were much more reliable. The anonymity of the financial relationship between shareholder and company could literally pay off in this respect. This may well have been one of the primary reasons that women adapted and adopted early to the Financial Revolution. Women found advantages to dealing with impersonal companies, rather than with family members or unrelated individuals.

Women also embraced the new opportunities of the Financial Revolution for other reasons. Lotteries, which were popular with both men and women, were fun and exciting for all. They seem to have functioned as a "gateway" investment for new public investors. With the advent of the State lottery, fun came to be coupled with a solid investment. And through lottery brokers who divided tickets into shares, even laboring women could invest. While contemporaries may have made fun of women investors, typifying them as spinsters or widows looking for a dowry and a husband, in the end female adventurers may have had the last laugh. The State lottery enabled women to invest and gain a modest income stream. As we saw, this was particularly useful for older, unmarried women. They made government funds and annuities a key part of their retirement planning. Government investments such as Lottery Annuities, and by the mid-eighteenth century, Consols, provided a much needed safe and secure place for unmarried women to lodge their money in their elder years.

By focusing so much on the blue chip stocks, or the big three—the East India Company, South Sea Company, and Bank of England—of the Financial Revolution period we have ignored the other companies, not to mention the government fund options listed in the stock price columns of London's eighteenth-century newspapers. And interestingly, the percentage of female subscribers and shareholders were higher in these latter investment options. By focusing on the full range of public investment options made available by the Financial Revolution, women's participation becomes even clearer. Focusing on a wider range of public investments also reveals that individuals from a wide social spectrum invested in public stocks and securities. Women who invested in the State lotteries and government funds came from a wider swath of society than the aristocratic women investors in the Royal African Company, for instance. Female creditors of the government were primarily made up of women from the ranks of the urban classes, middling sort, and gentry, but even some lower-status women such as servants and laborers.

The significant role that Englishwomen exercised as financial agents for their families is one of the biggest findings to leap off of these pages. We know that early modern women were household managers, budgeters, and consumers, as well as partners in trade and business with their spouses. They extended the skills they exercised in these roles to the public world of finance and investing. Wives sometimes took on the role of family financial planner. As we saw in the case of Grisell Baillie, this was due to her superior skill in investing, something acknowledged by her husband. In the case of Sarah, Duchess of Marlborough it was both skill and a practical division of labor— her husband was often at the front and busy with military affairs—so the couple delegated investing to Sarah. What is perhaps more surprising is that wives under coverture held their own investments and chose their own stocks. Sometimes, as in the case of Cassandra, Duchess of Chandos, it was husbands who authorized and allowed separate stock portfolios, but in other cases it seems that wives invested in stocks without their spouses' full knowledge. The participation of femes coverts in the world of early financial capitalism was much more common than I expected at the outset of this project.

Less of a surprise is the active involvement of single and widowed women in public investing. But even here, the role these women played as financial agents for their kin, both male and female, is notable. Not only did spouses agree on who was the better financial planner and designate that role to them, but extended families often looked to a particular relative for financial advice and assistance. And this relative was commonly an older, single woman. Mary Barwell, Cassandra (Willoughby) Brydges, and Hester Pinney invested for sisters, brothers, and nephews. Their families depended on them for financial news from London, for stock tips and advice, and for doing the financial chores of collecting dividends and interest. But these women functioned as more than financial servants; Barwell managed tens of thousands of pounds for her brother and got involved in East India Company politics to serve his interest. Hester Pinney became the financial secretary and agent for a man to whom she was not related. The financial ability of these women was recognized by their family, friends, and business associates.

This book has provided a much clearer picture of the investing practices, strategies, and behaviors of individual women who put their capital into public investments. Many women became interested in public stocks and securities after inheriting them. Heiresses, however, were not passive investors. As we have seen, women like Gertrude Savile and Mariabella Eliot altered the stock portfolios they inherited, transferred stock into their own names, sold off stocks they received from others, and bought and traded new ones. Another of the surprises of this research has been finding out that most female public investors preferred to be diversified in their holdings. Rather than investing in just one public stock or security, those who did put capital into public investments usually chose at least three or four of them.

Another significant finding is that women did not necessarily eschew risk. Women like Barbara Savile speculated in various ventures, such as the Royal Fishery and the York Buildings companies. However, many of the early corporations that women eagerly put their money into turned out not to be the best investments. While scholarship has primarily focused on the South Sea Bubble, we have done so to the detriment of noticing how many other bubbles ensnared and affected average investors. Hundreds if not thousands of women invested and lost capital in the London Orphan's Fund, the Mine Adventurers Company, and the Charitable Corporation. The London Orphan's Fund affected between 1,000 and 2,000 London orphans, male and female; women comprised nearly 30 percent of shareholders in the Mine Adventurers Company, and one third of the investors in the Charitable Corporation. These were the highest rates of female ownership in a joint-stock company for the first fifty years of the Financial Revolution. These shareholders had to appeal to Parliament to bail them out, and in the end they only got shillings on the pound back on their original investments. The first half-century of the Financial Revolution was not for the faint of heart, and yet as we saw, women only increased as a proportion of public investors over this period.

Finally, this work restores women's role and agency to the history of early British financial capitalism. Between one fifth and one third of investors in joint-stock companies, the Bank of England, and the national debt were women. Women's capital was critical to the success of Britain's imperial wars, global trade, and colonial endeavors from the late seventeenth to the mid-eighteenth century (and beyond). Some women were cognizant of the political influence they wielded through their money. As we have seen, women like Mary Barwell and Eleanor Curzon were active in company politics, with political voice and vote. The role of women such as these in shareholder elections adds a new chapter to the history of women's voting rights. Women could vote for the leaders of global multi-national companies but they could not vote for their local MP. The political influence that came from financial holdings was clear to some women. Sarah, Duchess of Marlborough, for instance, was all too keenly aware of how her control of the Marlborough Family trust could alter the interest rates of the entire nation. But not all women investors may have been as intentional as Sarah Churchill when it came to aiding the nation through their money. Whether intentional or not, however, women investors, especially in the aggregate, were functionally "financial patriots." The capital of British women helped make London the capital of the world.

With this book we are also able to start charting a chronology of women's public investing across the early modern and modern eras. The research of Mark Freeman, Robin Pearson, and James Taylor shows low rates of female shareholding in British and Irish companies in the late eighteenth and early nineteenth centuries.[1] They found that during the 1780s to 1820s women comprised less than 15 percent of shareholders in companies. Female participation began to pick up again after 1830 with the proliferation of new investment options in provincial banks, canal, and then rail, companies. Freeman, Pearson, and Taylor posit that the late eighteenth and early nineteenth centuries may have

---

[1] Mark Freeman, Robin Pearson, and James Taylor, "Between Madam Bubble and Kitty Lorimer: Women Investors in British and Irish Stock Companies," in *Women and their Money 1700–1950: Essays on women and finance*, ed. Anne Laurence, Josephine Maltby, and Janette Rutterford (London: Routledge, 2009), 95–114.

been a low point for women's public investing. This book certainly adds to their argument. Rates of female shareholding were higher pre-1750 than they were from the 1780s to the 1820s. As we have seen, women who put their capital into the Bank of England, South Sea Company, East India Company, and the Mine Adventurers Company averaged between a quarter and a third of investors by the 1730s and 40s. This was twice the rate of female shareholding in the 1780s. So what led to the drop in female participation in public investments after the end of the period of this study? One scenario is that women moved their capital out of companies and into government funds. Freeman et al. did not look at the national debt, where the rates of women investors remained higher. What is clear, however, is that women moved into public investments early on during the Financial Revolution and the first seventy-five years of this new era in finance saw relatively high rates of female participation; rates that perhaps were not equaled again until the mid-nineteenth century.

While this book has gone a long way in illuminating the engagement of Englishwomen with the financial opportunities opened up by the Financial Revolution, I hope it will not be the definitive work on the subject. There is still much research to be done and more questions to be asked. Much of this story has been an English one. More work needs to be done to uncover the extent of Scots, Irish, or Welsh women's experiences of the Financial Revolution. Scotswomen and Irishwomen are largely absent from subscriber lists up to 1750, although the former had their own Bank of Scotland and the Darien Company in which to invest. Did Scotswomen stick to these options out of "financial patriotism"? And what of women on the continent? Dutch women especially would provide a suitable comparison to the investing practices of Englishwomen. We know many of them invested in English companies and the Bank of England. They should have also invested domestically and in the Dutch East India Company, or VOC. French women's role in the Mississippi Company and its fall would also provide a compelling comparison to women investors' experiences in the South Sea Bubble.

We also need more gender comparative work on the behaviors and strategies of public investors. In working on female investors I came to realize how little work has been done on individual male investors. Scholars have not pored over men's account books and stock portfolios in any systematic way. My sense is that men and women of the middling sort and the gentry shared many of the same attitudes toward and experiences of investment during the early years of the Financial Revolution. Class may have trumped gender to some extent for investors with capital.

There were some questions I was not able to answer in this study. Amongst family papers and correspondence I found precious little discussion of why women invested in particular stocks and securities. They were stubbornly silent when it came to explicitly stating their motivations and investing strategies. I had to instead infer motivations from their actions. I also was not able to find any instances of women describing voting in person at General Courts or shareholder elections. Examples may be buried somewhere in correspondence or Company minutes, but I turned up nothing in my quest.

Similarly, I found no examples of women discussing the companies in which they were invested and how these companies made their money. Thus, I found no women investors expressing concern (or complacency) with the colonial policies of the British government or the South Sea and Royal African companies' involvement in the Atlantic slave trade. It is worth noting that the percentage of women who invested in the Royal African Company was one of the lowest rates of stockholding I found for women during the early years of the Financial Revolution. But this seems to have had more to do with the difficulty of breaking into the elite and tight-knit circle of investors who held that Company's stock, rather than any moral qualms on the part of female investors. Englishwomen, like men, showed no greater or lesser social conscience when it came to seeking the potential profits enabled by the Financial Revolution. New financial opportunities, profits, and steady rates of return seem to have been at the forefront of the minds of these female investors, just as they were for men. Money makes the world go round.

Bibliography

Manuscript Sources

Bank of England Archives
AC 27/104, 3% Annuities, 1726
AC 27/131, 134, 3% Annuities, 1731
AC 27/143, 3% Annuities, 1743
M1/6–9, Original Subscription Books, 1697

The British Library
Add. MS. 61472, Blenheim Papers
Add. MS. 70348–9, Portland Papers
Add. MS. Trumbull Papers

Harvard University, Baker Library, Harvard Business School
South Sea Bubble Collection

Huguenot Library, University College London
E1/1 Extracts from Wills (1725–)

London Metropolitan Archives
M/093/444–45 (1777)
ACC 1017/925, 1016–20 Ledger of investments, Mariabella Eliot

Mapledurham Archives
MA, Bound Original Letters
MS DD Blount Papers

Nottinghamshire Archives
DD/SR/219, 225, 234, Savile of Rufford Papers
DD/SR A4/45–46, Gertrude Savile Accounts, 1736–58

The Folger Shakespeare Library, Washington DC
V.b.292, Sarah Cole's Arithmetic Exercise Book, 1685

The Huntington Library, San Marino, CA
Hastings Papers
Herbert Family Papers
Stowe Collection, Brydges Correspondence
Stowe Temple Brydges Papers
Stowe Temple Grenville Papers

The National Archives, Kew, U.K.
C 46 Million Bank Documents
E 401/1991–1992, Pells Receipts
E 401/2018, Pell's Receipt Book, Long Annuity, 1707
E 407/166, Register of Tallies, 1708 Annuity Loan
NDO 1/1, National Debt Office, Life Annuities, 1745
PROB 11/, various

University of Bristol, Special Collections
DM 58, Pinney Papers

Printed Primary Sources

The Accomplish'd Housewife: Or, the Gentlewoman's Companion (L, 1745).
Advice to the Women and Maidens of London (L, 1678).
The Allegations of the Turky Company and Others Against the East-India-Company (L, 1681).
Anselment, Raymond, ed., *The Remembrances of Elizabeth Freke, 1671–1714*, Camden Fifth Series vol. 18 (Cambridge University Press/Royal Historical Society, 2001).
Arithmetic Made Familiar and easy to Gentleman and Ladies, Being the Second Volume of the Circle of the sciences, etc. 2d. ed., (L, 1748).
Asgill, Mr., *The computation of advantages saved to the publick by the South-Sea scheme... with a Postscript* (L,1721).
Brodie, Alexander, *A New and Easy Method of Book-keeping, or Instructions for a Methodical keeping of Merchants Accompts* (L, 1722).
The Case of Lady Elizabeth Master (L, 1721).
The Case of the Annuitants Stated, And Compar'd with other Creditors of the Government (L, 1720).
Characters of Several Ingenious designing Gentlemen, who have lately put in to the Ladies Invention (L, 1695).
The Connoisseur.
A Continuation of a Catalogue of Ladies, to be set up by Auction, on Monday the 6th of this Instant July (L, 1702).
Cowper, Charles Spence, ed., *Diary of Mary, Countess Cowper, Lady of the Bedchamber to the Princess of Wales, 1714–1720* (London: John Murray, 1864).
Cowper, Sarah, *Diary*, vol. 5, 1710. *Perdita Manuscripts*. www.amdigital.co.uk
Croker, John Wilson, ed., *Letters to and from Henrietta, Countess of Suffolk and her Second Husband, the Hon. George Berkeley. From 1712 to 1767*, vol. 1 (London: John Murray, 1824).
Daily Courant.
Daily Gazetteer.
The Daily Journal, or The Gentleman's and Tradesman's Complete Annual Accompt-Book (L, 1763).
A Dialogue Between a Gentleman and a Broker, Concerning the Funds (L, 1737).

A Dialogue between Francisco and Aurelia, two unfortunate Orphans of the City of London, Guildhall, November 3, 1690 (L, 1690).

Diluvium Lachrymarum [Flood of tears]. A Review of the Fortunate & Unfortunate Adventurers. A Satyr in Burlesque, Upon the Famous Lottery, Set up in Freeman's Yard in Cornhill (L, 1694).

An Epistle. From a British Lady to her Countrywomen. On the Occasion of the Present Rebellion (L, 1745).

The Female Tatler.

Fielding, Henry, *The Lottery, A Farce,* 2d. ed. (L, 1732).

Ford, Edward, *Fair Play In the Lottery, or, Mirth for Money. In several witty passages and conceits of Persons that came to the Lottery* (L, 1660).

The Gentleman Accomptant: or An Essay to unfold the Mystery of Accompts (L, 1714).

Gentleman's Magazine.

The Glasgow Lasses Garland, composed of some excellent new songs (Newcastle upon Tyne, 1765).

A Good Husband for five shillings, or Esquire Bickerstaff's Lottery for the London Ladies (L, 1710).

Good News to the Distressed; or Proper Amendments to the Bill ... (L, 1734).

Grier, Sydney C., *The letters of Warren Hastings to his wife.* (William Blackwood & Sons, 1905).

Grundy, Isobel, ed., *Letters from the Right Honourable Lady Mary Wortley Montagu 1709 to 1762* (J. M. Dent & Co., 1906).

Hayes, Richard, *The Broker's Breviat* (L, 1734).

Howard, Eliot, compiler, *Eliot Papers, No. 1: John Eliot of London, Merchant 1735-1813* (L, 1895).

The Irish Register: Or a List of the Duchesses . . . of large Fortunes of England (Dublin and London, 1742).

Johnson, Reginald Brimley, ed., *Letters from the Right Hon. Lady Mary Wortley Montagu 1709-1762* (J. M. Dent & sons, 1906).

Journal of the House of Commons.

The Ladies Invention, being a thousand pounds for six-pence, to the fortunate, and the Triple Adventure Made into one Lottery (L, 1695).

The Letters and Journals of Lady Mary Coke, vols. 1-4 (Edinburgh: David Douglas, 1889).

"The Letters of Mr. Richard Barwell," *Bengal, Past & Present,* vols. 9-12 (1914-16).

A List of all the Adventurers in the Mine-Adventure. May the first, 1700 (L, 1700).

A List of the Names of the Adventurers of the Royal African Company of England (L, 1681).

A List of the Names of the Corporation of the Governor and Company of Merchants of Great Britain Trading to the South Seas ... (L, 1712).

A List of the Names of the Governour and Company of the Mine-Adventurers of England. November the twenty third, 1704 (L, 1704).

A List of the Names of the Members of the Corporation for Making Hollow Sword-Blades in England (L, 1705).

A List of the Names of the Subscribers of Land and Money towards a Fund for the National Land-Bank (L, 1695).

London Daily Post and General Advertiser.

London Evening Post.

London Journal.

The London Lottery (L, 1693).

A Lottery for Ladies and Gentlemen: Or, A New Million Adventure. Invented for the Benefit of Ladies that want Husbands, and younger brothers that stand in need of rich Wives (L, 1694).

The Lottery: Or, The Characters of several ingenious designing Gentlewomen that have put into it (L, 1740).

Martin, Jeanna, ed., *A Governess in the Age of Jane Austen: The Journals and Letters of Agnes Porter* (Hambledon Press, 1998).

A Master-key to the Rich Ladies Treasury, or the Widower and Batchelor Directory . . . by a younger brother (L, 1742).

Midriff, Sir John, *Observations on the Spleen and Vapours: Containing Cases of Persons of both Sexes, and all Ranks, from the aspiring Director to the humble Bubbler, who have been miserably afflicted with those melancholy Disorders since the Fall of South-Sea, and other Public Stocks* (L, 1721).

Mortimer, Thomas, *Every Man his own Broker: Or, a Guide to Exchange Alley* (L, 1761).

Mowbray, D. *The Report of the Gentlemen Appointed by the General Court of the Charitable Corporation* (L, 1732).

Osborn, Emily F. D., ed., *Political and Social Letters of a Lady of the Eighteenth Century 1721–1771* (Dodd, Mead and Co., 1891).

The Particulars and Inventories of the Estates of the late South Sea Company Directors, 3 vols. (L, 1721).

Post Man.

The Present State of the Unhappy Sufferers of the Charitable Corporation Consider'd. With Reasons humbly offer'd for their Relief (L, 1733).

Private Correspondence of Sarah Duchess of Marlborough, 2d. ed. (New York: Krause reprint, 1972), 2 vols.

Public Advertiser.

The Records of Love: or, Weekly Amusements for the Fair Sex, v. 1–9 (L, 1710).

A Report from the Committee to whom the petition of [the creditors and subscribers of] York Buildings . . . was referred (L, 1735).

The Report of the Commissioners appointed to examine, state, and report, who of the Sufferers in the Charitable Corporation are Objects of Compassion (L, 1733).

Savile, Alan, ed., *Secret Comment: The Diaries of Gertrude Savile, 1721–1757,* The Thoroton Society Record Series, vol. 41 (Nottingham, 1997).

A Scheme for a New Lottery for the Ladies: or, a Husband and Coach and Six for Forty Shillings (L, 1732).

Scott-Moncrieff, Robert, ed., *The Household Book of Grisell Baillie,* Scottish History Society, 2nd series, vol. 1 (Edinburgh, 1911).

Sherburn, George, ed., *The Correspondence of Alexander Pope,* 2 vols. (Oxford, 1956).

A Short History of the Charitable Corporation (L, 1732).

The Tatler.

Tolson, Francis, "A Poem on his Majesty's Passing the South-Sea Bill" (L, 1720).

The universal library of trade and commerce (L, 1747).

Universal Museum.

Waller, William, *The Mine-Adventure Laid Open; Being an Answer to a Late Pamphlet, Intitled, A Familiar Discourse, &c. published by William Shiers* (L, 1710).

The Wheel of Fortune: Or, Nothing for a Penny, Being Remarks on the drawing the Penny-Lottery (L, 1698).

Whitehall Evening Post or London Intelligencer.

Online Sources

"Anne Finch's unpublished poetry taken from manuscripts and rare books" <www.jimandellen.org/finch/finchtexts.html>

British History Online <www.british-history.ac.uk>

London Lives <www.londonlives.org>

Old Bailey Proceedings Online <www.oldbaileyonline.org>

The Papers of Benjamin Franklin <www.franklinpapers.org>

Secondary Works

Albree, Joe and Scott H. Brown, "'A valuable monument of mathematical genius': *The Ladies Diary* (1704–1840)," *Historia Mathematica* 36:1 (2009): 10–47.

Anderson, B. L., "Provincial Aspects of the Financial Revolution of the Eighteenth Century," *Business History* 11 (Jan. 1969): 11–22.

Ashton, John, *The History of Gambling in England* reprint (Montclair, NJ: Patterson Smith, 1969).

Balen, Malcolm, *The Secret History of the South Sea Bubble* (London: Fourth Estate, 2002).

Bowen, H. V., "Investment and Empire in the later Eighteenth Century: East India Stockholding, 1756–1791," *Economic History Review* 42:2 (1989): 186–206.

Bowen, H. V., *The business of empire: the East India Company and imperial Britain, 1756–1833* (Cambridge: Cambridge University Press, 2006).

Bowen, H. V., ed., *The Worlds of the East India Company* (Rochester, NY: Boydell & Brewer, 2003).

Bowen, Huw V., "The 'Little Parliament': The General Court of the East India Company, 1750–1784," *The Historical Journal* 34:4 (Dec. 1991): 857–72.

Brewer, John, *The Sinews of Power: War, Money and the British State, 1688–1783* (New York: A. Knopf, 1989).

Carey, Daniel and Christopher Finlay, eds., *The Empire of Credit: The Financial Revolution in Britain, Ireland, and America, 1688–1815* (Sallins, Co. Kildare: Irish Academic Press, 2011).

Carlos, Ann, Erin Fletcher, and Larry Neal, "Share Portfolios in the Early Years of Financial Capitalism: London 1690–1730," *Economic History Review* 68:2 (2015): 574–99.

Carlos, Ann M., Jennifer Key, and Jill L. Dupree, "Learning and the Creation of Stock-Market Institutions: Evidence from the Royal African and Hudson's Bay Companies, 1670–1700," *The Journal of Economic History* 58:2 (1998): 318–44.

Carlos, Ann M., Karen Maguire, and Larry Neal, "Financial Acumen, Women Speculators, and the Royal African Company during the South Sea Bubble," *Accounting, Business & Financial History* 16:2 (July 2006): 219–43.

Carlos, Ann and Larry Neal, "Women investors in early capital markets, 1720–25," *Financial History Review* 11:2 (2004): 197–224.

Carlos, Ann M. and Larry Neal, "The micro-foundations of the London capital market: Bank of England shareholders during and after the South Sea Bubble, 1720–25," *Economic History Review* 59:3 (2006): 498–538.

Carlton, Charles, *The Court of Orphans* (Leicester: Leicester University Press, 1974).

Carruthers, Bruce G., *City of Capital: Politics and Markets in the English Financial Revolution* (Princeton: Princeton University Press, 1996).

Carruthers, Robert, *The life of Alexander Pope: Including extracts from his correspondence.* 2d. ed. (London: Henry G. Bohn, 1857).

Carswell, John, *The South Sea Bubble* (Gloucester: Alan Sutton, 1993).

Carter, A. C., *Getting, Spending, and Investing in early modern Times* (Assen, Netherlands: Van Gorcum, 1975).

Carter, Alice, *The English Public Debt in the 18th Century* (Historical Association, 1968).

Chandaman, C. D., *The English Public Revenue 1660–1688* (Oxford: Oxford University Press, 1975).

Clapham, Sir John, *The Bank of England: A History* (New York: Macmillan, 1945).

Cohen, Jacob, "The Element of Lottery in British government bonds, 1694–1919," *Economica* n.s. 20 (1953): 237–46.

Cope, S. R., "The Stock Exchange Revisited," *Economica* 45 (1978): 1–21.

Corfield, P. J., ed., *Language, History and Class* (Oxford: Oxford University Press, 1991).

Costa, Shelley, "The Ladies' Diary: Gender, Mathematics, and Civil Society in Early Eighteenth-Century England," *Osiris* 17 (2002): 49–73.

Cowles, Virginia, *The Great Swindle: The Story of the South Sea Bubble* (New York: Harper, 1960).

Cummings, A. J. G., *The York Buildings Company: A Case Study in Eighteenth-Century Corporation Mismanagement* (University of Strathclyde dissertation, 1980).

Davies, K. G., "Joint Stock investment in the Later Seventeenth Century," *Economic History Review* 2nd ser., 4 (1952): 283–301.

Davies, K. G., *The Royal African Company* (London: Longmans, Green, 1957).

Dickinson, H. T., *A Companion to Eighteenth Century Britain* (Oxford: Wiley-Blackwell, 2008).

Dickson, P. G. M., *The Financial Revolution in England: A Study in the Development of Public Credit, 1688–1756* (London: MacMillan, 1967).

Earle, Peter, *The Making of the English Middle Class: Business, Society and Family Life in London, 1660–1730* (Berkeley: University of California Press, 1989).

Erickson, Amy L., *Women and Property in early modern England* (New York: Routledge, 2002).

Erickson, Amy Louise, "Coverture and Capitalism," *History Workshop Journal* 59 (2005): 1–16.

Ewen, C. L'Estrange, *Lotteries and Sweepstakes* (London: Heath Cranton Ltd., 1932).

Froide, Amy M., "Hidden Women: Rediscovering the Singlewomen of Early Modern England," *Local Population Studies* 68 (Spring 2002): 26–41.

Froide, Amy M., *Never Married: Singlewomen in Early Modern England* (Oxford: Oxford University Press, 2005).

Froide, Amy M., "The Religious Lives of Singlewomen in the Anglo-Atlantic World: Quaker Missionaries, Protestant Nuns, and Covert Catholics," in Daniella Kostroun and Lisa Vollendorf, eds., *Women, Religion and the Atlantic World, 1600–1800* (Toronto: University of Toronto Press, 2009), 60–78.

Froide, Amy M., "Learning to Invest: Women's Education in Arithmetic and Accounting in early modern England," *Early Modern Women: An Interdisciplinary Journal* 10:1 (2015): 3–26.

Gallais-Hamonno, Georges and Christian Rietsch, "Learning by Doing: The Failure of the 1697 Malt Lottery-Loan," *Financial History Review* 20:3 (2013): 259–77.

Gates, Barbara, *Victorian Suicide: Mad Crimes and Sad Histories* (Princeton: Princeton University Press, 2014).

Glaisyer, Natasha, *The Culture of Commerce in England, 1660–1720* (Woodbridge: Boydell Press, 2011).

Green, David. R. and Alastair Owens, "Gentlewomanly capitalism? Spinsters, widows and wealth holding in England and Wales, c. 1800–1860," *Economic History Review* 56:3 (2003): 510–36.

Greenberg, Janelle, "The legal status of the English woman in early eighteenth century common law and equity," *Studies in 18th Century Culture* 4 (1975): 171–81.

Hancock, David, "'Domestic Bubbling': 18th-Century London Merchants and Individual Investment in the Funds," *Economic History Review* 47:4 (1994): 679–702.

Harris, Frances, *A Passion for Government: The Life of Sarah, Duchess of Marlborough* (Oxford: Oxford University Press, 1991).

Holderness, B. A., "Widows in Pre-Industrial Society: An Essay Upon their Economic Function," in Richard M. Smith, ed., *Land, Kinship, and Life-Cycle* (Cambridge: Cambridge University Press, 1984), 423–42.

Homer, Sidney and Richard Sylla, *A History of Interest Rates*, 4th ed. (New Brunswick, NJ: Rutgers University Press, 2005).

Hoppit, Julian, "The myths of the South Sea Bubble," *Transactions of the Royal Historical Society* 6th series, 12 (2002): 141–65.

Howson, Geoffrey, *A History of Mathematics Education in England* (Cambridge: Cambridge University Press, 1982).

Hunt, Margaret, "Wives and 'Marital Rights' in the Court of Exchequer in the Early Eighteenth Century," in Paul Griffiths and Mark S. R. Jenner, *Londinopolis: Essays in the Social and Cultural History of early modern London* (Manchester: Manchester University Press, 2000), 107–29.

Ingrassia, Catherine, *Authorship, Commerce, and Gender in Early Eighteenth-Century England* (Cambridge: Cambridge University Press, 1998).

Knoppers, Laura Lunger, ed., *The Cambridge Companion to Early Modern Women's Writing* (Cambridge: Cambridge University Press, 2009).

Laurence, Anne, "Lady Betty Hastings, Her Half-Sisters, and the South Sea Bubble: family fortunes and strategies," *Women's History Review* 15:4 (2006): 533–40.

Laurence, Anne, "Women Investors, 'That Nasty South Sea Affair' and the Rage to Speculate in Early Eighteenth-Century England," *Accounting, Business & Financial History* 16:2 (July 2006): 45–64.

Laurence, Anne, "The emergence of a private clientele for banks in the early eighteenth century: Hoare's Bank and some women customers," *Economic History Review* 61:3 (2008): 565–86.

Laurence, Anne, Josephine Maltby, and Janette Rutterford, *Women and their Money 1700–1950: Essays on women and finance* (New York: Routledge, 2008).

Lemire, Beverly, *The Business of Everyday Life: Gender, Politics, and Social Practice in England 1600–1900* (Manchester: Manchester University Press, 2005).

Keay, John, *The Honourable Company: A History of the English East India Company* (London: Macmillan, 1991).

McGowen, Randall, "Making the 'Bloody Code'? Forgery legislation in eighteenth-century England," in Norma Landau, ed., *Law, Crime and English Society, 1660–1830* (Cambridge: Cambridge University Press, 2002).

Miroski, Philip, "The Rise and Retreat of a Market: English Joint Stock Shares in the Eighteenth Century," *Journal of Economic History* 41 (1981): 559–77.

Muldrew, Craig, *The Economy of Obligation* (Cambridge: Cambridge University Press, 1999).

Murphy, Anne L., "Lotteries in the 1690s: investment or gamble?," *Financial History Review* 12:2 (2005): 227–46.

Murphy, Anne L., "Dealing with Uncertainty: Managing Personal Investment in the Early English National Debt," *History* 91:302 (April 2006): 200–17.

Murphy, Anne, *The Origins of English Financial Markets: Investment and Speculation before the South Sea Bubble* (Cambridge: Cambridge University Press, 2012).

Murray, David, *The York Buildings Company: A Chapter in Scotch History* (Glasgow: J. Maclehose, 1883).

Neal, Larry, *The Rise of Financial Capitalism* (Cambridge: Cambridge University Press, 1990).

Newton, Lucy and Philip Cottrell, "Female investors in the First English and Welsh Joint stock Banks," *Accounting, Business, and Financial History* 16:2 (July 2006): 315–40.

Newton, Lucy A., Philip L. Cottrell, Josephine Maltby, and Janette Rutterford, "Women and Wealth: The Nineteenth Century in Great Britain," in Anne Laurence, Josephine Maltby, and Janette Rutterford, eds., *Women and Their Money 1700–1950: Essays on Women and Finance* (Abingdon: Routledge, 2008), 86–94.

O'Day, Rosemary, *Cassandra Brydges (1670–1735), First Duchess of Chandos: Life and Letters* (Woodbridge: Boydell Press, 2007).

Okin, S., "Patriarchy and Married Women's Property," *Eighteenth-Century Studies* 17 (1983–4): 121–38.

Ottaway, Susannah, *The Decline of Life: Old Age in Eighteenth Century England* (Cambridge: Cambridge University Press, 2004).

Paul, Helen, *The South Sea Bubble: An Economic History of its Origins and Consequences* (London: Routledge, 2010).

Pelling, Margaret, *The Common Lot: Sickness, Medical Occupations and the Urban Poor in Early Modern England* (London: Routledge, 2014).

Perl, T., "The Ladies Diary or Woman's Almanack 1707–1841," *Historia Mathematica* 6 (1979): 36–53.

Poska, Allyson, "Gender, Property, and Retirement Strategies in early modern North-western Spain," *Journal of Family History* 25:3 (July 2000): 313–25.

Raven, James, *Publishing Business in Eighteenth-Century England* (Woodbridge: Boydell and Brewer, 2014).

Richards, R. D., "The Lottery in the History of English Government and Finance," *Economic History* 3 (1928): 334–55.

Richards, Richard, *The Early History of Banking in England* (London: Routledge, reprint 2012).

Roseveare, Henry G., *The Financial Revolution 1660–1760* (New York: Longman, 1991).

Rumbold, Valerie, *Women's Place in Pope's World* (Cambridge: Cambridge University Press, 1989).

Scott, William, *The Constitution and Finance of English, Scottish and Irish Joint Stock Companies to 1720* 3 vols. (Cambridge: Cambridge University Press, 1910–12).

Sharpe, Pamela, *Adapting to Capitalism: Working Women in the English Economy, 1700–1850* (New York: St Martin's Press, 1996).

Sharpe, Pamela, "Dealing with Love: The Ambiguous Independence of the Single Woman in Early Modern England," *Gender & History* 11:2 (July 1999): 209–32.

Shepard, Alexandra, *Accounting for Oneself: Worth, Status and Social Order in Early Modern England* (Oxford: Oxford University Press, 2015).

Spicksley, Judith, "'Fly with a duck in thy mouth': single women as sources of credit in seventeenth century England," *Social History* 32:2 (May 2007): 187–207.

Spicksley, Judith, "Usury legislation, cash and credit: the development of the female investor in the late Tudor and Stuart periods," *Economic History Review* 61:2 (May 2008): 277–301.

Spring, Eileen, *Law, Land and Family: Aristocratic Inheritance in England, 1300–1600* (Chapel Hill, NC: University of North Carolina Press, 1993).

Staves, Susan, "Investments, votes and 'bribes': women as shareholders in the chartered national companies," in Hilda Smith, ed., *Women writers and the early modern British political tradition* (Cambridge: Cambridge University Press, 1998), 259–78.

Staves, Susan, *Married Women's Separate Property in England, 1660–1833* (Cambridge, MA: Harvard University Press, 1990).

Staves, Susan, "Pin Money," *Studies in 18th Century Culture* 14 (1985): 47–74.

Sutherland, Dame Lucy Stuart, *Politics and Finance in the Eighteenth Century* (London: Bloomsbury Academic, 1984).

Thomas, Janet, "Women and Capitalism: Oppression or Emancipation? A Review Article," *Comparative Studies in Society and History* 30:3 (1988): 534–49.

Thomas, Keith, "Numeracy in early modern England," *Transactions of the Royal Historical Society* 37 (1987): 103–32.

Tittler, Robert, "Money-lending in the West Midlands: The Activities of Joyce Jeffries, 1638–49," *Historical Research* 67:164 (1994): 249–63.

Todd, Barbara J., "Fiscal Citizens: Female Investors in Public Finance before the South Sea Bubble," in Sigrun Haude and Melinda S. Zook, eds., *Challenging Orthodoxies: The Social and Cultural Worlds of Early Modern Women* (Farnham, Surrey: Ashgate, 2014), 53–74.

Todd, Barbara J., "Property and a Woman's Place in Restoration London," *Women's History Review* 19:2 (April 2010): 181–200.

Wennerlind, Carl, *Casualties of Credit: The English Financial Revolution 1620–1720* (Cambridge, MA: Harvard University Press, 2011).

Yamamoto, Koji, "Piety, Profit and Public Service in the Financial Revolution," *English Historical Review*, CXXVI:521 (Aug. 2011): 806–34.

Index